THE
EVERYTHING.
GUIDE TO
PAST LIFE EXPERIENCE

Dear Reader,

I was honored when I was asked to write this book. I have had many glimpses into past lives, for myself and for those clients I have read for as a professional psychic medium. I have witnessed the power that is innate and therapeutic—a catalyst for change—and I have seen how learning from past incarnations has enhanced lives. I have witnessed people co-creating a wonderful future when they recognize what lessons from the past have been shaping their future. This book is a gift to you from the world of spirit, and I want to show you the way to a brighter future by clearing the karma of the past.

 I have a running joke with my wife, Joanne, that she has had more past lives than you could possibly imagine—a pilot, a singer, a dancer, and a surgeon. I cringe at the thought.

 Nevertheless, I know deep within, and from my own spiritual team of helpers, that our past incarnations have shaped the present moment. Lessons have been learned (or not, as the case may be), and this could be the reason you experience certain influences, traits, and potential hurdles in your life. What I find astonishing is that you can be your own health therapist. With a little help from your own spiritual team and the knowledge contained in this book, you can go on the journey of lifetimes and see firsthand what has shaped your present moment.

 From my own experiences as a medium and with the aide of my colleagues and my guides, I offer you the opportunity to shape the now by learning from the past. You are meant to be reading this book at this moment, if only to be taken on a roller coaster of historical influence.

Jock Brocas

Welcome to the EVERYTHING® Series!

These handy, accessible books give you all you need to tackle a difficult project, gain a new hobby, comprehend a fascinating topic, prepare for an exam, or even brush up on something you learned back in school but have since forgotten.

You can choose to read an Everything® book from cover to cover or just pick out the information you want from our four useful boxes: e-questions, e-facts, e-alerts, and e-ssentials.

We give you everything you need to know on the subject, but throw in a lot of fun stuff along the way, too.

We now have more than 400 Everything® books in print, spanning such wide-ranging categories as weddings, pregnancy, cooking, music instruction, foreign language, crafts, pets, New Age, and so much more. When you're done reading them all, you can finally say you know Everything®!

QUESTION

Answers to common questions

FACT

Important snippets of information

ALERT

Urgent warnings

ESSENTIAL

Quick handy tips

PUBLISHER Karen Cooper

DIRECTOR OF ACQUISITIONS AND INNOVATION Paula Munier

MANAGING EDITOR, EVERYTHING® SERIES Lisa Laing

COPY CHIEF Casey Ebert

ASSISTANT PRODUCTION EDITOR Jacob Erickson

ACQUISITIONS EDITOR Lisa Laing

ASSOCIATE DEVELOPMENT EDITOR Hillary Thompson

EDITORIAL ASSISTANT Ross Weisman

EVERYTHING® SERIES COVER DESIGNER Erin Alexander

LAYOUT DESIGNERS Colleen Cunningham, Elisabeth Lariviere, Ashley Vierra, Denise Wallace

Visit the entire Everything® series at *www.everything.com*

THE
EVERYTHING®
GUIDE TO PAST LIFE EXPERIENCE

Explore the scientific, spiritual, and philosophical
evidence of past life experiences

Jock Brocas, founding member of American Society for
Standards in Mediumship and Psychical Investigation

adamsmedia

Avon, Massachusetts

I dedicate this work to my wife and soul mate, Jo. Her love and support is more than I deserve, and I thank God for bringing her to me. I also dedicate this book to my guide Ellie, thank you! A special thanks goes to the editors at Adams Media, who were some of the best I have worked with.

An Everything® Series Book.
Everything® and everything.com® are registered trademarks of F+W Media, Inc.

Published by Adams Media, a division of F+W Media, Inc.
57 Littlefield Street, Avon, MA 02322 U.S.A.
www.adamsmedia.com

ISBN 10: 1-4405-2670-2
ISBN 13: 978-1-4405-2670-1
eISBN 10: 1-4405-2727-X
eISBN 13: 978-1-4405-2727-2

Printed in the United States of America.

10 9 8 7 6 5 4 3 2 1

Library of Congress Cataloging-in-Publication Data
is available from the publisher.

This publication is designed to provide accurate and authoritative information with regard to the subject matter covered. It is sold with the understanding that the publisher is not engaged in rendering legal, accounting, or other professional advice. If legal advice or other expert assistance is required, the services of a competent professional person should be sought.

—From a *Declaration of Principles* jointly adopted by a Committee of the American Bar Association and a Committee of Publishers and Associations

Many of the designations used by manufacturers and sellers to distinguish their products are claimed as trademarks. Where those designations appear in this book and Adams Media was aware of a trademark claim, the designations have been printed with initial capital letters.

This book is available at quantity discounts for bulk purchases.
For information, please call 1-800-289-0963.

Contents

Acknowledgments

I would like to acknowledge those people who have helped me compile the book and who have shared stories or written case histories. I am thankful to:

Joanne Brocas; Ian Lawton; Camilla Persson; Mani Asvadi and Jasmin S.; Jennifer Hillman; Andrea Greenwood; Christine De Nucci; John Sinclair, Clinical Hypnotherapist and musician; and the editors at Adams Media who were understanding when I fell ill and missed my deadline.

The Top 10 Tips for Exploring Your Past Lives

1. Learn this easy series of words that have the secrets of manifesting within them: Perceive—Believe—Conceive. This is the base you need to achieve success in all the exercises.

2. Ensure you have a suitable journal during your journey of the soul that you can take all your notes in.

3. Do not rush in where angels fear to tread. Your excitement might get the better of you and you will be tempted to try to complete everything as quickly as possible. Take your time.

4. Eat high-vibrational foods and try to maintain your health by exercising. It is very good practice to try to increase your healthy living.

5. Drink plenty of water to cleanse and purify your body.

6. Begin a daily or weekly regime of meditation no matter how short. Even ten minutes a day will give you great results.

7. Be aware of the breath and learn to control your breathing. Remember, everything exists on the breath and without it we would not exist.

8. Always wear loose-fitting clothing so that you are not restricted when you attempt any of the exercises.

9. Be aware of the dangers associated with any altered state or meditative practice. Always have suitable protection in place.

10. Do not attempt any of these exercises if you have a history of mental illness.

Introduction

BEEN HERE BEFORE? INEXPLICABLY drawn to a particular culture such as the ancient Egyptians or the Druids of old? Perhaps you have been there also and experienced all that life had to offer with its highs and lows.

There is a fascination with past lives, and occasionally in the news you'll hear of individuals claiming past lives. But haven't you felt that you have been elsewhere before—a kind of déjà vu feeling? Specialists such as mediums, hypnotherapists, and regression experts have found the issues and life choices you are presently dealing with are related to past lives. The choices you make have a dramatic effect on the karma you carry forward from your past life that affects your present circumstances. Is there a reason why your relationships fail? Why are you experiencing those yearnings from a different race or culture? How about reincarnation, do you believe in that? If indeed you had a past life that has shaped your present, do you feel you will come back to another time and space? Most religions have some kind of explanation for reincarnation and will say it is neither true nor false.

The truth is that what we consider as paranormal is in fact very normal, and studies have shown that people do have detailed knowledge of past incarnations. You will investigate some of these later in this book, and you will see some of the experiences others have had. The knowledge that you will glean from this guide, of seeing and learning from your past incarnations, will help to shape your present and your future.

In this book, you will gain the skills and knowledge needed to have a glimpse into your past lives. You'll learn from past mistakes that have created barriers and blockages of the future. Hopefully, much of what you learn will be able to be validated by historical registers and documentation, so you can prove your past life by confirming the information you receive. You should have some fun along the way while having a glimpse into your previous lives. Perhaps you will find this process enlightening and life changing, or it may answer questions as to why you are experiencing events in a certain way now. This concise and informative guide will take you on your journeys of many lives. Have fun looking at the past and learn through past mistakes or missed opportunities.

Did you know that you have a guide and an angel? Do you want to meet them? These are special beings who are there to guide you through life. They are your conscience when you need it and will keep you on the right track if you listen. However, did you also know those special relationships that you have with them existed before your incarnation on this timeline? Did you know they have experienced all you have—with you in all of your lifetimes? Enhance your relationship with them to a more communicative level, and you will realize the influence and guidance they can assert with a gentle nudge. With this realistic newfound awareness of your spirit friends, you can be taken on a journey—facilitated by them—that will give you a glimpse into your previous incarnations.

Perhaps you will learn from your lessons of the past so that you can shape your future. If this is your desire now, then you are reading the right book and it is no coincidence why you have it in your possession. In this guide, all the tools are provided so that you may indeed revisit the past and make the now a wonderful experience.

This easy-to-read and easy-to-learn-from book is your first step in releasing your innate potential. You may have issues in your life that need to be faced now, or you might just be interested in where you have been before. There is an old Buddhist saying: "The past is gone, the future has not arrived, and the only time to live is now." How true, but what of the lessons that have shaped your now? You can make the present moment more wholesome if you learn from your failures of the past.

CHAPTER 1

A Brief History of Past Life Regression

Have you ever considered your life in the past, what it was and who you were? This chapter is where you will learn a little bit about the history of regression and past lives and how it affects you. The chapter will examine the typical scenarios that may play out and the type of lives that you may associate with. Perhaps you were famous, perhaps not, or maybe you were some kind of warrior. You will also be introduced to the individuals who are considered the pioneers in past life regression and therapy.

Times Gone By

Past life regression is by no means a modern concept. It has existed in some form or another for thousands of years and is even alluded to in the Bible and other religious writings. People have believed in reincarnation and past lives in every race and religion, including the Hindus, Buddhists, Hebrews, Celts, Christians, and Egyptians. The list is by no means complete, and you could go on researching and adding to it until you have compiled a volume of books. While the concept of past lives has been included in all major religions, it may be coined or phrased differently.

ESSENTIAL

Past life regression is enjoying rapid growth as a new method of health and healing despite skeptical claims. Individuals are enjoying a new level of health and well-being by facing the issues that hold them prisoner; these are past-life lessons.

The fascination with our past is endless. Think back to your childhood history classes. Have you ever become interested in a particular historical time and imagined yourself living in that era? Maybe you manifested your dreams in your mind—playing out your ultimate fantasies in adventure and love.

The Buddha and Past Lives

Buddha recounted thousands of his past lives, but only 550 have been written in the *Jataka Tales*, which are a series of writings depicting the previous incarnations of the Buddha. No one knows why only 550 have been written about in detail; perhaps these were the only ones that could be recounted at that time. He would ask his disciples to explore their own past lives to gain an understanding of the life-and-death reality of impermanence. According to his teachings on the subject, one attains enlightenment when one becomes free from the bondage of life and death and its associated issues.

He believed that we continue as an expression of the essence of life or as an energy form manifested in something else. For instance, to illustrate that energy permeates everything, he would make the analogy that an extinguished flame is not destroyed. The flame would continue its existence as a form other than its original. As the flame burned it would create heat and also smoke, which would rise and join with other universal energy. Therefore, it would become part of the clouds and other elements and continue its expression in another form.

FACT

The *Jataka Tales* are a series of writings that were primarily concerned with the past lives and reincarnations of the Buddha. What is interesting to note is that lives were not only recounted in human form but also depicted in tales of animal incarnations, too.

It is for this very reason that he gently guided his students to look at their past incarnations through the practice of meditative principles. The Buddha believed that meditation would free a person from the material perceptions of life by learning of the true reality from the past.

Christianity and the Afterlife

Christianity maintains that the soul separates from the body and leaves after physical death. But so much conjecture exists as to where that soul actually goes or resides, or indeed if it comes back for another tour, so to speak. This is understood as the afterlife, and this concept exists in some form in other spiritual practices.

ALERT

The belief in the afterlife exists in almost all spiritual disciplines. The afterlife is what mediums understand as the world of spirit and the spirit world. It is this world that you will also tap into in order to gain information from your past incarnations. Mediums are able to raise their vibration enough to communicate with those who live in the spirit world.

From information that has been derived from various texts, and from wisdom that has been imparted by the spirit world through entranced mediums, we know that Christians believe that the soul is received by heavenly beings such as angels, guides, or loved ones. The individual is then given a "life review" of all lessons learned and failed within each incarnation, and the soul is able to judge itself.

Other Looks at Past Lives

The ancient Egyptians believed that it took a person 3,000 years to complete all the lives that she had to live, developing and preparing for a new life in the heavenly realms during each individual incarnation. The ancient Greeks attested to these many lives, and noted philosophers such as Plato and Pythagoras explained past lives and reincarnation in their texts. Pythagoras claimed to be incarnated many times as a warrior, prophet, peasant, and prostitute.

In Hinduism, there is a great belief in reincarnation and, therefore, past life incarnation. Sri Krishna said in the Bhagavad Gita, "As a man, casting off worn-out garments, takes new ones, so the dweller in the body, casting off worn-out bodies, enters into others that are new." He also said, "The misdeeds of our past lives torment us in the form of illnesses or ailments."

In the Tibetan beliefs, there is a plethora of information on the subject of past lives and reincarnation. One of the most important pieces of literature to come from Tibetan wisdom is the *Tibetan Book of the Dead*, which was read to individuals as they were dying or as part of the funeral ceremony. It was thought this work would be a kind of guidebook and compass to the afterlife. As these newly arrived spirits get used to the spirit world, they are faced with the choice of preparing for another life or releasing all attachments to an earthly existence and continuing the path within the spirit realms.

As you can see, issues in past lives have been a standard belief of many spiritual systems. Nevertheless, these religions have failed to see or teach the benefits of understanding your past. There is a spiritual law that covers this belief and the understanding of why these issues occur, and that is the law of cause and effect, which is also understood as karma. You will learn about karma in Chapter 6.

Probable Past Lives

Now, take a look at some of the past lives that you may have had or may be aware of. Through history, mankind has had many different cultures. Most people know about the culture or traditions of the ancient Egyptians, African tribes, Middle Eastern societies, and the cultures of Europe, Japan, and China. Perhaps because you've read about these particular cultures and learned about them in school; maybe you feel consciously drawn to a certain place and time.

It is possible that you might recall a life in a time and place that you have never thought of, like an unknown South American tribe or a servant in a Victorian household. This could be the beginning of a wonderful learning experience if you accessed those memories. This is why you have this book now; you will learn as you go through it how you may access those hidden memories of your past. If you recounted any of these lives through your visualizations or by regressing yourself or with a professional, and had information that you could validate, that would certainly support the belief that you were there and experienced that previous life. Many people suspect that they have existed before, and sometimes flashbacks of a past life can come at any time of the day or night. You do not have to be in a state of meditation or deep trance; sometimes these experiences can happen all of a sudden, though they often occur when you are just in a calm and relaxed state.

QUESTION

What does it mean if I am drawn to a particular culture?
The chances are very high that you have had an incarnation in that culture. If you have photos and artwork from a culture, or if you are drawn to the food, clothing, or lifestyle, it is highly likely that you've been there before.

You may be inexplicably drawn to a particular culture from the past, such as the Samurai—a warrior culture. Perhaps you were in Scotland during a famous battle; this may explain why you have such a need to surround yourself in everything that appertains to the particular culture. You would, for instance, have pictures, clothing, or items from the past on display in your home now. Maybe you just love the particular food from that culture, and to an extreme, perhaps you are looking for a wife or a husband from the culture you are drawn to. This would definitely allude to having experienced that culture in another time.

Was I Famous?

One thing that you must tread carefully with is the belief that you were someone famous in another incarnation. This seems to be more of a desire, and imagining that you were something better than what you may be now is controlled by a deep need to fulfill a yearning for fame and fortune. Therefore, you must be aware this may be a way of filling a desire or a missing part of your life and is very often coming from the ego self. It's not a bad thing, just something that you should have an awareness of—for when the desire arises from the subconscious mind, you can control it.

ALERT

Beware of creating an egotistical alternate reality that is borne of desire and not real. This may make you feel better but essentially will only be an escape from the truth. If you wish to change and learn from your past lives, you must be prepared to face those difficult realities once more. Learn that your daydream may bring comfort, but do not perceive it as reality.

There is nothing wrong with creating an alternate reality in your mind if you have a deep desire to be something you are not; it is a kind of a daydream state that will create an air of happiness for a short time. The truth is, most people were not as famous in the past as they would like to believe. Most people led normal lives. Nevertheless, there are people who have regressed and have found themselves with some sort of famous connection. It is essential to validate these claims in some way before accepting the revelation.

Perhaps you just have a fascination with a long-lost time and a place, person, or event at that time. This does not mean that you were that famous person; it does suggest that you may have lived in that person's era and might have memories connected with that time and place. It may also suggest that you have some form of karmic tie with a particular event in time. This may be the reason that you have blockages or cannot get past the fascination with the historical revelations of that timeline.

Identifying Real Connections

There is a slim chance that you were actually famous in another past incarnation. This can be confirmed under a professional regression where evidence is collected and verified after the regression. Suppose you constantly dream of someone famous—say, an Egyptian Pharaoh—and you constantly have the experience of feeling guilt surrounding this dreamlike state that you find yourself in from time to time. Perhaps in that state you carried out terrible acts against your fellow man. You will relive these acts in your mind. Maybe you see yourself committing these atrocious acts again in your dream state; note your feelings. If these feelings of regret or other such emotions are awakened when you are near a visual or auditory experience connected with that life, you most probably were that person or very close to that person during that space and time. Therefore, this would be an excellent point in the proceedings to identify issues, such as a deep need for forgiveness, in order to move on in life.

Children and Past Lives

Typically, thoughts of a past life come to the fore from your children and you ignore them, casting them off as a figment of the imagination. Often, children will recount details that seem so out of the ordinary that it makes you stop and think. For instance, imagine you took your child on a daytrip to a historical place and out of the blue your child begins to recognize and recount the historical facts from the past with astonishing accuracy. What should you think? You have no way of knowing the facts or the history, but it all seems real enough, and so with your interest piqued, you begin to check the information and find that it is accurate. Certainly, every time a child says something unusual does not mean she is recalling a past life. However, you will know and feel the difference in her statements. Some things the child will reaffirm will be too close to the truth; you will feel it and discern the information.

A point to note: Parents will often disregard what children are saying as the product of pure fantasy or an overactive imagination, sometimes chastising the child for being so dramatic. However, have you ever considered what they are saying and how detailed the events, people, and surroundings they describe actually are? An imagination that recounts so much pure detail needs further scrutiny and should be investigated rather than refuted. Your child can often be the catalyst that you need to investigate your own past incarnations. There will definitely be some kind of soul connection with you both and the rest of the family. Your child could have been your father or mother or sibling in another incarnation.

Charlie's Experience

Charlie was a young boy whose dad was in the military and mother was in the medical service. They were normal in every way. One evening, Charlie and his mom and dad were watching a historical documentary on TV, though Charlie was more interested in playing with his toys rather than paying attention to everything that was being shown on the television. However, at a certain point during the documentary, Charlie came out with a bold statement: "I was there. The clothes we had were different, and I remember my friend James who was with me. We had to go to an old house near the area to get help and shelter after the battle." You can imagine how that would sound to mom and dad. They were flabbergasted, not because of what he said, but the detail in which he described everything of that time without any prior knowledge. The father actually knew a little more on that particular history and recognized some facts that his son came out with as true. If tested, those facts would stand up to scrutiny.

QUESTION

How do you deal with your child who recalls a past life?
You must treat the child with love and compassion, and do not discount anything until you have investigated the matter more fully. Ignoring the child could cause her suffering, and you may actually learn something from the experience.

Charlie's parents began to take a serious interest in what he was talking about, and slowly over time more information was revealed. Charlie's dad recorded the information meticulously and had it validated. Charlie was coming out with information that he couldn't have known. When the information was eventually validated, it ruled out any other possibility other than that he had surely been there before. His parents found this difficult to accept. They were concerned and began to think their son was strange; they feared for his safety and took him to their local pastor.

The pastor further exacerbated their fears when he said that a demonic presence was in the child and was giving out the information they were receiving. He maintained that Charlie would have to go through a deliverance, which is an evangelical form of exorcism, to rid him of the heinous beast. Both parents agreed and Charlie was brought to the church at the appropriate date and time.

The deliverance was a frightening experience for the young child and he sobbed during the whole procedure, with his mother clinging to him for dear life. After the service, blessings were said and it was confirmed the pastor had done battle with the forces of darkness. All was well, or so he claimed.

ESSENTIAL

There have been occasions where a misguided pastor has mistaken a past life recall for something more sinister. It is important that you are not swayed by ignorance, for there can be far greater damage by acting on ignorance. Past life recall is not evil in nature, and certainly the memories that are recalled are in no way created by an evil influence.

Young Charlie was a little scarred from this experience and had retreated into his shell for a while, and this convinced his parents that the pastor had done the job. As things settled over a period of time and Charlie began to get some of his confidence back, he began to come out with further details and more evidence of his past incarnation. He managed to scare his mother by saying they had been related in the past and that she was a man. The information seemed far beyond that of an imagination coming from a child at play. Once more, mom and dad looked for an explanation of the seriousness of the situation and what their child was going through, who evidently seemed happy enough.

Charlie's mom decided to take him to John, a local psychiatrist and clinical hypnotherapist. John suggested that Charlie may be experiencing past life events and that his spirit was so old and advanced that he could remember past incarnations. John suggested that he meet with Charlie to talk with him and work with him to identify if this was the case. John continued to see Charlie on a regular basis and began to work with him, gradually and gently extracting evidence. When he finally got the trust of the young boy, he was able to put him into a relaxed enough state where he could regress him further to collaborate the information. His mother gave witness and testimony to the regression and was absolutely amazed at the revelations that came from the young boy.

ALERT

Such a regression may induce feelings and negative emotions from the child's parents and could cause the parents to feel detached from their child when they find out certain information. It is important that you recognize that the information does not change the relationship that you have with your child now. It is beyond material perception.

The parents eventually concluded their son was a rather special child and that he did in fact have a past life that they could access through his memories under regression and validate the information that was brought forth. The revelations were so compelling that both parents also agreed to be regressed by John and the information collated and validated to see where the soul connection lay. The product of all this research actually had a dramatic effect on all their lives. It was as if an amazing healing had taken place, and issues that plagued them in the past no longer had any significance or effect on them. In short, they led a happier life. They were able to see the bigger picture and recognized what the catalysts were that caused issues within their lives in the present. This knowledge enabled them to make informed decisions and take the correct path in life.

Before You Start

There are a few things that you need to consider before you start this journey. First, you need to be aware that there is a chance that you will not have experienced any other incarnations other than what you are living now. So what does this mean? Does it mean that you are so highly evolved that you have learned all and may be perfect? Or does it mean that you are less evolved and uninteresting? No! It could mean that you are a new soul experiencing your first incarnation. Therefore, you have nothing to learn from other incarnations because this is your first, so you will have no karmic debt to pay. Furthermore, the chances are that you will not be much interested in historical events of any sort as all your lessons may just be beginning, so you will not be drawn to particular cultures or be as emphatic in your search for answers relating to a particular historical time.

It must be noted that another explanation is also necessary, and this is tied to the world of spirit and your guides and angels, which you will learn about in Chapter 13. The possibility exists that you have been disallowed to view your past existence on a specific timeline. You may be in the process of repeating lessons, or you might be so emotionally disingenuous that to show you the mistakes or missed opportunities of the past would be spiritually damaging. Therefore, it will not be allowed and will be blocked from your consciousness. Whether you are a new soul or an older one with your lessons being curtailed by your guides and angels, do not be disheartened in any way. Throughout the book you will learn how to deal with these possibilities, and should you find yourself at a stumbling block, you will learn how to navigate through it and see what other potential benefits there are.

You Are Not Leaving Your Body

There is a fear that exists with the unknown, and so individuals fail to take part in anything that involves alternate reality. Do not be concerned. When you take part in the exercises and tasks in this book, you will not be possessed, and you will not be leaving your body in any way. Get that fear out of your head now, and you will progress further as you delve into the trancelike states and the hypnotic conditions that are a prerequisite to the exercises.

Don't worry—you are not under threat of being turned into a chicken or a barking dog, and don't worry—you will not suffer physically.

You may laugh at the previous statement, but you would be amazed at the perceptions many hold with regard to hypnosis. Some believe that because people are prone to suggestion in a hypnotic state, they will feel compelled to do whatever anyone suggests—kind of like a stage magician's show. Have you ever gone to a hypnotist stage show? Most stage hypnotists will make some poor soul act in a way that is demeaning and very silly. Unfortunately, this particular type of entertainment also tars the professional and ethical hypnotists with a bad image. This just is not true, and should you regress yourself or take part in a professional regression, you will be completely safe.

ESSENTIAL

If you have a history of psychiatric or other associated mental disorders, you must not regress yourself under any circumstances. You must consult a professional and identify if it would be appropriate to do so. This is for your safety and that of others too.

The truth is that you will be in some control the whole time, and the control you relinquish under hypnotic conditions does not take over your mind and personality; you will be releasing strong clairvoyant imagery that will tell your story from a detached view. You will learn about this form of clairvoyance in Chapter 9. You will learn how to interpret what you see so that you will have insights and answers to issues or blockages in your life right now.

Leaders in the Field

Consider the many professions that exist in the world. Each profession has leaders, pioneers who have gone above and beyond to challenge the weak perceptions that exist in this vague universe. These individuals have pioneered new research in their chosen fields and some have been laughed at and jeered, yet they have provided some of the most important advances in the modern world. The same parallels exist within the field of past lives and the regressive aspects of past lives. There are professionals who have been the catalyst for past life regression who were maligned, such as Edgar Cayce (the Sleeping Prophet). Yet Edgar Cayce, through his trance readings, has provided some of the most startling revelations connected to past lives.

When people discuss past life regression as a therapy in the modern-day world, one name is mentioned often: Dr. Brian Weiss. Dr. Weiss is the author of many books on the subject of past life regression and its application in modern-day healing modalities. He is at the forefront of exploration and past life therapy today. Dr. Weiss is a psychotherapist who accidentally fell into the realm of past lives when one of his patients spontaneously began to recount her past life and associated experiences. At first, Dr. Weiss was incredibly skeptical, yet this self-induced skepticism was eroded when the patient began to channel an intelligence that gave empirical evidence regarding Dr. Weiss's family and his loved ones who had passed on to the world of spirit.

Dr. Bruce Goldberg is another modern pioneer of past life research and like Dr. Weiss is the author of many past life books. Dr. Goldberg has carried out over 35,000 past life regressions and had some amazing successes to date. He continually researches and lectures internationally on the subject of past life regression. His book, *The Search for Grace*, was the basis for a movie made by CBS. He has appeared in the media many times and is often the guest of choice when hosts are looking for a professional to discuss past life regression therapy. Dr. Goldberg developed the field of progression hypnotherapy in 1977, along with the superconscious mind tap, a healing technique using hypnosis. In his own words, he states:

> *For thirteen years I was a practicing dentist using hypnosis on my dental patients, while maintaining a separate and full-time practice using hypnosis to regress patients into their past and future lives. As my reputation spread, I gave up my dental practice and became the country's only full-time hypnotherapist specializing in past life regression and future life progression (a field I developed).*

Edgar Cayce

Edgar Cayce was noted as one of the best psychics who ever lived. He came from a staunch fundamentalist Christian family and was brought up in the ways of the Bible, and this caused him to question his faith after his beliefs were challenged while in trance. Edgar was not an intelligent boy, and he also suffered from poor health. His unique abilities were discovered when he was induced into a hypnotic state in order to get information regarding his state of health. While in the hypnotic trancelike state, the young Edgar began to channel information regarding past life incarnations and otherworldly knowledge beyond the perception of the average human being. This went against everything that Cayce was taught as a Christian, and it shocked him deeply. However, he continued to work in the trance state when he realized that he could help to heal individuals' lives as he began to trust in the accuracy of his readings. Cayce conducted over 15,000 individual readings, which have been documented and can be viewed at the Edgar Cayce Foundation in Virginia today.

Scientific Research

There is a great deal of conjecture surrounding studies into past life regression, and this is primarily due to the need for anomalous tangible physical evidence, which is impossible within the earth plane today. This is a similar parallel to the scientific exploration into the continuation of consciousness in afterlife experimentation carried out by several institutions. Therefore, the only way that one can measure the anomalous intelligence that is collated is by carefully testing a regression exercise, but under scientific conditions and under proper scientific protocols. (The protocols ensure there is no room for fraud or false information, and ensures the integrity of the test.) The information lends itself to similar collaboration and so can be validated when analyzed. Therefore, after the testing is completed, the information must be properly validated if it is to withstand scientific scrutiny.

The saying of a world-renowned spiritual leader can sum up the reason for this research and why we would want to understand our past lives:

Reconciliation is to understand both sides; to go to one side and describe the suffering being endured by the other side, and then go to the other side and describe the suffering being endured by the first side.

—THICH NHAT HANH

CHAPTER 2

Ever Felt Like You've Been Here Before?

Imagine that presently you are on a trip with your family in a far-off destination, such as Japan. The more you integrate within the culture, the more you have a deep knowing that you have experienced this place before; perhaps you have that feeling that you have been there before. Maybe you experience some kind of fear that you have never felt before. This chapter will explain why you may be feeling the way you do in these situations. You will also learn the meaning of déjà vu and how it may be applicable to your journey—so do not dismiss it as fantasy or something weird.

That Déjà Vu Feeling

You've probably heard of déjà vu before, but perhaps you thought nothing of it or remained skeptical as to its real meaning and origin. *Déjà vu* comes from the French language and means "to have already seen." This is a literal translation, but it has a different sort of feeling when it comes down to the experience within conscious experience.

ESSENTIAL

You might have a sense of familiarity when visiting a historic place. Just being in the energy of this place will cause you to pick up the subtle nuances that still exist within the energy of the site. Emotions and energy of events will be held within the auric energy, and this is what you will perceive. This perception will be the catalyst to releasing the memories contained.

If you have ever felt that you have experienced an event or a time or a place before, then you have more than likely just experienced déjà vu. The truth is that many experience this often in their lives, but few actually recognize the feeling. The word that adequately describes this feeling or concept would be "familiarity," and this feeling of something familiar could come over you at any particular time. For instance, say you are on a business or recreation trip to the Highlands of Scotland and you decide to tour one of the castles in the town or area that you are visiting. On entering you feel something familiar. At that time, you may feel like you have been there before or that you have had some kind of experience there at the time that represents its history. This would be déjà vu, and there is probably some truth in the feeling you have just experienced. For the most part, most people will already have experienced several incarnations, and so it is within the realms of probability that you will at some point experience a déjà vu feeling. Even if you are drawn to go on vacation somewhere just because you like the idea of sun, sea, and sand, it is probable that you may have experienced the local culture before.

Inexplicably Drawn

Many of you will be drawn to a particular culture and will not know the reason why; you just seem fascinated with Indians, or those of the Middle East, or another culture. You might just contribute this to a keen interest because of some film you may have enjoyed or a fantasy that makes you feel better than you feel today. There are those, however, who are attracted to a culture and have no real explanation as to why. They may not even be drawn to the culture as portrayed in the cinematic view and would not go out of their way to watch anything pertaining to that particular lifetime. On the other hand, they may actively seek out ornaments, trinkets, and other items that denote that culture. This individual will have a sense of belonging, and possibly even of comfort, by having these items around him or on display within his home. This individual would be a good candidate for past life investigation. There is a very high probability that the reason he is drawn is because he has had some kind of experience with this lifestyle.

ESSENTIAL

Have you ever wondered why you have all those statues of Egyptians or Indians or Samurai around your home? Take another look at your pictures and the way you have decorated. Why do you listen to music from another era, even though you aren't old enough to have experienced it firsthand? Maybe this is because you have a past incarnation in that time frame. It's time to find out your real history.

Past Life Magnetism

Your desire to visit a particular foreign place is an example of past life magnetism. Past life magnetism is a theory (proposed by author and psychic medium Jock Brocas) that explains why you would be drawn to visit a distant land with no former or current connection to it. An individual may have a deep desire to visit a far-off country with no knowledge of it, no connections, or no experience of it. She just knows that she has to go there for some reason and will do anything in her power to get there, even if this means borrowing finances or changing life goals. The need to integrate is so strong that nothing will hinder her in the quest. This may even affect the relationships and the life choices she is faced with. This is a past life magnetism.

Repulsions

There is a chance that repulsions you are feeling to food, a situation, a culture, or an area could also be an inclination that you have had a past life history there, or that a past life fear has resurfaced in your present life and exists to a certain food or object. As previously discussed, you may be drawn to a particular culture. However, you could also have a deep-seated reason for disliking another culture. This could be the result of negative experiences you had in a past life within that culture. You could have experienced events that may have been terrifying, negative, or hurtful in many other ways. Perhaps people of this culture raided your village, and the invading marauders killed many of your friends and family. It could be that you were abused or mistreated by someone of the culture that you now carry a repulsion for.

Fears

What is fear? Fear can be understood through the acronym False Emotion Appearing Real, and this is very true, yet we are not born with fears. Fears are learned through experience of some description. They become a learned experience, a reaction to some stimulus, like Pavlov's theory. This theory is based on conditioned behavior that denotes a certain stimulus, which would cause an associated reflex within the subject.

Say your fear of water has a basis in a past incarnation. There are many who fear water, and that itself does not necessitate a belief that the fear you experience has roots in the past. However, if the fear had other fears associated with it, then a connection to a past life episode could be a possible explanation. Consider this example. If you had a fear of water and could not be around the sea or a swimming pool, then you could rationalize the explanation for the fear. But if you were also afraid of boats and anything to do with sailing or travel on water, then you might accept that the fear could have its roots in a past incarnation. Perhaps you drowned after falling off a ship in a past life.

FACT

Ivan Pavlov was a behaviorist. His studies were based around human behavior and the patterns that cause stimulus. Pavlov's theory was the hypothesis that behavior could be measured yet thought could not, and therefore stimuli from an outside environment would cause an appropriate physical reflex. Perhaps the greatest experiment that Pavlov is known for was the result of a stimulus directed at dogs. He would show one dog some food and the food would result in the dog salivating. Therefore, he noted that an external stimulus would cause an appropriate physical reaction. Pavlov then theorized on many other reflexes in behavioral patterns, such as the blinking of the eyes and other reflexive conditioning.

Some people have a fear of certain types of foods, and though this could be explained by a past trauma, if the food were of a foreign culture and they would normally eat other foods of that culture, chances are they may have experienced a negative event associated with that food. Perhaps they choked on that particular food and have carried that ingrained emotion with them into that life. The fear of heights affects many individuals, yet this type of fear can be explained as a past life event.

QUESTION

What is fear?
Fear is simply an emotion, but that emotion is often borne out of illusion. The fear is therefore not real. Fear can be used productively when its reality is identified; the negative energy can be enhanced and transmuted into something far more positive.

Hatred

The truth is that many of the fears you feel will have an associated trauma in the past, but this could also include negative feelings toward a different culture—a culture in which you experienced something negative in a past life. If you feel repulsion for a particular culture, there is the possibility that you have suffered at the hands of the culture in question. Rather than continue to feel resentment, which would inevitably cause further blockages in your life, it would be better to revisit the past and to learn to heal from it. Why cause any further suffering to yourself or others?

Trauma

It is said that traumas can last for lifetimes, that humans carry trauma with them. Individuals can also carry trauma with them from the recent past to this lifetime. A great deal of problems that may be associated with the ability to form meaningful relationships either in the home, in love, or at work can be attributed to past trauma. Someone who has experienced some form of abusive relationship will have tremendous difficulty in settling into a meaningful relationship with a partner or even in a close circle of friends. This is because of the trauma of the negative event. What if the individual has not experienced any form of abuse in this lifetime yet still comes up against barriers that cause problems within her relationships? The probability remains that it could be attributed to a past life trauma.

Physical Attributes

Dr. Ian Stevenson, MD, (who passed in 2007) researched perceptual studies and most notably past life cases while he was at the University of Charlottesville in Virginia. He maintained that individuals may even carry the facial features and scars of past life trauma. If someone had recounted the way she died, and if it was at the hands of a murderer or from an accident, the individual would very often show signs of that tragic passing in this lifetime. This would be revealed by scars that had no explanation as to their origin other than the way that the individual passed in the past life incarnation.

Phobias

Phobias are characterized as a fear of something, often an irrational fear involving a deep-seated dislike for a particular animal, such as spiders or snakes, or confined spaces or heights. The fear is real and can cause a great deal of discomfort for the individual. However, because most phobias are fears of some sort, they are an emotion that you can control.

Medical professionals and scientists look at phobias rather differently, and they often break them down into sections, such as simple phobias and complex phobias. To the scientist or medical professional, a phobia is a simple type of anxiety disorder. To the past life professional, phobias are widely considered as simple fears and complex fears. Simple phobias or fears are those previously discussed, such as spiders, snakes, or heights. They can be attributed to past lives as well as negative occurrences in the present incarnation. The complex fears are the ones that could be categorized as most likely associated with a past life incarnation. These are very deep and often emotionally and physically disabling. They may not be just one particular phobia but could include a group of phobias together. Not just a social phobia but more related to events and situations that involve simple fears.

ALERT

Do not think that all fears are the result of some past life trauma that has caused your conditions in your present existence. You may have a fear due to something that happened to you in this existence. For example, you may have burned yourself when you were younger, and this would be carried forward to your present.

Past life regression can often give you the keys to unlocking your phobias and fears. It shows you the reasons why you feel the way you do when associated with, or in direct contact with, an object or particular event. Therefore, understanding your past lives can aid you in healing your fears and phobias that affect you now.

Memories

Individuals who are experiencing past life episodes will often have their first encounter due to a past life memory. This past life memory will often be instigated during the sleeping process or will come as a flash of inspiration. While the individual sleeps, she will often have vivid dreams that recall past life events, places, and people with amazing accuracy. These memories are not just tied to the sleeping state and can come in subjective clairvoyant vision in the mind's eye at any given time.

In his book *Unlearned Language*, Dr. Ian Stevenson tells us of a case of past life memory recall. The case is about a young boy who suddenly and unexpectedly began to recount a life he lived before, in a town near to where he lived in the present. He told his parents where he lived before, and this included exact information that could be verified. His parents decided to investigate his claims and took him to the city that he described. Unbelievably, the child found his way to the previous place that he lived before. When he got to the property in the area, he recognized a woman there, and this woman would have been his wife in the previous incarnation. The young boy then recounted details to the woman with amazing accuracy, which she verified, and then to everyone's amazement, he gave her strict instructions to follow to find buried money that he put there. She followed the boy's instructions and found the sum of money that he had buried there previously.

Stimulated Memory

There is another phenomenon, called stimulated memory, that is a memory that is activated from a déjà vu feeling. Perhaps being at a certain place at a specific timeline can be the catalyst for the memory to resurface. Dr. Ian Stevenson again details a particular case where a woman had an instant memory recall outside a building that she visited.

Laure Raynaud was a French woman who had rebelled against religion in her earlier years; she claimed there was no heaven or hell and instead told her parents that individuals were reborn instantly in another body. She became an alternative therapist and specialized in a form of hypnotherapy. A physician, Gaston Durville, employed Raynaud in Paris. Raynaud often spoke about past life memories she was experiencing. She described the house where she lived, claiming that it was in a sunny climate and had large arched windows. She described the terrace that surrounded the house at the top and claimed that she lived there in the last century. Durville was obviously very skeptical of the young woman's claims, though when he was faced with strong evidence, he published the report on Raynaud.

Memory Recall in Italy

Durville sent Raynaud to treat a client of his in Genoa, Italy. Raynaud traveled there by train, and as she got closer to her destination, she began to experience the déjà vu feeling to which she had so readily become accustomed. This time, the familiar feelings were far greater and she knew that she had been there before—that she had lived there in a past life. When she was in Genoa, she shared her feelings and inquired if there was a building that was exactly the same as she had seen in her visions. Her host took her to a house that was supposed to match the description, but as Raynaud approached she explained that this was not the property that she had been aware of. As they drove farther through the countryside they came upon a mansion, and Raynaud instantly had memory recall. Everything was exactly as she had described. Probably the most convincing piece of evidence was to come, as she remembered the place where she was entombed. This memory recall was a further stimulus from seeing the house, and she had not experienced this memory before. Stevenson states, "She said that she was certain that in the previous life her body was not buried in the cemetery, but in the church itself." Durville investigated this statement through the church records and found some astonishingly accurate evidence. The mansion belonged to Benjamino Spontini, whose wife, Giovanna, was in fact buried in the church at Notre-Dame-du-Mont in a private ceremony. This is the evidence that eventually convinced Durville to publish the report based on Laure Raynaud's past life. It is perhaps one of the best cases to understand how past life evidence can be gained and verified in official records.

Famous Cases

There are two famous cases to discuss: Edgar Cayce's evidence of Jesus' past lives, and the past lives of Paul Kurabin. There is an element of interrelation and parallels in both. Edgar Cayce staunchly denied past lives due to his Christian background, but he gave much evidence in his readings of not only his own past lives but that of Jesus of Nazareth. He maintained that Jesus had many incarnations on a soul level and that his atonement by suffering the crucifixion was for the sin that was committed in the Garden of Eden. Of course, this can all be symbolic and have a hidden or deeper meaning. For instance, during one particular trance address, the trance controls (the guides able to overshadow and control the individual's mental and psychic faculties during a trance) known by Cayce said, "Yes, they are here"—which suggested there was a group of them. While Cayce was in the trance state, they revealed that Jesus was known as Amilius. He was reputed to be the expression of the Divine Mind and the Christ soul before the soul was incarnated into human form as depicted in the first book of the Bible (Genesis). The spirit team also maintained that Jesus was the being who lived during the time of Atlantis and was immeasurably responsible for the evolution of the human race by creating a physical form that souls could incarnate into, thus releasing humanity from the bondage of being apelike.

Jesus then became Adam, who was the first son of God; the Christ soul as depicted once more in Genesis. The same spirit team then stated that Jesus was the incarnation of Enoch, who was a human soul that was reputed to have risen to the heavens to receive the secret mysteries: "And Enoch walked with God: and he was not, for God took him" (Gen. 5:18–24). Then Jesus was Melchizedek, who was the high priest and king of Salem (Jerusalem). It is interesting to note that Melchizedek was depicted also as an angelic figure in the Dead Sea Scrolls.

In the Bible, it states that Jesus was the "high priest after the order of Melchizedek" (Ps. 110:4).

There are many more incarnations of Jesus as various figures depicted in the Bible, and these teachings would seem to parallel others in other texts, such as the book of Enoch and other religious scrolls.

Jesus is an important figure in history, but what about the normal men and women? There are many cases of normal people having a past life as someone famous. Paul Kurabin of New York experienced a past life as Major General George Pickett, who fought in the famous battle of Gettysburg. It is interesting to note that Paul experienced this using all of his spiritual gifts to identify his past life.

Also, there has been some discussion that would suggest that John F. Kennedy may have experienced a past life as Abraham Lincoln, as their karma seems to have been repeated almost identically in each case. When you study the facts, you will find there are amazing parallels in each life. There are amazing similarities in physical appearance to both presidents, and each was assassinated by an individual who shared the same characteristics as the other—even in appearance.

CHAPTER 3

Why Explore Past Lives?

There are tremendous benefits in taking time to delve into your past lives. In doing so, insights will be revealed to you that you may not otherwise consider in this life, and helpful information will be presented that you can learn from. This will be revealed to you in order to help you now in your current existence. In this chapter, you will learn the reasons why you would want or need to explore your past incarnations. You can learn more about your character, health, soul qualities, weaknesses, and the strength of your spirit gained from each singular life already experienced. Each lifetime builds on the lessons that have been learned, or not learned, during prior incarnations. These lessons may include (and are not limited to) spiritual growth, or lack of it, the development of soul qualities, or no improvement in the growth of the soul.

Soul Qualities and Past Incarnations

Soul qualities are those that shine through in your personality, nature, and character. Consider these important facts: Are you loving, gentle, kind-hearted, and do you have a peaceful mind? In contrast, do you feel anger, frustration, suffer ill health, and lack any inner peace in your daily life? You can look to the past to enlighten yourself and learn what you need to keep working on or why you may be suffering in the manner that you experience in the now. Furthermore, you may continually grow through any issues that reflect similar situations today that have been already experienced but not overcome.

QUESTION

What is the soul?
The soul is your essence; it is the eternal part of you that contains your spirit, your spark of the divine. It has all the qualities that made the universe and is in a continual state of growth. It is the eternal spark of divinity that can never go out, and it cannot be destroyed. The soul is the real self.

It can take many lifetimes to achieve a spiritual understanding in a certain lesson such as unconditional love and forgiveness, or other lessons such as trust, patience, tolerance, and kindness. Each lesson will be repeated through many lifetimes in a multitude of ways. This is so that every angle is covered in learning the complete aspects of what it means to be forgiving, patient, and tolerant. If you fail these lessons, you will have to continually go through them again and again until you learn—you cannot escape from this spiritual law. This is the reason why we may have to repeat our experience in a similar manner and repeat our cycles. The good news is that you have many chances to perfect your spiritual goals because you have eternal life, and this equates to more than enough time to achieve the desired results. But imagine if you have to experience something entirely negative. Is it not better to learn now than to continually experience that which may be bad in your life?

Committing to Soul Growth

Failure, therefore, is not something that can have any real hold on a person because there are always new lifetimes to continue on with until you fully mature through spiritual growth. Every single person on this planet is spiritual because, at our very nature, we are spiritual beings having a human experience and not humans having a spiritual experience. The difference between people is that they are all at different levels of soul growth and vibration. Some are immature souls with many lessons to learn and are only just starting out, others are halfway up the spiritual ladder (so to speak), and others are mature souls with a great level and understanding of spiritual truths. These often become spiritual teachers on the earth plane, guiding others along their life path and aiding them in reaching understanding and enlightenment.

ESSENTIAL

There is no such thing as failure. This is a perception only and a case of missed opportunities for growth. This is exactly the same as mistakes, for these are illusions also. If you look at these instances as an opportunity to grow and to learn, then you will not let the perceptions of failure and mistakes drag you down.

All of a person's past lives equate to the level of soul growth this person now holds in this incarnation. Consequently, this means that you keep on growing and learning continually, and when something is understood spiritually, the experience or lesson leaves only for something else to present itself to study, comprehend, learn from, and experience in the physical realm of the earth plane. The quicker a person is able to grasp that he has a spiritual responsibility to grow and serve others in each lifetime, the easier he will make his current existence and will set good karma for future lifetimes. Committing to spiritual growth is taking responsibility to mature as a soul, and unwillingness to take responsibility to spiritually mature will hold you back. This refusal of soul growth will just bring more powerful lessons to you in this life or your next, until you wake up and realize your spiritual potential and your true spiritual authority.

The Answer Is?

The past lives you already experienced hold the answers to those particular parts of your current life that you are having difficulty with, known as blocks or energy blocks or restriction of the soul's growth. Being aware of what you need to work at, and then applying the spiritual knowledge to these energy blocks, will help them to disperse and heal the connection they hold to the past life issue. This will then prevent you from taking it with you in a future life incarnation. Many things that are not overcome will be carried over to a new incarnation, and will continue to do so until the spiritual lesson is understood deep within your soul.

FACT

Past lives very often contain the hidden catalysts that cause your present conditions. Your fears are often caused from a past life incident, and even the relationships that you have now are orchestrated due to your past life lessons. This is the reason why visiting that life once more will help you to make the right life changes now.

Illness can be carried over from one lifetime to another, fears and phobias can be carried over, and unfinished business and the cycle of karmic balance will also be carried over. The reason you are where you are in this moment in time is due to all of your current actions, thoughts, and feelings that you have had in this lifetime so far, but also it is because of all prior actions already taken in all other lives lived. Problems experienced in this lifetime cannot be solved entirely by searching for answers in the present. Therefore, one can find solace and solution from researching your past incarnations.

Do You Really Want to Know?

Many people feel anxious about finding out more about their past lives, in case it is revealed to them that they were evil to others. They also may find out that something terrible befell them, such as being murdered or hurt in some awful way. Karma bonds people together, and any actions that have affected others by your own hand will bind you with them until good deeds are repaid and balanced. So many people made mistakes in the past, and these mistakes will keep repeating themselves until applying spiritual growth in each experiential event breaks the karmic cycle. This will ensure that you do not allow patterns to repeat themselves.

Negative Behavior

Humans can be stuck together in many negative patterns of behavior, such as the victim and the perpetrator, or the lover and the adulterer. These negative patterns bind them together. All of these are human factors and errors that belong to the earth plane, but when you apply higher spiritual solutions to them, then they will begin to dissolve and heal. Take a look at a few examples of people being bound together and who carry their circumstances from their past lives to their present.

Affairs

Many people who have affairs with others in this lifetime have been on the other end of the affair in a prior lifetime. This is the karmic wheel at work, and the two lovers are entwined together in each successive lifetime until lessons are learned and unconditional love prevails—not lust, passion, and temporary desires for selfish human gain. The lover is free to love anyone who is single but happens to fall in love with someone married; the married person allows this to prevail, and so they begin a karmic cycle that will continue on until higher spiritual choices are applied to the situation.

Any lie, false living, deceit, or intentional wrongdoing in a person's life will not only affect that person but will cause hurt and sorrow to others, so karmic debt will be accruing. This is why there is no excuse to allow human pleasure to override living the spiritual way. The spiritual way will bring blessings that will last longer than any temporary selfish earthly pleasure. Each lifetime will bring more difficult lessons, and the cycle will repeat until eventually one or both persons will gain spiritual insight into the error of their ways. This kind of spiritual insight can be applied to all other areas that you may be questioning now, such as: Do you really want to know why you are experiencing so much trouble in your love life? Do you really want to know why your finances are nonexistent? Do you really want to know why your health never seems to improve or why you were born with a condition that still affects you now?

The answer to these questions can help to alter the circumstances of your current existence, so, yes, it is not only helpful to know, it is also wise to know. Do not let your fear or anxieties stop you from looking into the past, because knowledge is powerful when you have the information needed to cause subtle changes in your current life.

Abuse: A Case Study

Pat had suffered abuse at the hands of relatives in the past (in this incarnation). Pat also had a terrible fear that haunted her, and she always felt she had witnessed a murder when she was young. Pat was shocked to find that she was murdered at some point in her past and that her abuse cycles had something to do with her past that presented itself in the present time. This feeling grew and would not leave her.

Pat then consulted a friend named Christine who was a past life therapist. Her friend suggested that evidence may lie in the past and that her answers could be revealed to her during regression. Pat then agreed to undertake the past life journey. Christine set the time and day, and when that day came, she settled Pat comfortably and began to take her into a hypnogogic state, the state of mind immediately prior to being fully asleep. This process of past life regression only accesses memories contained within the being, and at no time will any false image present itself. Therefore, if nothing negative was witnessed, then it would be safe to assume that Pat's feelings would have been falsified.

ESSENTIAL

Please remember that if you have ever suffered any form of abuse, it only takes one decision to stop that abuse and create a new cycle for yourself. Visiting your past life will help you take a subjective point of view and empower you to make the requisite changes in your life.

Pat was taken through a visual scene and asked to choose a gateway to walk through. She was asked to note the date—she clairvoyantly saw that it was 1942. Pat immediately saw herself as a child with the name of Elizabeth and stated that she was five years old. Further along in the regression, she became aware of a man that she was frightened of; this man stood before her and she felt this was the man who wanted to hurt her or who had hurt her. Further evidence was gained from the regression, and Pat was brought out due to her becoming upset.

A second regression session was set up, and as with the first, Pat went through the same process. Pat was asked to look for a gateway that had the number 1940 on it and to go through. She did this and was immediately faced with an older brother called Georgie; she witnessed herself and the brother playing with his wooden train set. She had a sister by the name of Anna, who shared her bed and was slightly older than Elizabeth now—she was five years old. Pat described her siblings, and this was noted; other details were offered without any prompting from the therapist. She said her mother's name was Margaret and did not see her father much. Elizabeth then stated that she liked to play in the garden but hated going alone due to the shadows she would see.

Pat continued the regression and had immediate recognition of many verifiable facts. She knew she had died at the hands of the man she saw previously. Pat had further evidence when she met with a medium who was friends with Christine and had no prior knowledge. The medium confirmed she had suffered abuse that followed her from a past life and that the man who had abused her in this life was the same man who reincarnated in this life to face his misgivings. Pat also had lessons to learn of forgiveness and compassion and was able to free her bonds that tied her to past life karma. This case is still ongoing!

Financial Ties

Financial issues are by far one of the most problematic issues of our time, no matter if it is within the close family unit or across global economies. Unfortunately, it seems that financial concerns drive the materialism in the world today. It is often burdened with the greed of man and the desire for power and control. This energy is almost as heinous as murder in the past incarnations that you may or may not have suffered from. Your financial issues, concerns, and drive can be a force of its own that is driven from past incarnations and past karmic responsibilities. These ties are often continued into your present life and represent lessons to be learned because past lessons were missed. It could also be past karma catching up with you, and inevitably this is a debt that must be paid.

The Benefits of Learning about Past Lives

There are so many benefits of discovering specific happenings located in your past lives. The principle and basis of past lives analysis is to identify the issues and causes of your ailments, diseases, and blockages within the present moment by revisiting the past. This visitation can, at times, awaken you to the events that may have been the catalyst to a specific fear, disease, or other problem that may be affecting you in the present moment, and it gives you an understanding of what may be causing issues in your life within the present time.

Healing

One lady had a terrible fear of water in her current life, and no matter what she did to help ease her fear, she could not go anywhere near water without breaking out into a panic attack. Finally, someone suggested she seek help from a hypnotherapist who had studied past life regression. The hypnotherapist soon located the overwhelming fear she had of being near water and discovered that in a prior incarnation she and her baby had drowned at sea.

This woman had such a dramatic death experience that she carried the fear deep within her soul and now her soul was alerting her to potential danger whenever she was around water in this lifetime. As her consciousness was able to pinpoint the cause of her fear, the past life therapist was able to help her heal from her trauma and move through her pain, forgiving herself and letting go of all the anxiety that was tied with her old death. Healing can happen when the cause of the symptoms is located and found, and if you cannot find the cause in your current existence, then it is wise to see if you can locate it in the past.

Real Soul Mates

Soul mates belong to a group of souls whom you already know from life between lives and when you rest in the spirit world. Real soul mates are connected to an eternal love bond that exists between them. They have such a strong bond and connection that if both soul mates are born on earth at the same time at different ends of the world, they will find each other. Soul mate love is like no other; it is unconditional, deep, everlasting, and, of course, spiritual. Another name associated with soul mates is twin souls; again, this is an interpretation of two souls entwined together with divine love for each other. It is not just human, man-made love. You do not always incarnate with your soul mate, but that does not mean that you can't still find happiness in your love life, especially if you learn from the mistakes you may have made in past lives. There is someone out there for you, and you will attract the person to you based on your own level of soul growth and spiritual vibration. Destined soul mates are those who have agreed to meet up prior to incarnation in this lifetime. You choose whom you will marry, have children with, and have the life partner that you will share companionship with for the duration of your life on earth. Of course, all the best-laid plans can go astray when free will plays out in a person's life—good intentions can be overcome by the indulgence of instant gratification.

ALERT

Even if you have not found soul mate love in this incarnation, that does not mean there is no soul mate for you. You can still have love in this life that will be fulfilling and happy. Soul mates exist through many lifetimes and are destined to be together.

Recognizing Your Soul Mate

Look at the person who swears that she is in love with her soul mate, but her so-called soul mate just happens to be married to someone else but is engaging in a long-term relationship with her as well. What you see is a person who is in sweet denial about the person who she believes is her soul mate. Her real soul mate would not hesitate to realize his mistake in being married to someone else and would end his loveless marriage so that he could be with his real soul mate. Soul mates would never live a lie with another person, preventing them from being fully connected to their one real love. Sweet denial is so strong that the person is prepared to wait it out, because she is so sure that one day her soul mate will leave his partner and come to be with her. What is happening is they are creating a karmic triangle that, if not broken and healed in this lifetime, will carry the players and all parts with them into another lifetime. Soul mates do not cheat, and they will go to great lengths to be together sincerely, as their love goes beyond the bounds of human passion.

QUESTION

Is there more than one soul mate for an individual?
This is a good question, and one that invokes many answers. In truth there is only one true soul mate—the other half of you. But there is such a thing called soul love, which is when two souls of the same group are brought together due to similar vibrational attraction.

When someone is stuck in believing she is with her real soul mate but is actually in a deceitful relationship, she will be preventing real love from finding her in this lifetime, unless she faces the pain of the fact that she is with the wrong person. She needs to end the relationship and move forward so that she can heal from the pain of her mistake and be free to attract the right kind of love. Real soul mate love exists, and it is written into your life that you will find and be with your soul mate—but you can also make silly human mistakes that prevent or delay this from happening. This is also free will.

How do you know when you meet your soul mate? You will know at the level of your soul; you will also feel like you have known him forever; you will feel at ease in his presence; you will feel like you can trust him deeply; you will feel fulfilled, and again as previously mentioned, you will know deep within your soul. Do not be disappointed if you believe your soul mate is not with you now, as you can begin to make those subtle changes that will open the door for your soul mate to enter. If you believe your soul mate may be in the spirit world and that is the reason you feel lonely in this lifetime, then know that you are still able to find spiritual love with another soul who resonates on the same level of spiritual growth as you do. You can begin to attract him to you when you stop feeling lonely and know that there is someone out there for everyone.

Making Connections

Connections between souls exist because of the soul group to which they belong in the spirit realm of life between lives. A soul group will consist of a number of souls varying in different levels of soul growth with the objective of helping each other to evolve and grow through each lifetime. The reason some souls will be of higher spiritual growth is for the purpose of guiding those who may have less awareness in accomplishing victory in their lessons on the earth plane. The whole of the group will agree on issues to be overcome and worked on in each new lifetime prior to incarnation. Someone who was your mother in a past life could be your daughter/son in this lifetime. There are so many different roles that someone from your soul group can agree to fulfill for you, to learn preplanned experiences on earth.

Family Soul Group Connections

Past lives are connected to the reincarnation of your continued soul group. You have lived many lives with these spirits and have agreed to help each other spiritually evolve. Sometimes some members of these soul groups will agree to incarnate, experiencing difficult life circumstances for the purpose of bringing specific lessons to all concerned in the family group.

For example, say that a family line on earth lacked all kinds of awareness of spiritual principles or ignored the fact that a higher power exists all around them. This lack of awareness can be because of spiritual ignorance, and so a spirit is born into the family with the intention of bringing this awareness out in them. This may not be easy, as the spirit may have his work cut out because he feels like the black sheep of the family, or he just feels so different from the rest of the family group. This bloodline will be enhanced from spiritual growth that is being brought to help them if their free will allows them to change their ignorant ways. Spiritual connections will continue to exist until all things are worked out from family lines. Such issues that are carried on continuously in the family line are anger, abuse, betrayal, hardheartedness, and any kind of negative traits that are not healed from one family to the next.

QUESTION

What is a soul group?
A soul group is a group of spirits or people (as in spirit people) of the same soul vibration. They have existed for all time, and each individual soul has agreed to be of service to those souls that need them within their soul group. In terms easy to understand, if you can imagine the ancient North American Indians, they lived in tribes, and each member supported the other and lived in harmony according to universal law. This model is similar to a soul group.

Other Soul Group Connections

Connections between souls can happen at any time throughout your life, and maybe you have previously agreed to connect at a specific age along your life path to fulfill a certain purpose, and then you can both go your separate ways. Small connections like this happen often, such as with neighbors, friends, and strangers who cross your path. Others are longer lasting, such as marriage, best friendships, and long-term relationships. There is always something to learn from whomever is in your life at present so you should look for the lessons that each person can bring. You may have finished with an old love relationship, but ask yourself: Did she bring out the best in you? And are you a nicer person because of what she brought to the relationship? You will always learn from another person in your life. Maybe the other person inspires you to be more joyful, carefree, openhearted, responsible, or just to be yourself. It is important to keep working on yourself when you notice these spiritual qualities within another.

It's a Kind of Magic

Carl Jung first coined the term "synchronicity," which is when two seemingly coincidental events join to make an event a meaningful one. Synchronistic events happen, and it can be like something magical has occurred. Two souls just happen to be in the right place at the right time, and sparks fly as they are drawn together. This can be the start of a long-lasting, loving relationship. There are no such things as coincidences; coincidental events, circumstances, and meeting certain people can come your way due to a kind of magic. These are auspicious times, and when heaven moves to bring magic into your path, this is when you need to take action.

Emotional Attraction

Sometimes you meet someone and you will feel a strong emotional attraction to the individual. This does not have to be a romantic inclination, as it can be friendship too. Have you ever met someone for a few moments and you feel like you have known that person all of your life? If so, this is called soul recognition, which means at the soul's level you already know each other, but at the human level you fail to realize who it is you are with. This can also happen in the opposite way. If you find someone who gives you the creeps or someone you have taken an instant dislike to, maybe you are recognizing them from a prior existence and there is still some karmic connection between you. This can also be explained as some type of negative vibrational attraction through the magnetic field.

CHAPTER 4

Piercing the Veil of Reality

You will now move into the realms of past life regression; it is here that you will truly begin your journey. This is the crossroads at which you stand, the veil between reality as perceived with your physical attributes and the perceived reality that you are entering now, where you will use your other senses. You will learn what it means to receive the visions of the past and weigh your expectations of what is actual reality. The perceptive veil is extremely thin—read on to learn about this veil and how to break through it. It's all about perception.

Dealing with Past Life Expectations

The reality of your past lives will differ from your expectations because your expectations are often rooted in fantasy or desire. One does not resonate with the other. Individuals often have expectations of life and of their status, situations, or of perceived ideas that are not in line with their present reality. The expectations remain out of the ordinary and not within their normal everyday reach—within the present moment—so the expectations of the past may be steeped in fantasy. This fantasy illusion is eradicated immediately when you enter the realm of the time traveler and visit the past to gain insight and answers.

Quantum Explanations

There is a difference in life between needing, wanting, and desire. Two of these emotions (want, desire) are driven by the emotional ego, so you must recognize the difference: The universe will always give you what you need and that which is in harmony with your current vibration, not necessarily what you want or desire. This may seem a little absurd; to explain the meaning behind it, consider quantum physics in a layman's way. You emit a frequency, a vibration rather like the note you hear when striking a piano key. After you have struck this key, the sound waves travel and affect people in different ways. If a crystal glass is placed at the other side of the room, it will respond to the vibration by ringing in response to the note—this is resonance in its simplest form. Similarly, you emit a vibration, and what you attract in life depends on the rate of that vibration. Therefore, the universe will only respond to the harmonic frequency that you emit in the present moment, and so in this particular field of resonance, you attract what you give out. This means that if you are consistently telling the universe that there is not enough to go around, or that you are always a victim, this is what you will experience.

The Law of Attraction

You attract what you need because of the resonance of your frequency under the universal law of attraction. However, desire and wanting are ego-driven emotions and are not in synch with the universal laws or universal harmony. So, you see that your expectations are not in line with what you need, and as a spiritual being in the present, all is in resonance to your emitted frequency. Your expectations are almost always higher than what you will attract. That is not to say that you cannot expect anything and bring it into conscious awareness if it is in line with your spiritual makeup, which you may understand as destiny and what may be included in your spiritual life.

QUESTION

What is the law of attraction?
The law of attraction is a spiritual law that is perfect in operation. To understand this law, it is easier to learn the phrases "What you give out, you get back" or "What you omit, you attract." This has a close relation to the law of karma but is rather easier. By using the law of attraction, you work with the universe to attain what you most desire or what matches your vibration that you omit. It means you attract to you what your vibration is at the time, whether it is life lessons or material worth. The point is that all must be in line with your spiritual point of attraction or vibration. For more on this subject, see *The Everything® Law of Attraction Book*.

Recognizing your spiritual point of attraction will help you to reduce your expectations when you begin to investigate your past life history. This is because, as you begin, you will undoubtedly expect far more due to your lack of knowledge and understanding. So how do you recognize this point of attraction? Well, in truth, it cannot be taught, as it is beyond a conceived notion or idea and can only come from an inner "aha!" moment. Nevertheless, you have this book to be your light and guide to navigate the problems that others have experienced, and working carefully through it will help you to reach that moment in the present when it arrives.

Expectations Revisited

Now, revisit your expectations; they probably will not be in line with what you may receive. You may expect to hear and see spirits, or to have amazing epiphanies, or to see images similar to those you may have witnessed in Hollywood movies. You may even think that you were Jesus or King Herod, or have another idea based on pure fantasy. These expectations are not real and are often born of environmental fantasy rather than experiential fantasy. (Experiential fantasy can be switched on through visual experience such as a movie or recognition of your innate powers.) You have to enter into the journey with no expectations and allow yourself to paint your own canvas by unlocking the memories of your past in your superconscious. These memories will come to the surface naturally and you will view them from an objective point; the memory will not be forced and will often be what you least expect. Perhaps you were expecting to read the word "subconscious," but this is entirely different, and you will learn about those levels of consciousness in Chapter 7.

The Real World Versus the Lucid Vision

The real world differs from the world you may perceive through lucid visions, yet you must understand that *real* is only a perceived idea that is learned by others' perceived notions and beliefs. What if the lucid perception is in fact the reality and what you term as "real" is in fact an illusion? The veil between illusion and reality is thin indeed, and therefore it is only a matter of perception versus understanding; the scales of perception can easily be weighed one way or the other.

An atom is a tiny thing, but you cannot see it with your physical eyes. There has to be an instrument that allows you to see this thing, and this instrument is a microscope that is so advanced it can view the atom in its present condition. The atom vibrates at a certain frequency, and that frequency attracts other atoms that are harmonious with it. The atom binds with those it is in resonance with, and the binding and vibration together gives us the perception of something solid and tangible. This means that what you perceive with your physical eyes can be broken down to its constituent atoms; it is only the resonance and binding phenomena that allow you to perceive this tangible thing. It could be suggested that what you see with your physical eyes is in fact an illusion. In essence, therefore, reality is only a perception, and the veil of that perception is thin.

When you begin to meditate and delve into your past lives, or you access your soul's blueprint for information pertaining to your soul's path, your personality and traits, and your soul's lessons, you would be wise to recognize that your perception is your reality and your reality is your perception.

Lucid Visions

Lucid visions are exactly that—lucid, which literally means rational and clear. So it is like being there in that moment and experiencing what you are seeing as tangible and realistic. Lucid visions can be likened to watching a DVD of your favorite movie in 3D and feeling like you are there—experiencing all the emotions that conjoin to dance with your senses. The vision awakens the deep-seated emotions within your consciousness such as happiness, sadness, and compassion. It is like having a conscious experience in the here and now and having that experience affect you on an emotional level.

Lucid visions can be broken down into two states of conscious experience. There is the conscious lucid visionary experience and the dream state experience of lucidity. Physicist and former director of Project Stargate, Dale E. Graff, who has continued his study into dream state psi (psychic sensory information) and conscious psi, coined these two states of consciousness.

Dreaming

Everyone dreams, and research indicates that you dream at least eight times per night, perhaps more or less depending on your emotional state. Most fail to remember their dreams, and the ones that you do remember are almost always of some importance. These are the lucid dreams that seem so real and tangible that they are etched onto your conscious memory. A lucid dream is so real that when you awake from it, you feel rather disoriented, just as if you feel you are in a different reality. You will learn more about the dream state and the methods used to recall and investigate your past lives through your dreams in Chapter 11. You can also wake up and remember a dream that seems so silly and stupid that it is more amusing than anything, and this would most probably be the result of your conscious thinking mind overworking before you sleep. The dream state recognition experience is different.

Cultural Taboos of Psychic Exploration

Unfortunately, the world is fraught with taboos that are brought on by lack of understanding, ignorance, and, most of all, fear of the truth. Most of what is considered wrong is again only a level of perception. Much of modern society is dogmatic, and one man's dogma may be entirely different from another's. Because of this division, misconstrued perceptions and beliefs between cultures have resulted in conflicts and wars.

ALERT

Before you jump to conclusions or follow preconceived perceptions, you must recognize that religion is not a divine gift given by the creator; instead it is man-made. At no time did enlightened beings such as Jesus, Buddha, or Mohammed come and say that they were going to start a new religion. They came to teach lessons of love, forgiveness, and compassion.

Delving into the psyche to gain insights and information is considered blasphemous in most religions and belief systems. Your own belief system may even suggest that it is entirely evil to investigate anything that may be perceived as paranormal in nature. If you only accept whatever you are told by another individual who claims to have "the answers," it could result in the manifestation of problems, which cause suffering, hatred, and a separation from society and reality. You are supposed to turn to your belief system or seek enlightenment and guidance from the head of your belief system. However, how can you be helped if the representative's perception is weak? And what if that person is also misguided, just a product of dogma?

ALERT

You must remember that religion is a man-made thing, which means it is man's interpretation of something. Be wary of interpretation that is born from ignorance and the desire for material power. You must ensure that you do not follow blindly what anyone tells you is right. Turn to your inner spiritual authority and discern if it sits well with you. If it does, accept it; if not, discard it.

A wise philosopher once said, "Perception is strong and sight is weak," but the truth is that perception can only be strong if you do not allow sight to govern your perceived ideas and notions. Jesus of Nazareth stated that all answers are within, as is the kingdom of God. This means that any problem that may arise in your life can be dealt with effectively by going within and seeking the answers or the way to resolution. Surely this is also a green light that shows you that you are not delving into anything paranormal or evil. Buddha, Mohammed, and many others also stated the same thing, but perhaps phrased it differently.

What Is Reality?

Are you living in a world of illusion, or is what you see the only reality? This journey will obviously challenge your own beliefs, as you will begin to perceive a world that is different and may not conform to old beliefs and perceptions. You have learned that what you are seeing is energy, energy that is illusionary and transitory. How does it make you feel? Look at something that is tangible and can be touched with your body and seen with your eyes. Examine your emotional state at that precise time, and then train your mind to accept that it is not really there; it's an illusion brought on by the dance of energy. It will never be destroyed—it can only be manipulated—and the energy can change its current form into another form that you may perceive differently. This statement should empower you as you begin to realize that you cannot be destroyed and may only resume another form.

Impermanence

Energy that cannot be destroyed is what is understood as impermanence. The energy changes but it still exists. Now, delve into this impermanence: see where it may lead and how it might explain past lives. Imagine a candle; as the candle burns away, it will radiate heat all around it and will emit light. The heat and the light are energy in a different form but still exist as atoms, as does the candle. Therefore, it could be said that all constituents are as one and do not exist separately. As the candle burns down, the wick in the center burns away and is sent into the atmosphere as light wisps of smoke. The smoke will rise and go up into the atmosphere, joining with all the elements of nature. It will go into the air and become the clouds, and so as the energy changes, it will become the rain and continue its cycle, falling once more onto the earth. At this point it will nourish the land and the flora and fauna will grow. Beautiful flowers will emerge and bloom as a result of the nourishment in the ground that came from the atmosphere that contained the burned candle. A bee visits the wondrous flower and collects the pollen that makes the honey and creates wax. This is the cycle—the wax then becomes the candle once more. You can see from the example that the cycle is one of impermanence, nonduality, and oneness. The atoms that are contained are atoms and only change form. They are not destroyed, and so in the impermanence of nature there is formlessness, which reconstituted by atomic energy becomes an illusion of form and therefore continues and cannot be destroyed.

QUESTION

Why is impermanence so important?
The reason is because energy cannot be destroyed. If energy could be destroyed, then creation would discontinue and matter would have only one linear life expectancy. This also would cause a catastrophic chain reaction. If disaster struck, then life could be destroyed and would not continue to flourish and grow. Therefore, there would be no reason to live and learn. Life is eternal, and therefore energy is the life force.

Form Follows Form?

The aforementioned example is just that—an example—to show you how impermanence does not stop you from becoming reconstituted as something else or another form of the same subject. And so, as you pass from this world onto the next, you will see that you only change form, and so you can reform in another form at another time. This is the simplest example that may explain how one could possibly exist in many lifetimes. One point to note is that just because the candle changes form due to its spent energy, it does not cease to be a candle. The same point can be made with your existence: You do not stop existing.

So the illusion is only your perception, because you are real and your energy is real. Your impermanence, which is an important factor, is also real—you can change form and can exist once more in another form. This other form does not have to change its base makeup; you may not incarnate as a butterfly, but you can reincarnate as someone else.

Can Past Life Regression Cure You?

Humans are naturally inquisitive and in constant investigation, looking for cures for diseases or ailments or solutions to problems in their lives. Cures suggest that you heal something or treat an illness through to a successful conclusion. It also means to resolve a problem, to preserve something, or to make something stronger.

As previously discussed, revisiting your previous incarnations can heal you from your emotional turmoil, your fears and your weaknesses, from the past that you may have carried with you to the present moment. Can it heal you from disease? Well, that depends on what event could be connected to the manifestation of the emotion that created the disease. Consider that you are treating your problems in the present by learning from the past. Then you are treating to arrive at a successful conclusion. This is also a means to solve a problem, preserve something, or make something stronger. Visiting your past incarnations and learning from the missed opportunities or lessons that you have taken part in will help you to resolve issues that may be the result of past experience. Those issues may be solved in the present moment by a simple act of self-realization. Take these entire factors into consideration; discovering your past life experience most definitely can be a cure when understood in the correct context.

Learning from Your Past (Life)

What you should be hoping to do is to learn from the past by simply examining your past issues that may have arrived in your present moment or your present incarnation. Why are you an angry individual, why do you act the way you do, and why have you not been able to change the mistakes you may keep making within your relationships? Could there be an answer as to why you have the addictions that may be destroying you in this lifetime? But what does this learning from the past mean? When you consider history, you should arrive at the conclusion that you may have learned from past mistakes, but you would be gravely misguided.

ALERT

An unfortunate circumstance of man's ego means that we fail to learn from past mistakes. One only has to investigate milestone events in history to deduce that history certainly does repeat itself. This repetition of the event or essence of the event in a timeline is because as a human race we fail to learn from the missed opportunities to grow. This is humanity's own cycle of abuse.

The reason is that some of the lessons humans have learned involve some kind of evolution, but as a human race, the cycle of abuse continues in this lifetime, and humans are repeating those mistakes that have been made in the past. For instance, how many wars have there been from those same ego-driven desires, such as the need for wealth, power, and control? These wars are still continuing in the present—again due to the same desire for wealth, power, and control. This has a domino effect on your financial status, and, like a vicious cycle, more suffering and pain circulates. This suffering can spill over to your personal life. You also can deduce that, as a race, there seems to be a distinct lack in learning from others' experiences.

CHAPTER 5

Reincarnation—Is It True?

Reincarnation has been discussed for centuries and has been alluded to in many belief systems. There is no scientific basis of fact for reincarnation. Instead, one has to measure the information that is transmitted in writing or by word through some form of intermediary such as a medium, a hypnotherapist, or an enlightened being. This being, other than the hypnotherapist, would have already incarnated on the earth plane before and now returns in the present moment to teach. In this chapter you will learn about reincarnation and will be provided with ideas, perceptions, and theories that will allow you to make an informed decision and arrive at your own conclusions with regard to the potential and reality of incarnation.

What Is Reincarnation?

Reincarnation is not just a fancy word used by New Age followers and members of religious cults; nor is it a far-out idea that has just arisen in recent times. The fact that the concept of reincarnation has existed for thousands of years and is alluded to in cultures that follow no religious creed or doctrine as well as those that do should make you consider that there must be something to this theory.

ALERT

It is said that reincarnation first became a concept in ancient Egypt, though there is no proof of this. Perhaps it was the first time that it was taken seriously—the Egyptians believed they would reincarnate at some point when the soul had established itself through its various journeys and lessons.

Imagine that when you pass from this earthly existence you will be reincarnated into another existence. Some believe that you incarnate into another body, while others believe that you incarnate into another existence—not just a human form but perhaps an animal, as alluded to in the Buddhist traditions. No matter what you believe, the easiest way that you can understand reincarnation is to view it as a means of living again as someone else or something else. "Reincarnate" is understood as "rebirth," meaning a rebirth of the soul and its faculties—but in a new vessel. This means that the soul, or what you think is "you," is not destroyed but reincarnates with all the scars and lessons that it has gained from the past. This is another reason why you would want to revisit your past incarnations—to learn from them.

Religious Beliefs and Reincarnation

As mentioned previously, religion has its own perceptions and belief in reincarnation. People tend to believe in reincarnation as a second chance to right the wrongs that they have done in the past, and so this ideology sits very well. In Christianity, this is a divided issue, primarily due to inconsistencies in sacred texts. For instance, Jesus intimated that John was previously Elijah, which obviously suggests that he was reincarnated as John the Baptist.

The following passage in the Bible supports this belief:

For all the prophets and the law have prophesied until John. And if you are willing to receive it, he is Elijah who was to come. (Matt. 11:13–14)

Matthew continues to write and shows that Jesus further supports the statement by saying:

And the disciples asked him, saying,

"Why then do the scribes say that Elijah must come first?" But he answered them and said, "Elijah indeed is to come and will restore all things. But I say to you that Elijah has come already, and they did not know him, but did to him whatever they wished. So also shall the Son of Man suffer at their hand." Then the disciples understood that he had spoken of John the Baptist. (Matt. 17:10–13)

Clearly, Jesus was talking about the possibility or the belief in reincarnation; however, other areas of the New Testament contradict this belief. Hebrews 9:27 states, "and in as much as it is appointed for men to die once, and after this becomes judgment." Surely this is a rebuttal to the belief in reincarnation. However, you must consider that as there is no death in the sense of a finality of the mind, body, and soul, it could be suggested that a person only dies once when he finally goes home to his rightful place—when he becomes one with God (or the creator) and is no longer a separate consciousness. Each statement can be taken to mean many different versions of a truth, and this is why there are so many concepts and changes in perception.

Corinthians reveals what is supposedly a secret mystery known only to a few: "Listen, I tell you a *mystery*: We will not all sleep, but we will all be changed" (1 Cor. 15:51). Again, this suggests that immutable fact that one cannot die and therefore will only change, which is the belief in reincarnation. It would seem the Christian belief system is very divided when it comes to reincarnation, yet other religions have a more understanding view.

Judaism and Reincarnation

Now examine the Jewish religion and see where the parallels lie. The Jewish historian Flavius Josephus writes that the Pharisees were a Jewish community who believed in reincarnation. They believed that souls of evil men would be punished after death to dwell in Sheol (hell) for eternity, and the souls of good men would be removed and enter into other bodies with the power to be reborn again in another incarnation. He further states that the Sadducees, which were more puritan in their beliefs, rejected the belief that was held by the Pharisees. They believed only in Sheol and so concluded that there was judgment: evil souls dwelt there, and good souls went to their version of heaven.

If you study the New Testament, you will deduce that many individuals thought that Jesus was the reincarnation of one of the prophets. Similarly, they believed the same with John the Baptist. Jesus made two distinctions: He maintained that there were differences in the peoples' belief, and he tried to rectify those old perceptions by making a distinction between spiritual reincarnation (rebirth) and physical reincarnation.

You should now be able to see that even with the concept of reincarnation, it comes down to two facets of the one concept. Spiritual reincarnation can mean the rebirth of the spirit or of the soul in an ethereal sense, and physical reincarnation would be the rebirth in another body in another dimension in time.

Buddhism and Reincarnation

The concept of reincarnation is closely linked with the spiritual law of karma in the sense that you reap what you sow, which is also a concept taught by Jesus in the New Testament. This seems to be a constant that exists throughout the Buddhist faith. Furthermore, in Buddhism, reincarnation takes on a new meaning but with similarities to Christianity. Buddha recounted many of his past lives, and 550 of them were written about and described. This shows clear evidence of the belief in reincarnation and past lives. Yet, there is a distinct difference in the understanding of reincarnation. The Buddhist principle of reincarnation is founded upon the premise of energy and the fact that energy can be reformulated into anything. This means that if you were to be reborn, you would not necessarily be reborn as another person; you could incarnate as an animal such as a lion or a butterfly—these were also the lives that were recounted by the Buddha himself.

FACT

Buddha was considered an enlightened being and achieved the enlightened state while he was searching for the root cause of suffering. His original name was Siddhartha Gautama, known as the Buddha, and he was born in the sixth century B.C. in what is now modern Nepal. His father was the ruler of the Sakya people. He married at the young age of sixteen. His father had ordered that he live a life of total seclusion, but Siddhartha eventually left his palace and went out into the world. He was confronted with the reality of the inevitable suffering of life, and after spent his time learning how to appease universal suffering.

There is another concept that can be linked with the premise of reincarnation: the concept of impermanence. Everything, according to the Buddha, is impermanent, for one state cannot remain the same for eternity; the very nature of energy is a process of change. This means that there are constant births and rebirths, which runs parallel to the conceptual belief in reincarnation. It could then be said that there is no coming or going, that one exists eternally. Therefore, death in itself means that one goes somewhere when one passes, and that same individual had to have come from somewhere. When the conditions are sufficient, then a being manifests, and that manifestation would mean the continuation of the experience in another form and with a consciousness of its own. When the conditions are no longer sufficient, beings do not exist. In the same way, this can be reincarnation and the process of birth and rebirth.

Hinduism and Reincarnation

In Hinduism, reincarnation takes on a different premise again but shows many parallels in its roots. According to Hinduism, the soul has to incarnate in many bodies to learn lessons and achieve a state of enlightenment. It is then believed that when this state is reached, the soul will return to its source and become one. This birth and rebirth process is covered in the understanding of creationism, which suggests when the creative process is switched on, the soul then hides behind a false personality called Jiva. This consists of the subtle body with an outer personality understood as mind, and Ego, which is the physical aspect. This subtle body and subtle mind has a discretionary intelligence, which succumbs to desires and external influences and impulses. At the end of the life cycle, the physical body and mind return to the earth, and the soul, or Jiva consciousness, survives. Depending on the experiences and lessons learned, the soul or Jiva either ascends to heaven or descends into hell. There it will stay until it pays back its karmic debt and is reborn into another incarnation.

Reincarnation for Native Americans

The premise of rebirth exists for North American Indians. The Indians' belief in reincarnation was centered on the interconnectedness of nature and Mother Earth, and the process of birth and rebirth was a natural facet of universal law. The Indian traditions were steeped in the belief of the spirit world and of what you may understand as the paranormal. There was a constant interaction of spirit communication between those of the world beyond and the human forms on the earth plane. This communication was achieved by trance communication, vision quests, and soul journeys the Indians would take.

Does Everyone Reincarnate?

Before this question is answered, look at what information is gleaned by the process of trance communication from those of the world beyond. Silver Birch was the trance control of a medium by the name of Maurice Barbanel in London. Silver Birch had experienced his earthly incarnation as a North American Indian and offered words of wise counsel to millions of individuals through his communications, which appeared in print and in audio form. Silver Birch also offered information of an evidential nature, which gave him added creditability. One thing to note is that the guide never asked for anyone to believe him; instead he asked that you try to test every piece of information that he gave for yourself. If it sat well with you and was validated in some way, you would have used your own free will.

The Hannen Swaffer Circle was the original circle where the famed spirit guide Silver Birch made his appearance through the medium Maurice Barbanel. Hannen Swaffer was a mainstream journalist in London. He set the circle up to investigate the reality of life hereafter, and the guide made his appearance one evening when Barbanel initially went to discredit the circle. Barbanel fell into a deep trance and when he came to, he apologized for falling asleep during the séance. To his amazement, he was told that he was in trance and his guide, Silver Birch, introduced himself to the sitters. The following conversation is a transcript of a sitting in the Hannen Swaffer Circle:

We were discussing reincarnation during a lull in one sitting.

Suddenly, in the middle of the discussion, Silver Birch's medium was entranced, and we found ourselves talking, not to an antireincarnation sitter, but to a proreincarnation spirit guide.

"I do not agree with you," said the spirit to Swaffer, who had been loud in his denial of the theory. "Tell me this," said Swaffer. "Why am I, so far as I can see things, the direct descendent of my ancestry?"

"Show me one of your ancestors who could have done the work you do," countered the guide.

"I belong to a different period," said Swaffer. "My grandmother was as dominant a character as I am."

"You talk of the things of the brain. I mean the things of the spirit."

"Well, then, tell me about my previous incarnations," said Swaffer.

"No, it does not matter," the guide replied.

"But you have reincarnated, whether you agree with it or not. Which one of your ancestors, do you think, gave you the power to be inspired?"

"One of my relatives, who died before he was twenty-eight, was one of the greatest poets who ever lived," remarked Swaffer, referring to John Keats.

"Yes, I know," the spirit said, "and that is carried forward in the blood-stream. But which one has swayed meetings?"

"He swayed people by thousands," said the sitter. "When he wrote, 'A thing of beauty is a joy for ever,' it went round the world."

"Tell me which one of your ancestors was an orator?"

"That I cannot tell you," admitted Swaffer.

"Tell me which one was born from among the low and the humble and walked with kings and princes."

"That is largely because of my occupation," said Swaffer. "They lived in the country and I live in London."

"But they were born in the country and you were born in the country."

"I have a young brother, twenty years younger than I am, who is one of the best journalists in Fleet Street," went on Swaffer.

"Does he sway the thoughts of millions?" asked the guide.

"No, but he might."

"But he does not."

"No, but I did not when I was his age," replied Swaffer.

"It is your physical body that comes from your physical parents," said the guide.

"Your soul is of the Great Spirit. The qualities of the soul are those which you unfold for yourself. Your material body is determined by heredity, by environment, by the health of the parents. Those things affect the things of matter, but not the soul."

"But, if there is reincarnation," urged Swaffer, "why do not human beings improve at a greater rate? They seem to me to improve as the conditions outside them improve."

"Yes, but the conditions improve only as human beings improve," said the guide.

"But they seem to improve at the same rate," objected Swaffer.

"No, it is because the spirit improves that the conditions improve," said the spirit.

"Yes, but the conditions react on the spirit."

"You are putting it the wrong way round," said the guide. "Improvement starts with the spirit and expresses itself in matter. It does not start with the expression in matter and then evolve the spirit."

"That is an argument about spirit, not about reincarnation," said Swaffer. "If we are constantly reborn, why cannot we produce men greater than Homer, Shakespeare, or Simpson? Why are not the types always improving? You only improve the types as you improve the conditions around the people."

"What you call types refer to the things of matter. I refer to the quality of the spirit."

"Is there today a man with a finer spirit than Socrates?" asked Swaffer.

"Oh, yes."

"Or Jesus of Nazareth?"

"No."

"Or Joan of Arc?"

"Yes."

"No, my logic rebels against reincarnation," remarked Swaffer.

"I know," said the guide, "and therefore you are right not to accept it."

"I am taught to accept only those things which can be proved to me," said Swaffer. "I accept you but I must not be expected to take from you things which rebel against my sense of logic."

"You have known me a long time," said the guide. "Have I ever asked you or anyone to accept that which your reason rejects?"

"No," admitted Swaffer. "Then I am told that when I evolve to a certain condition I shall be able to accept the theory of reincarnation naturally. Are the people who accept it more evolved than I am?"

"No," replied the spirit. "Sometimes they do it because it gives them an opportunity for thinking that they are frustrated. There are some of the evolved souls who know about their past incarnations. But you have reincarnated. So have I."

"Why, when you passed on three thousand years ago, did you not reincarnate?" asked Swaffer.

"I had, before then," said the guide. "I will tell you this so that you can understand. It is more important that your world should understand the laws of the spirit so that the things of the world of spirit can be brought to it. That is gradually happening. The next stage is that they will understand more about their past lives and their

relationships to their present lives. It is not so important as the other but I tell you that it is so. If you say you do not agree with me, I love you just the same."

"Red Cloud told me that I voluntarily reincarnated this time," said Swaffer.

"Yes, that is so," the guide replied.

"Why should I do it voluntarily, if it is a law?" asked Swaffer.

"There are many laws in operation," said the spirit, "and there are many people who do not know of the operation of the law until it is time for the law to operate through their lives."

"But why should I choose reincarnation if reincarnation is the law?" persisted Swaffer.

"You had the choice of going on in the world of spirit or doing as I did, forego some of my evolution in order to help your world," said the guide. "You chose to return. It was connected with all the troubles that you have seen in the past few years."

"How much of that job do you think I have done?" asked Swaffer.

"A great deal," was the reply. "Although you have not yet reached the end. That is why you were always told of the work you had to do."

Then the guide left, and the medium, coming out of trance, denied all the things his guide had said. For although the guide teaches reincarnation, his medium rejects the theory! The argument went on for an hour afterwards, with the medium arguing fiercely against the case his guide had built up.

From *Teachings of Silver Birch,* compiled and edited by A. W. Austen. Reprinted by kind permission.

Life Review

As the conversation illustrates, you will be able to deduce that there is a choice, and this is very important. You do not have to come back to the heavier vibration of the earth plane. Everyone will undergo what is called a "life review" when they pass. Perhaps this is what people are rather frightened of because, as it is understood, this life review will include every lesson you have gone through and every lesson you have failed. You will also see the results of your choices—whether good or bad—and how you may have treated others. Everything you have ever said, whether in love or in anger, will be reviewed. This may sound like nothing, but when you consider that you may suffer from guilt through negative actions, or that you may have treated your friends and loved ones with contempt, would you not have some trepidation about going through this life review?

Where Do You Go When You Die?

Where do you think you go when you die? The truth, unfortunately, lies within your perceptions and beliefs. It does matter what is written in these pages, because you will undoubtedly follow this analysis from where your belief stems from. Here, you will only find another perception or hypothesis, but it will give you cause for thought and may even change your old perceptions and beliefs. This could happen after you read the material based on evidence and communication from the world of spirit that is in line with similar teachings in other religious material.

ALERT

It is now widely accepted that when you pass from this life to the next, you make the transition to what is known as the world of spirit. This spirit world consists of etheric energy that makes up what is understood as a heavenly realm. It is more tangible and more beautiful than anything you could possibly imagine.

Jesus of Nazareth stated, "there are many mansions in my father's house." This was Jesus' teaching on the levels of the spirit world. It was the easiest way that he could use the analogy to break the news gently that a spirit world existed. Jesus mainly spoke in parables as this was the way that most people learned in that period. Within these parables would be hidden lessons, and it was the individual's responsibility to find these hidden truths, as a way to get closer to a kind of enlightenment. The mansions that he spoke of were a reflection of lower and higher planes of spirit that existed. The house was representative of the spirit world as a whole or the heavenly state that was considered the destination for souls.

When the soul throws off the cloak, which is the physical body on the earth plane, your soul and spirit will cross over to the realm of the spirit, and the determining factor in where you will go will depend on your state of overall vibration at the time. The more you spiritually grow and recognize your spiritual authority, the higher and lighter your vibration will be, and that will determine your level in the world of the spirit. Now there is also another factor that should be covered, and you may find this hard to understand. The law of karma, which will be discussed in Chapter 6, is the other determining factor. The amount of karmic debt that you accrue through actions, deeds, or through failed lessons will also have an effect. Nevertheless, if you have accrued good karma by carrying out good actions in thought and deed, you will have grown spiritually, and this will be an extra determining factor. The truth (as perceived by mediums and enlightened spiritual beings) is that you will go to the spirit world. Each religion has its own beliefs, and some religions believe that the soul goes somewhere other than a spirit world. For instance, in Islam, they believe the soul sleeps until a final judgment, which is similar to early Christian belief, too.

Is There a Choice?

When you have reviewed your life, you will then be faced with a choice. Do you come back and be of service to humanity, and at the same time rectify those lessons that you may have failed? On the other hand, you could decide to stay in the realm of spirit and not come back to the earth plane, choosing to be of service to those in the spirit world. However, one point to note will be that your job in the spirit world will be determined by your spiritual growth. Some individuals will also have a choice to come back to experience another lifetime. Consider for the moment that when you are in the spirit realm you will have a choice to develop your soul by experience. You are less limited in your sphere of experience to develop the soul by making choices to experience those things that will help you to grow. Growth is not easy, and it involves experiences that are difficult to comprehend.

Remembering Past Incarnations

It is now time for you to delve further, and part of this preparatory work is about recognition—not just of yourself but of the reality, expectations, and what remembering your past is all about. Past life exploration is about memory; this is why you access your memories of the past that will bring about the realizations that you may be seeking. Of course, these memories are within, and as many an enlightened soul has suggested, all answers are within. So by accessing your memories of the past, you are remembering your past incarnations.

ESSENTIAL

Many individuals have what is known as spontaneous memory. This is when they remember a past incarnation that was experienced with some lucidity. This memory can be invoked at any time when the person is in a peaceful and tranquil state. This can happen when you are walking or taking part in a relaxation.

By remembering these incarnations, you are ensuring that you are not releasing Random Egotistical Induced Images (REI). What you visualize and what you experience are coming directly from your past life memories and are not being induced by ego. This ensures that you are not creating what you desire to be, and it will also be another way to show how your past life may not be what you expected it to be. Remembering your past incarnation will help you to release the blockages that may exist on the earth plane in the present moment. Perhaps this is why many individuals experience that aha! moment and are able to move forward, living a happier and healthier life.

CHAPTER 6

Wheel of Karma

"You reap what you sow." "What goes around comes around." "The sins of the fathers." You've heard these statements time and time again. They may have come from someone that you do not get along with or a family member who feels that you have wronged them in some way, or you may have just read them somewhere. Wherever you heard them, they all are expressing the concept of karma, and this chapter is all about karma, that inescapable spiritual law—the bank that allows no debt. Scary, isn't it? Karma is an immutable law that, until now, you may have thought didn't seem so bad. Now it's time to face the reality: no one can escape karma, and the only deciding factor is whether you are spiritually aware or not. This will have a dramatic effect on the outcome of the karmic debt.

What Is Karma?

In Buddhist teaching, the law of karma is more in line with the spiritual law of cause and effect. For every event or action there has to be an appropriate effect. So no matter what you say, do, or think, there will always be an effect. The cause then can be an action, emotion, or belief that has an associated effect. In Buddhism, it is said: "For every event that occurs, there will follow another event whose existence was caused by the first, and this second event will be pleasant or unpleasant according as its cause was skillful or unskillful." A skillful event is one that is not accompanied by craving, resistance, or delusions; an unskillful event is one that is accompanied by any one of those things. (Events are not skillful in themselves but are so called only in virtue of the mental events that occur with them.)

Therefore, the law of karma teaches that same immutable law, which is the law of responsibility. So your actions are those that are manifested by the individual who carries them out.

The Karmic Bank

The best way to understand what constitutes karma is to imagine a financial institution such as a bank. The more you do good deeds and have good thoughts—perhaps you treat people in a nonjudgmental way—you create good karma, and that is deposited in your karmic account at the karmic bank. If, however, you carry out negative deeds, have impure thoughts, act in a judgmental way, or deliberately cause suffering, you are making withdrawals from your karmic account. Sooner or later, the sum total of your karmic balance will be negative, and you will have karmic debt should you do more bad than good. Now this is a debt that must be paid, and that balance will be carried on all levels and in all lifetimes. Karma is a spiritual law that is perfect in operation, and though in this life you may be able to hide away from those you may owe financially, you cannot hide from karma. At some time in the future (in this life or in future lives), karma will call to collect.

FACT

The law of karma is inescapable; there is no way you can get away with doing a bad deed on earth and not pay for it in some way. If everyone realized this, there would be less hatred and less negativity. In turn, this would result in a more harmonious place to live.

A Karmic Example

Consider an example of how karma will affect you. John worked undercover in the underworld and often set up deals and meetings to gain intelligence on drug operations in the state. It was getting near to Christmas and the salary he earned was pitiful—the dollars just did not seem to stretch. Not particularly spiritually aware at this point in his life, he was used to taking chances and risks not only in his job but in all areas of his life. He struggled financially, and this was primarily due to his wife, who had expensive tastes and liked to live a life that was beyond her means. During one particular operation, he was in a position to take an amount of money hidden with some drugs—$8,000—and claim that there was nothing there apart from drugs. In fact, there was $24,000 available, and three colleagues took the money, claiming there was nothing there. The three agents did not think there was anything particularly wrong with this because the state would have received the money anyway and the government would be the only one to benefit; in short, no one would know. They all agreed to split the money three ways and have a joyous and abundant Christmas. No one really felt guilty about what they had done—apart from John. This played on his mind, though with time the guilt went away and the little bit of awareness he had of wrongdoing dissipated.

ESSENTIAL

Thich Nhat Hanh said, "My actions are my only true belongings. I cannot escape the consequences of my actions. My actions are the ground upon which I stand."

A few years passed and John left his previous career. He became a security advisor and was doing well for himself, though he was now divorced. During a particular security detail, John acted courageously, and his reward was a very expensive watch that was given as a gift for services rendered. He never had a watch like this before and was worried that he would lose it or damage it. He took it to some appraisers to get it valued for insurance purposes. The appraiser stated that it would be worth just over $8,000. John was absolutely delighted and went home; however, he forgot to have it insured and carried on his everyday life and work.

ALERT

Be aware of all your actions, speech, and thoughts. No one can escape the law of karma and responsibility. All debt has to be paid, and sometimes this can result in having to undergo negative experiences over again. This is the immutable law in perfect operation. Therefore, having a true awareness of your actions, deeds, thoughts, and speech will help you to overcome and reduce any karmic debt that you may have while growing in mind, body, and soul.

Soon enough, John hit rough times through a series of missed opportunities and was totally in jeopardy, financially and personally. The only thing that he had to fall on was his watch, and in his desperation, he decided to sell his beloved gift. He put this on the Internet and waited for a suitable buyer. Soon enough a buyer was found and all seemed well. John thought things were turning around for him and decided to sell. He was told that because of the value of the item, it had to be sold in a special way. Money was to be held in an escrow account and when the goods were inspected and valued, the money would be released. You can now see where this is going! It was a setup, and John lost $8,000 in the transaction, including the postage and insurance he paid for. You should have already deduced that mistress karma paid John a visit.

How Does Karma Affect Me?

Spiritual awareness and karma operate almost in a parallel nature. As stated, no one can escape the law of karma, and you will be affected in some way due to your actions, though this also depends on your spiritual growth. The nature of your free will influences how karma affects you. If you have not gone through much spiritual growth and are naturally unspiritual on this earth plane, you will be bound in a material way to the material issues of the earth plane. Your free will then becomes an element of choice only, and you will make decisions based on your own conscious choice of what you are driven by, such as environment, religious belief, and desires or ego. In layman's terms, this means that if you carry out acts that may be negative in nature based on your desires, ego, and lack of spirituality, you will not be penalized quite as harshly as you would have if you were the opposite (if you were aware of what is right and true in the spiritual sense). Again, do not think this is an easy way out, because you will still be penalized, and it won't be a nice process.

However, consider the reality of things should you be far more spiritually aware. If you try to lead a spiritual existence and knowingly commit acts that are against your understanding of your soul's vibration, because of your decision to live more spiritually, you will have relinquished some of your free will. You will have recognized your innate spiritual authority and therefore have a great deal of knowledge and wisdom of what is right and wrong, which will be beyond a material basis. What does this mean? Have you ever heard that you will receive ten times what you expect? You will receive instant karma, should you be acting against the spiritual part of you, if you are aware of the consequences of your actions.

ALERT

If you knew the consequences of your actions, you would reconsider things. Imagine the instant karma you would receive if you acted in a negative way and were aware spiritually that your actions were wrong. Think seriously before you act.

This again can be summed up by the Sleeping Prophet, Edgar Cayce, who stated the following under trance conditions from those who were known as the Elders or Council (a group of personalities rather than one person):

Live with this in mind (and every soul may take heed): Ye shall pay every whit, that ye break of the law of the lord. For the law of the lord is perfect, it covereth the soul.

Whatsoever an entity, an individual, sows, that must he also reap. That as law cannot be changed. As to whether one meets it in the letter of the law or in mercy, in grace, becomes the choice of the entity. If one would have mercy, grace, love, friend, one must show self in such a manner to those whom he becomes associated. For like begets like.

Is My Family Affected?

The question should not be "Is my family affected?" but "How much will my family be affected?" Family in the sense of the word means those who share a bloodline; however, consider the bigger picture—the soul group or soul family.

As stated before, no one can escape karma; therefore, your actions will obviously affect those around you. The severity may depend on how much they have to go through with their own lessons. If, for instance, you have committed an atrocious act in a past existence, you will carry that burden of karma with you. It is not unusual that you will meet with the same soul in this incarnation to weigh up the balance of karma by having the choice to make your own decisions, which may or may not pay back the karmic debt you owe. There are times where the spiritual growth of the individual is not enough to awaken him to the suffering he has created, and so as with the immutable law, he will continue in the same abusive cycle, which may cause further suffering to those in the soul group. A good analogy for this would be the old saying, "One bad apple can spoil the whole barrel" —this is very similar to the law of karmic actions. You must understand that you cannot escape another spiritual law, which is, of course, the law of responsibility. All people must take responsibility for their actions, and whether or not they recognize this, karma will be meted. No one is above this law, either.

How Do I Balance?

Everyone wants to learn how to balance karma, and the truth is, it is easy if you know what you have done or how you may be suffering from someone else's actions. It is not just a case of doing good deeds, as in, the more you do, the less your karmic debt will be. There has to be an element of soul growth and self-recognition—you will not learn what you have done wrong unless you face the lesson again or you are able to grow spiritually enough that you can recognize how your decisions were not the correct ones to make. It is a simple case of awareness, as awareness is the key to transcending any emotions or karmic ties. Nevertheless, there is an element of the amount of good service you carry out for humanity, from your heart and not through self-gratification or the amount of suffering you help to reduce. Silver Birch once said the following about service:

> There is no joy and no service that can match helping others. In a world so full of darkness, where millions have lost their way, where there are countless numbers troubled and perplexed with sorrow in their hearts, who awake each morning in fear and apprehension of what the day brings—if you can help one soul to find some serenity and to realize that he/she is not neglected, but surrounded by arms of infinite love, that is a great work. It is more important than anything else.

Pinpoint the Issue

So how do we get to the root of the matter that may be affecting you in the present moment? That's why you are studying this book. There are many ways, and going back to your past incarnations is just one of the ways— perhaps one of the most important and most healing, if done correctly. You may already have some idea of what may have gone on. Do you remember the story of Pat, who had an inclination that she had witnessed something terrible? She had that memory etched into her soul, and in her awareness she knew deep inside that something was wrong. So perhaps these negative issues can be accessed in the present just by recognizing that intuitive feeling that will not go away. Maybe that little feeling that you have, and you just can't quite put your finger on it, will be that issue that may have the past life connection. Perhaps you have an inner dislike for a particular individual. If you were not brought up in an environment that exacerbated the problem, you might just find that the answers lie in your past incarnations.

Exercise: Achieving Growth

Now you are going to do your first exercise, and it does not involve going into any meditative state; this exercise is going to be one of inner awareness. It should hopefully release those negative issues that are harbored deep within you. By releasing these issues to your conscious mind, you will be making the first step in achieving a basic level of awareness. When you have reached this level of awareness, you will recognize what you have done or what emotions may be affecting you in the present moment.

You will need a notebook and a pencil or pen. The exercise will involve you writing feelings and asking your inner self what you need to work on. So you see there are two aspects to this exercise: The first is one of inner work—releasing your emotional problems—and the second is when you ask what you are going to work on.

Writing Your Present

First, you must find a place where you will not be disturbed, somewhere quiet and peaceful. You may wish to play soft music in the background if you are not used to a silent atmosphere. Now you must set the intention, which is just telling yourself what you are going to do and what you hope to achieve. You will do this by way of repeating the following statement (or, of course, you can write it):

I am about to delve into the deep caverns of my hidden experiences. I ask that a blessing may be put upon me and that all my emotions, feelings, and weaknesses are shown from my deepest hidden depths, if only for a short time, to awaken my awareness. I will be viewing these from a detached place and know that I am safe and secure and will not be affected emotionally.

Ensure that when you say this or write it that you take some time to let the words settle into your mind; say them with feeling, and say them slowly.

Take your pen and your piece of paper, close your eyes, and slowly ask yourself to release what is blocking you or what emotions are affecting your present moment. Write down the first words that come to your mind. It is fundamentally important that you do not take too much time in between what you are writing. For instance, if the words are coming through fast, such as anger, resentment, solitude, abuse, or stealing, do not think about them, just write them down as fluidly as you possibly can. What you will begin to see is a pattern of emotions, feelings, and blockages that have some connection to the way you have been painting the canvas of your life, and these issues may or may not have a past life connection. Don't think for one minute that those words shown earlier are what you will get; these are just examples to show you how it must be done.

Now things are going to change just a little. Now you are going to ask what it is that you need to work on. You might then get other words, such as kindness, compassion, anger, abuse, and so on. The difference is that you will find that some words are exactly the same as the others, and some will be entirely different. While you can learn from all of these, the words that are parallel or the same will be the strongest issues that you need to work on.

What Have You Learned?

Let's say for instance that "anger" came up on both accounts. You now have the awareness to recognize that you have an issue with this emotion. Perhaps you will even begin to see when that anger is sparked within you, and you will have the awareness to make that free will choice of how to deal with it. Will you react to the anger, or will you cool the flames of the anger by knowing there is much more at play than you could have imagined? Will you see the futility of the anger and that the emotion is just energy that is negative in nature and can be wasted by feeding it? You should decide to channel that energy in a different way in order to have a positive outcome.

You see, this is about awareness and having the common sense to recognize when something is wrong or right on an intuitive emotional level. It is a kind of discernment.

Consider for a moment that you have been abused some way in this life. The blockages that you may have identified will be connected in some way to that abuse. You might find out that you can identify a pattern of behavior that will be associated with the abuse. This identification of the pattern will be the first step that you can take toward rectifying any potential upsets or failures in your life. All of the issues will affect you in many ways in all areas of your life. These issues will affect your relationships, your work, your family, and anyone else you come into contact with. This will be a seed that was planted when you were being abused, and now that you have an awareness of the cause, you may be able to change the effect.

ESSENTIAL

Do not lie to yourself and think about your answers before you write them. It is fundamentally important that for this exercise you write down the first words that immediately come to your mind. In this way, you will restrain your ego from giving you disinformation.

But what if you were the abuser? Perhaps these associated words will act like a treasure map to your psyche. You will understand that you were abused and now you have become the abuser. This would be a good reason for you to investigate your past life. Furthermore, those emotional blocks you may have identified could arise when you meet a certain person—maybe that emotional tie is where the abuse may lie in a past incarnation.

The important thing to note is that a simple exercise of word association from a spiritual point of view can be the catalyst to change. You will be given a map that shows you where the blockages in your psyche are; the knowledge to clear them is also contained within, and so the mind and body connection becomes your elixir.

CHAPTER 7

States of Consciousness

This chapter is very important for you to understand because delving into the different levels of the mind and consciousness is integral to past life regression. Consciousness
is a word that has been mentioned in previous chapters—
you may think you understand it, or you may already have
a preconceived idea of what it meant by the context in
which it was written. Be assured that it is much deeper than
you originally thought, and this should be an enlightening
lesson.

What Is Consciousness?

Consciousness is a state of being in the sense that without it you would not be nor exist nor have such faculties that allow you to make choices. Conscious experience is what you can perceive with your physical attributes such as your senses, but there are various levels of consciousness. The main faculty of consciousness is awareness and experience, yet this perception is a much-argued point of conjecture between science and philosophy. There seems to be a vast canyon between the two, yet one constant remains, and that is the perception or experience of awareness. In Japanese philosophy there is a word, *mushin*, which means "no mind"—this is supposed to be the ultimate conscious reality, to have nothing material harbor the conscious experience and to just be in the moment between life and death. So is this reality in the true sense of the word? No!

QUESTION

What is consciousness?
Consciousness is your existence, your awakened moment. It is the reality between your now and the present. It makes you have an awareness of being alive in the present.

The reality is that consciousness defines your existence, but what you may not understand is the mechanics of your thoughts and feelings. What is the mind? Where is the mind, and is it separate or a part of your consciousness? Your conscious perceptions are what portrays the world to you, or how you see it through physical faculties. The higher awareness, however, is still a consciousness, similar in meaning and yet a different sphere of experience. It can be thought of as an objective experience, which can be perceived by the physical attributes of the human form, or it can be considered a subjective experience, meaning that some form of mind function or universal energy under its own consciousness and volition creates it. Without consciousness, humans would not exist, and this existence is only perceptible because humans have consciousness.

The Science of It All

How does science see consciousness? There are two camps of science that look at the studies of consciousness in its different spheres. The first is the science of the brain, or neuroscience, where scientists are looking at the material perceptions and functions of human form through brain and neuron interaction. The second is the science of the mind (religious and spiritual science) where they look at the mind as an energy form and study the faculties and abilities they consider to be a part of the mind. It must be noted that not many people actually understand the realities of the mind, and studies into the mind and the mind/body interaction are still being investigated. Therefore, it is difficult to label either approach as right or wrong because both perceptions have their own understandings.

QUESTION

Where is the mind?
This is a question that still eludes scientists and philosophers. It seems to be widely accepted in some camps that the mind exists as an external reality to our physical form under its own consciousness, yet it remains a part of who you are. Where it exists, no one knows, but from a medium's perspective, it is claimed to be part of the divine essence of universal consciousness. It is the higher self and the real you.

The science of the mind is broken down further into cognitive theory and spiritual theory. There are further theories, but for now, and for a more simplistic approach, this book will cover these two major theories. Cognitive theory places your consciousness as a facet of the brain and the interaction of the human body. So even though many would deny this facet of human interaction, you can place desire and emotion as part of this.

Spiritual theory places the consciousness as both a subjective and objective experience. The experience is one that sees us existing in a universal continuum, governed by a higher order or personality such as a divine being or entity. This consciousness is also part of you, and so you are attuned to the same. Perhaps this is where humans can place the mind and the soul as one.

Levels of Consciousness

The levels of consciousness that exist within you comprise the conscious mind, the subconscious mind, and the superconscious mind. All three minds are interconnected, and one affects the other in varying degrees. The subconscious and superconscious minds, however, are parts of the mind that will function and of which your waking consciousness will be unaware. The subconscious is a powerful force in your life, and the superconscious is even more so. It is likened to your divinity and connection to the creating force of the universe. It is therefore important to get to know your levels of consciousness through study, contemplation, and self-examination of who you are at a soul level. You can think of the three levels of consciousness as radio stations; each station offers its program for the day and is working simultaneously with the others. Information is passed along in both directions from the superconscious to the conscious and vice versa. The difference is the superconscious is the connection to the divine essence and therefore is the gateway to receiving divine guidance.

The Conscious Mind

The conscious mind is your waking state or your alert mind; it is known like this because you have to be fully awake to be aware of your surroundings and to be conscious of making certain choices or performing any tasks in your daily life. This is the mind that makes you feel truly alive in the present moment. Yes, you can daydream and your mind will then wander or travel to whatever it is you are imagining, but when you think rationally, you are using your conscious mind; therefore, it could be understood as the mind of choice. The conscious mind makes full use of the five senses that belong to the material world and govern your life in a physical body. For instance, you are alert to seeing, hearing, sensing, tasting, and smelling whatever fills up your daily existence through the conscious mind. You will use your conscious mind to rationalize and analyze thoughts, ideas, and concepts so that you can figure it all out and consciously follow through to create what you thought about or what you may have chosen at the time.

The Subconscious Mind

Your subconscious mind does not require any sleep as your conscious mind tells the body it is time to rest. The subconscious carries on working even when you are asleep; your eyes blink and you breathe without conscious thought—it's all natural. Everything you have ever learned, thought, and felt is stored within your subconscious mind, and this information will then form into the belief systems that you have about anything in your life today. The subconscious is responsible for the working order of your bodily functions, the blood flow, the healing that happens when you cut or graze your skin, and the act of perspiration to keep you cool when your core temperature rises. All of this is done behind the scenes, so to speak, of your conscious mind.

When something emotionally upsetting occurs, the information is stored in the subconscious mind, and this information will be brought to the attention of your conscious mind whenever you are in a situation that could cause you the same kind of emotional reaction. Your goal is to heal and move on from this pain rather than to keep recreating the pattern that has been stored in the subconscious mind. Memory is stored in the subconscious, and these memories are what you will take with you into a future life. It is also these memories that you will access to review the issues in your past life. In doing so, you will change the program, and a more positive program will take its place.

Thus, you will have healed from the past by learning what is harboring the development of your present. This is how a hypnotherapist will be able to help address issues such as bad habits from smoking or drinking, or low self-esteem issues. A hypnotherapist merely uses suggestion that will sink into the computer of your subconscious to change the patterns of negative behavior that you may be suffering from. This process will help you to change the programs that you have believed to be true, even though they are destructive, and change them to a healing pattern that cancels out the old negative patterns.

The Superconscious Mind

The superconscious mind is the mind that is directly connected to the source of your being, the divine creator God, also known as the universal consciousness. This level of the mind can be reached through a process of stilling the mind by meditation or the power of prayer. This level holds great creative potential that can be filtered down to the conscious mind through the subconscious mind, by the process of thoughts, ideas, and inspirations to get your attention. The power that exists at this level of consciousness is full of unlimited creative potential that is available to you as a person who is made of mind/body/spirit. It is the divine facet of universal harmony and easy to understand as the direct line of communication to God or the creating universal force (or whatever you follow with your beliefs). Jesus the Nazarene and many other enlightened souls were so highly evolved that they were able to bypass the subconscious mind and go straight to the divine authority they recognized. This is perhaps characterized by the miracles they performed and the fact that Jesus stated, "no one can come to the Father except through me" (John 14:6). This statement alone shows that the Christ consciousness and the universal creating force were as one, and he confirmed that all were his brothers and sisters. Again, Christ taught that you are a spark of that divine essence; therefore, he bypassed the subconscious and was able to display amazing divine powers.

QUESTION

What are the levels of the mind?
The levels of the mind are broken into three consecutive parts of the whole. You have the conscious mind, the subconscious mind, and the superconscious mind. If you imagine the analogy of a ladder going up to the sky, the higher you go, the lighter and faster the vibration, and the easier that information can come to you.

Many people are unaware of the amazing help they can receive from this higher power source, if only they took the time to relax and move through their busy conscious awareness. Spiritual growth requires time spent in conscious awareness, thus knowing it is a higher power (God) that is behind the creative good and positive results of your life. Do not be an unconscious traveler along the path of your life; dig deeper and discover the potential that is available to every person alive today, but realize the path is not easy.

Silver Birch stated:

If spiritual mastery could be easily attained, it would not be worth the having. The prizes of the spirit have to be earned by arduous labor, but once gained they cannot be lost. The wealth of the spirit is eternal, the wealth you acquire on earth can only have a temporary possession for you. Spiritual mastery is not easily attained. Neither are the prizes of the spirit speedily gained.

A Matter of Trust

Trust is a spiritual quality that expects you to believe in something before you see the results. It is closely related to faith, but trust requires you to allow someone or something to do what you hope for. Trust is an essential element in accessing different states of consciousness. Imagine you are about to be hypnotized for a past life regression. You need to trust in the process, even if you do not understand how, why, and what is going to happen. Trust will need to be placed in the therapist to be able to do her job properly because all you can do is surrender to her instructions. If you do not trust the therapist, then you would not be able to relax enough, and the regression will not work out.

You also will be putting your trust in the guides within the spirit world, for when you delve into the path of your past lives, you will have to trust in the process and those of a higher power to walk along that path for you. If you cannot learn to trust, then you will fail at your first hurdle. A medium has to go through a very long process of learning to trust the spirit and the guides that may be working with the medium. This does not happen overnight and neither will this process, but the journey itself is not only engaging but very joyous and beneficial.

Another way in which trust matters is when you have prayed or asked a higher power (God) for help in your life and you do not know when this help is going to show up. You need to trust that God has heard your request and that behind the scenes you are being helped. Trust is something that you cannot fix or make, but you have to feel and believe inside of you. You may also need to trust in yourself to make better decisions and life choices because you might have made many mistakes before now and may not believe in yourself anymore. If this is the case, then you need to pick yourself up and dust yourself off and trust that you will now have another chance to make new, different, positive, and healthier choices. Get rid of the guilt, blame, and all other negative emotions and trust that you can do what you need to do to make a difference in your life.

Meditation

What do you do when you are so stressed with all the worries, trials, and tribulations that life throws at you? Do not express your emotions in a negative way. Instead, there is a safer option that is better than any medication you could take: meditation. The benefits of meditation can be found in the improvement of your physical health and the emotional and mental well-being of your soul. Meditation can also aid your spiritual growth and understanding of who you are at a deeper level of existence. A person who has a very stressful life would benefit from learning how to meditate because in doing so he would relieve so much of that pent-up stress and tension from daily life. Everyone has times of anger, frustration, and irritation, and all this negative energy is draining and can make you feel fatigued. Meditation is energizing and can help to clean away the mental and emotional tension. It can relieve headaches caused by overanalyzing your life's problems.

ESSENTIAL

You don't have to meditate in a lotus position; in fact, you can meditate while walking in the forests and in the countryside. You can meditate in the bath or in the shower. When you are training in the gym or in your martial art class or yoga class, you are learning to meditate. The truth is there are many ways you can meditate, and you do not have to follow other dogmatic perceptions.

Meditation has been known to help to lower blood pressure, as it causes physiological changes in the body and in the hormones due to the heightened state of relaxation. In fact, many big corporations allow their staff time to meditate; because of the improvements in their working life, they are healthier and happier people to work with. Meditation can energize you, and it can help you align with a higher power so that you receive inspiration and information to help you along the next part of your life. If you make meditation part of your daily life, if only five minutes a day, then you will soon notice a tremendous difference and you will desire to do more.

What Meditation Isn't

Contrary to popular thought, meditation is not about sitting in the lotus position or chanting some kind of mantra to export you to the other realms. You certainly do not have to sit for hours on end to gain any benefits, and it will not make you a target for bad spirits. Meditation is actually a very simple process, though the issue that will block your success is the endless mind chatter that will continually carry on during the first stages.

The mind chatter is comprised of your everyday thoughts, such as you need to go shopping, you need to pick up your children, or you need to pay the bills. This constant barrage of random thoughts takes you away from your meditation process. Inevitably, anger ensues, and you begin to doubt that you can actually achieve anything or can be successful in any of your attempts to meditate. The secret is to not to try to get rid of these thoughts, for they are a natural phenomenon. What you need to do is recognize them for what they are and just accept they will come and go. If you do this and do not allow it to get to you, meditation will become easier and you will be successful. Bring your awareness back to your breath every time, and slowly you will eradicate the mind clutter.

FACT

Most individuals give up when they begin meditating due to experiencing the constant activity within the mind. What is important to understand is that the constant mind chatter is a necessary process to go through. It is the first lesson that you will be faced with, and if you pass this lesson, you will become very successful at experiencing that inner calm that seems so elusive.

You can meditate anywhere, and you do not necessarily have to sit in a still position constantly. Before you move onto the meditation exercise, think of other ways you can meditate and write them down on a piece of paper. Do not worry if you think what you write is silly.

Meditation therefore does not need to be something to get worried about, nor is it anything that is hard to do. Meditation should become part of your daily routine. It can be a wonderful fulfilling experience for you to do, and it will change your life for the better. The word *meditation* itself sometimes puts people off, and this is no reason to stop; if this is one of your blockages, call it something else, like your "inner peace time."

Exercise: Meditation

You will now take part in a meditation exercise, and please note that you will be going through a protection exercise to allay any fears before you go into your meditation. Do not worry; you will be totally safe, and if you bring out any fears, you will hold yourself back.

Get yourself ready and wear loose-fitting clothing. Find yourself a quiet spot where you will not be disturbed. If you wish, you could select some gentle music to play in the background. This may be helpful, but you must ensure that you do not play anything too heavy or with a large beat or you will not reach the levels your brain waves require for the meditative state. Without this heavy music, it will become far more alert.

ALERT

It is important to be comfortable when you meditate. When you are comfortable, you are providing the optimum conditions that are conducive to a good meditation. If you are uncomfortable, your conscious mind will try to work out why you are uncomfortable. Your comfort is your meditative success.

Find yourself a comfy chair to sit in but make sure that you are erect enough that you can keep your spine and torso relatively straight. Sit in the chair and begin to take deep breaths in through your nose and out through your mouth. As you breathe in, visualize white purifying smoke coming into your body; see the white smoke coming down from the heavens above and enter through your head. Witness as the purifying smoke runs all through your body, picking up all negative vibrations and negative energies that may be blocking your path. When you have felt the smoke has been all around your physical body picking up the negative energies, take the smoke, which will now be gray in color and heavy with all the blockages that have been inside you. Visualize the now-gray smoke leaving on your exhale and being sent back into the atmosphere to be transmuted. You are feeling much lighter and cleaner. Now visualize a beautiful white ball of light before you. It is the most amazing light that you have seen, yet it does not blind you. Walk toward the light and enter it, feel its radiance surround you, and know this bubble of white light is always around you.

ESSENTIAL

Remember that you are protected at all times when entering the white light; ensure that you do not let any doubt creep into your mind. Remember the intention and manifestation motto: "First you must perceive, then you must believe, only then will you conceive." This statement is a secret of the universe given to the author by his spirit guides. It is important that you do not let any thoughts of failure or fantasy enter your mind.

Imagine that you are now walking along a beautiful winding path through an enchanted forest. Feel the sunshine on your face and witness the beauty and majesty that Mother Nature has to offer. You are totally safe here and the animals have no fear of you; see them dance and play in this glorious place. As you walk along the path, you hear the gentle trickling of a stream in the distance. The sound brings you comfort and you decide to walk toward the stream. At the edge of a stream is a large seat that is carved into a tree, and you decide to walk toward it and sit down for a while. The sounds of the birds chirping and the animals that are around are very comforting. The sun shines through the trees and cascades all over the area; shimmering sparkles of light cover the water, and you are totally safe and relaxed.

Sit here for a while and enjoy the area and all that the universe has to offer. Allow your thoughts to drift away, and make note of anything that comes to you.

After you have been there for a while, start to realize that you have learned a great deal, and that any suffering that you may have experienced before has been allayed. Get up from your seat and look around the area once more. Walk along the forest path and note the sound of the water is becoming faint in the distance. As you walk along, you know that you have had a wonderful time being in the universal garden. At the end of the path is another white light, a kind of doorway. Go toward this doorway and walk through. You now find yourself back in the room that you were in, and now you should become aware of your body in your chair and your breath. Slowly and surely open your eyes and take one last deep breath. You are now recharged and lighter in energy.

Congratulations, you have just completed your first meditation. It wasn't hard, was it? You can see how easy the process is, and it's just a case of visualization. Yes, you may find that your mind will wander, and you may come out of your meditation faster. Don't worry, that is all part of the process, and even the world's top meditation experts have gone through the same thing time and time again—and probably still do. If your mind does wander and brings you out, just realize this is normal and you will find it easier to return to your special place in the spirit.

Altered States of Consciousness

There is a great deal of conjecture regarding altered states of consciousness, especially in the world of the medium—in the scientific world, it is more about neurons, cycles, and equations. It is important to learn what an altered state of consciousness means in an easy-to-understand way so that you can take it in and process it further and so that you are able to reach these particular states of conscious awareness.

The first thing you need to grasp is that the altered state is very much the state of the alpha, beta, theta, and delta waves, which give varying levels of conscious awareness. The mind and the body seem detached, and the individual has no conscious or awakened experience of the physical senses. Many methods, and even some that are induced by the use of substances, can be used to enter into each altered state; however, the use of chemical substances will cause far more serious implications not only for the mind but also the physical body.

The alpha, beta, theta, and delta waves are manifested in areas of the brain. They are part of a system that is electromechanical in operation, and each corresponding wave has a particular role and function. The differing waves relate to the levels of conscious or unconscious experience. This also means that the brain is able to generate electrical power, and it is this power that also stimulates muscle movement as well as awareness. All of these waves operate on a frequency, much like your auric field and a radio transmitter.

Alpha Wave

The alpha wave is the frequency that is primarily associated with the contemplative or meditative experience. When you take time to sit and meditate, or to relax and contemplate, it is the alpha state that you will be in. The brain wave is slowed down considerably to enable this altered state of consciousness. This is not just associated with meditation, but it is often induced when you finish a certain task that involves deep concentration and then relax by perhaps going for a gentle stroll.

FACT

Jess Stearn, noted journalist and author, came to believe in the paranormal subject matter that he wrote about. His best-known books are biographies of Edgar Cayce (*Edgar Cayce: The Sleeping Prophet: The Life and Works of Edgar Cayce*, and *A Prophet in His Own Country: The Story of the Young Edgar Cayce*), but he also wrote about reincarnation (*The Search for the Girl with the Blue Eyes*) and alpha state thinking (*The Power of Alpha-Thinking*).

Beta Wave

The beta wave is the fastest wave frequency and is induced when taking part in a great deal of mental activity. For instance, this would be similar to an alert or heightened state of conscious awareness, such as a soldier on patrol in a dangerous location, or alternatively when you are driving and following directions. Someone who is teaching would also be in the beta state. It could be said that the beta state is the working state.

Theta Wave

The next slowest frequency is the theta wave, and this is the frequency of daydreaming. The individual who is engaged in a task and then takes time off to daydream and manifest images of hopes, desires, and wishes will be in the theta state. Anything that is repetitious in nature, such as showering or bathing, can also induce the theta state. This is when the flow of information—such as ideas or communication from the higher self or perhaps an outside influence—can happen. The activity of driving is in the theta state; you have learned the process and naturally do it without having to consciously think about it.

Delta Wave

The delta wave is the state you enter when you are sleeping deeply, and science would maintain that no thought processes are actually being manifested. It has been noted that rapid eye movements, or REMs, are a widely accepted phenomenon that supports that small episodes of dreaming take place.

It is important to recognize what state you may be looking for. The alpha and theta brain waves are the optimum frequencies that you should aim for to get to the altered states of consciousness where you can meditate or go into a deeper level of trance.

Methods of Entering Altered States

There are various methods to enter into the altered states of consciousness. These methodologies can be learned by going through certain processes to achieve the altered state, though there are other approaches that are induced by accident through the use of drugs or illness. It has been suggested that individuals who are susceptible to energy, or have a higher vibration, can go into an altered state very easily. This may be a hypothesis as to why some people seem to skip time and have no conscious recollection as to what has happened. It is like the mind having a driver of its own, but it's not the physical you.

Drugs and Alcohol

Taking chemical substances or being overindulgent in alcohol consumption can be a catalyst to inducing an altered state, though the particular state is often unwelcome and can be negative in nature. It is a common fact that shamen of Indian nations and ancient tribes induce these altered states by taking some substance in a controlled manner. This means that the intent has to be formed to experience the altered state via the use of the substance, and when this is achieved, they enter with an expectation. Nevertheless, an individual who unknowingly chooses this route will very often cause more damage in mind, body, and soul. The effects on the auric field are devastating and can result in spirit attachment.

Meditation

Meditation has existed in one form or another for thousands of years, and there are countless books and training courses throughout the world that teach meditation. Spiritual beliefs and religions all have meditation in some form, though it may be titled differently. There is also an air of mystery surrounding meditation, but, as noted before, meditation is a simple thing to learn and continue using daily. The objective of meditation is to quiet your conscious mind to allow yourself to enter the appropriate state of consciousness associated with the meditative experience.

Brain Wave Entrainment

Another method of entering the altered state is brain wave entrainment, which, as its title suggests, trains the brain. This technique uses audio sounds or flashing lights, or a combination of the two, to aid you in entering the appropriate state associated with the sound or sequencing lights. This allows the frequencies of the lights or sounds to take your brain waves down to the state required but in an almost mechanical way.

Levels of Trance

This is possibly the most used altered state of consciousness and is often associated with the world of the paranormal. Trance can be induced by hypnotic techniques and is often used by clinical hypnotherapists to make suggestions to change someone's learned behavior. Mediums utilize the trance state to allow communication from the spirit world by allowing a spirit to mold their mental energies with the entranced medium. Some individuals believe that there are various levels of trance, ranging from a light trance to deep trance; however, it has been suggested that light trance is mainly an ego thing, and the medium's personality shines through. Deep trance is when the medium is in a deep altered state and the spirit entity is able to control the medium's faculties of the mind in order to communicate. When in deep trance, all physical perception is detached.

CHAPTER 8

The Dangers of Exploring Consciousness

Many people have this subject on their minds but are often too scared to voice an opinion or to ask any questions, for fear of ridicule from family members or from religious leaders. The fear of possessions or going mad are often born of ignorance and associated with religious myth and folklore. In this chapter, you will learn about any associated dangers so that you will be able to come to your own conclusions rather than accepting others from potentially ill-informed individuals.

Possession

That very word often strikes fear into the hearts of many; there is nothing more fearful than thinking that your body may be taken over by some grotesque demonic entity or wandering spirit, leaving you helpless and under the will of the entity. The truth is that will not happen during past life regression; the worst thing that you can do is block yourself from making any progress through your own fears. However, that is not to say that there are no dangers. As with anything in life, there are dangers that are easy to stumble upon if you do not know where they may be. This is no different in the spirit world, and when in the altered state you must be aware of these dangers. Even though you may not be able to perceive anything with your physical eyes, it does not mean that there are no dangers. However, it must be noted that the dangers that lurk are not as bad as you would immediately think— especially when you are not delving into the land of the medium. First, you should consider possession, what it really is, and how frequently it really happens.

ALERT

Note that you are entering the dark waters of the psyche and you must have respect for the waters. You must learn to navigate just as a sailor would navigate the rough seas of the world, for in those rough seas lie hidden dangers that you must be aware of. Put your protection in the hands of the higher power you believe in.

What you have to understand is that God or the universal creating force (whatever your belief) has created good and evil in order to maintain a quid pro quo and to ensure lessons are learned; therefore, there is control over each, for as the creator was responsible for creating them, they remain under control of divine authority. We are all a spark of the divine essence that permeates the universe, and therefore we have this divine authority within us. This means that you have all those ingredients that the creator has but only to a lesser degree. This can be likened to being the fragment of a diamond, or imagine it as a cake and you are a slice. The constituents are the same, and a lesser facet does not take anything away from its makeup. Humans therefore have an innate divine authority that we can call upon. The only way that a real possession can occur is by divine authority or by invitation, which has to be an execution of free will and under a blood rite. Then a possession will develop over many years and not just days or weeks. There are five stages of possession, and these stages can happen over a very long time and are not easily recognized. These stages are as follows.

Invitation

This stage is the first stage of any possession and is normally orchestrated through an act of free will, for instance, becoming involved in satanic worship or inviting through the use of a spirit board, without any understanding or discernment. It is no easy thing to invite an entity into your aura or body, and normally this invoking or invitation will be during a blood rite.

Infestation

Infestation is where the host's body and mental faculties will begin to be subjugated and come under the will of the entity. The individual will then carry out acts of a negative nature that are not within the true nature of the individual. At this level, the demon will start using what may seem like normal signs that a paranormal event is occurring, such as smells and growling like a dog. This is a sure sign the entity is evil. The demon may present itself as a loved one or even an angel in order to trick you, and this is where the discernment from your inner authority should come into play. The demon is doing this to gain trust, but it is important to note that it cannot by its very nature stand anything from the light.

Oppression

When this stage is reached the demon will have gained some form of control over the individual, and the individual will show signs of possession such as a disdain for anything holy or will become darkly depressed and suicidal. The demon will often show itself through the individual's acting out of character and displaying unusual signs.

Obsession

During this stage the individual is constantly under the control of the entity. The will of the individual is almost under the entity's total control, and the obsessed person will be truly removed from society in every way. The possessed person will often show greater paranormal gifts and will be psychologically controlled. This is similar to spirit obsession in spiritualism but has some unique differences as aforementioned. Spirit obsession in spiritualism is a lower form of spirit possession.

Diabolical Possession

This is the last stage of the act of possession, and in this stage one or many demons can infest the host. The will of the host is the demons' and normally under their command; however, short spells of freedom will be shown to trick anyone who may be investigating or trying to help the possessed. This stage is normally beyond the professional abilities of lay personnel and will involve spiritual intervention by a proper team. The demon now tries to kill the host by getting a surrender of the soul, which in actual fact it cannot have due to divine authority, so it settles on the death of the host and turmoil for those who may be close.

Good News

This is quite frightening, and reading it may cause you to rethink your position with regard to investigating your past lives. Possessions are few and far between and very rarely occur—the odds are 5 in 1 million in reality. Demons are under the control of divine authority under the creator and do not just take any human host they see fit. This would have to be an individual who may be spiritually weak and will undoubtedly be dabbling in occult practices, including taking part in blood rituals. It doesn't happen that easily, and when you investigate your past lives, you will be using your clairvoyance or clairaudience and not communicating with spirit entities; you'll be watching from a detached point of view and will be completely safe. Your will cannot be interfered with when looking back to the past, and you will be taking requisite precautions anyway. You will have a level of conscious control.

Can I change or irreparably harm myself through an altered state of consciousness?
There is a movie that deals with this subject: the 1980 classic *Altered States*. In the film, the protagonist experiments with sensory deprivation and hallucinogenics to achieve an altered state and then begins to devolve, physically and mentally. That is not possible in reality, but using drugs to induce an altered state usually has deleterious results.

Many years ago possessions were mistaken, and illnesses such as epilepsy were considered to be the work of the devil. How laughable this is when there is plenty of scientific and medical evidence to refute it.

Spirit Obsession

This is similar to possession; however, it is in no way a demonic entity or possession per se. Rather, spirit obsession is an intrusion into your auric field by a wandering or grounded spirit person over a long period of time. The spirit is driven to obsession through the need to feel alive once more on the material plane, and so the spirit will be attracted to and gain entry into the auric field of a spiritually weaker individual. This weakness can be brought about by drugs, alcohol, or consistently living out of a state of grace. The spirit will then try to influence your mind, and that is why some people who may be spirit obsessed will act "out of character." Now, do not get this confused with feeling low or depressed and not being you; it is way beyond that. Spirit obsession is far more prevalent on the earth plane than you would think. A great number of issues in personal lives may be attributed to spirit obsession, including violent encounters or criminal acts. This, of course, is only a hypothesis, but one that warrants further investigation.

What Is the Ego?

The ego is the part of you that denies your spirituality and instead wants to keep you in the material fears of the earth plane. It likes to keep the spiritual side of you subjugated. "Edging God out"—that is essentially what you are doing when you allow the ego to control your emotions. While you need your ego, you need to learn to control it, or it will dance to its own tune and will serve you up a huge dish of doubt. Your ego will be your nemesis and cause you to disbelieve anything you may be witnessing, perhaps making you feel like you should be better than what you witnessed or that it's all a load of baloney. The only way that you can control your ego is by realizing that you are a spiritual being and that you have control. You must learn that your ego is necessary, for it often teaches you lessons, and if you accept these, you can learn to recognize when your ego is at play. This awareness allows you to keep control of your ego; it becomes your friend rather than your enemy.

Controlling the Ego

You must look deep into the awareness of the ego and learn other ways to manage it. As discussed before, awareness is the most powerful way to control the ego, but it is not easy to learn how to become more aware. The path to having awareness is by learning a process called "mindfulness," which means living in and becoming aware of the present moment. It is about becoming aware of what you are doing or feeling in the moment. Being aware of your speech and how you treat others is learning to become more mindful.

Mindfulness in Practice

For instance, look at the process of simply viewing an object. Suppose in front of you there is a beautiful flower—what do you see? Individuals who are not aware of the present moment or the fact they are spiritual beings will only perceive what they see physically. Being mindful means that you will perceive its very essence; you will see its life, its energy. You will see how it has come through many cycles of life and death and that the universe has given birth to something so wonderful. You will also appreciate its vibrancy and its energy, and you will bear witness to what it may have gone through to get here in the present moment to you.

You show gratitude by being mindful, and you see beyond what others may only perceive physically. You are using your spiritual senses in conjunction with your physical senses alone; you blend the two together. This amalgamation allows you to feel the beauty in something at a deeper level—to show gratitude for what you are experiencing in the present moment. This is then a very powerful catalyst toward the discernment of awareness, and that recognition is what will be your secret weapon against your ego.

Look at your speech as a path to awareness and mindfulness, which ultimately controls the ego. Speech is very powerful; wars have started because of speech, and speeches have also brought peace. On a smaller scale, bad speech can cause much suffering to an individual and to groups. It is important that you learn to be aware of your speech. Thich Nhat Hanh (the Spiritual Teacher) says:

Aware of the suffering caused by unmindful speech and the inability to listen to others, I am committed to cultivating loving speech and compassionate listening in order to relieve suffering and to promote reconciliation and peace in myself and among other people, ethnic and religious groups, and nations. Knowing that words can create happiness or suffering, I am committed to speaking truthfully using words that inspire confidence, joy, and hope. When anger is manifesting in me, I am determined not to speak. I will practice mindful breathing and walking in order to recognize and to look deeply into my anger. I know that the roots of anger can be found in my wrong perceptions and lack of understanding of the suffering in myself and in the other person. I will speak and listen in a way that can help myself and the other person to transform suffering and see the way out of difficult situations. I am determined not to spread news that I do not know to be certain and not to utter words that can cause division or discord. I will practice Right Diligence to nourish my capacity for understanding, love, joy, and inclusiveness, and gradually transform anger, violence, and fear that lie deep in my consciousness.

Following these guidelines, which come from the five mindfulness practices, is one of the most potent forms of learning mindfulness and control of the ego. It is partly because of the ego that you will speak angrily, and through anger and ignorance humans create suffering. This is because the ego does not recognize compassion. True control of suffering in a lesser degree or reducing the suffering of an individual is true control of the ego in an outward way.

Fears Unleashed

If you cannot control the ego, you will manifest fears, and normally fears are what will cause failure or hinder progression in all aspects of your life. When you fear something, you are saying that you are powerless to control the outside influence that is subjugating you or attacking you in some way. These fears will stop you from taking that vital step that may make your life more harmonious and even productive. A lack of confidence tends to control the way you will react to a given situation. Fear of what people will think of you will cause you to make wrong choices that will inevitably cause suffering to yourself in the long run. You must realize that your fears are what you manifest by yourself—yes, you read right—you are the cause of your fears, which can be attributed to the environment you live in and possibly the dogma you believe. You may say you never had a choice in the matter, but, unfortunately, you have always had a choice—you just never used the power of that choice. Fear will keep you a prisoner, and you have been judge and jury and jailed yourself. The good news is that you have the key to get out.

ESSENTIAL

You create your fears yourself, and ultimately you will cause your own suffering. Having an awareness of what you are doing and how you are manifesting your own fears is self-empowering and can change your life dramatically. It is up to you, and you hold all the answers within.

Understanding Fear

You must understand what fear really is, and there is a great mnemonic that is offered once more as a method of etching it into your subconscious mind. Fear is nothing more than False Emotions Appearing Real; therefore, fear is nothing more than an emotion that is brought about by your ego. The fact that the fear is an emotion tells you that you have the power within to defeat it or to transmute it into a most powerful weapon. It is a matter of awareness and choice. You can empower yourself by believing you have the power to control and change your life by learning to be more mindful and controlling your fears. Think about this for a moment: Most individuals fear death; they fear the unknown and what may be there for them wherever they may go. In Chapter 6, you read that some individuals fear karma. Now, how empowering do you think it is when you realize that your soul cannot die—that you are eternal and indestructible? This is the nature of the universe, and it's a law that is irrefutable. Because of this, you will look at fear in a completely different way, and you will see that it is nothing that you should worry about, for you are an eternal spiritual being.

Calming Fears

So, if you have these fears, what do you do to calm them? There are many techniques that can be utilized to calm your fear. Perhaps one of the greatest techniques is meditation, and later on in this section you will learn a short meditation to battle your fears. For now, it is important that you begin to look at the breath. Why? Well, the breath is a key ingredient to learning how to control and release your fears. Everything exists on the breath; it is the reality of life, for without the breath you would not exist. The breath gives life and the breath takes life away at the end of your time on the earth plane. Everything exists on the breath, and within this is the reality of your life. For thousands of years, many spiritual and enlightened beings have taught the importance of the breath. As well as life, it brings health and healing. The breath can transform your emotions and take you to places that you cannot go in the physical realm. Within the breath is the catalyst to find the answers humans continually seek, and happiness exists in this space between life and death. The secret of calming your fears is also within the breath, for as you allow the breath to permeate your physical body, you will have the appropriate physical response, such as reducing your heart rate.

Removing Fears with the Breath

It is important to learn an exercise involving the breath and how to release your fears. The intention is the most important factor, and to set the intent, you will either say an affirmation or write your affirmation, such as, "I am now going within in order to recognize and release the fears that may be blocking my progress spiritually and in this life now; I transmute that negative energy and send it back to the universe to be used positively."

Protecting Yourself

Before you go into the exercise in its entirety, you will ask for protection from the universal consciousness, or if you believe in God, guides, or angels, from them. You will ask them to surround and protect you while you carry out the exercise. Again, the most important point is the intention that you set, and this will be done when you marry the belief and the emotion in any affirmation that you do.

You will not just protect yourself from wandering spirits or negative entities but more or less from negative energy that can have a dramatic effect on your energy field. Negative thoughts can have a dramatic effect on your life. Imagine if you were constantly being attacked and drained by negative energy—you would find it difficult to deal with any fears that may arise.

Exercise: Releasing Fears

You did an exercise similar to this in Chapter 7, but that was more of a meditative experience. Now you are going to go one stage further and actively participate in the exercise to allay fears by intention and active visualization.

There are two types of visualization that can be taught: active and passive. Active visualization means that you will be taking part in the visualization process and carrying out spiritually physical acts. Passive visualization is detached viewing where you are only creating and viewing the scene that you visualize; you will not be actively taking part in carrying out physical acts but will be transported to a scene where you will watch and view to gain further insights. Sometimes you will experience physical pulling and energy when you are actively visualizing. This is the case in the exercise you are about to do.

Find a quiet place to sit. Ensure you are wearing loose-fitting clothes and that you will not be disturbed for a period of time. Though you can normally do a meditation in a short space of time, this exercise will be predominantly longer so that you can really feel the difference in your energy.

Ask yourself to be surrounded by the white light, and as you did before, see this white light encircling you in a ball and creating a protective field around you. Now, take in deep breaths and as you breathe in, count "one, two, three, four, five, six" on your in-breath and the same on your out-breath. Ensure you do not force your breath. Everyone has a unique lung capacity, and one person may only count to four, or another may count a great deal more. The point is that you should be taking these breaths and asking yourself to relax every time you breathe out.

See yourself standing in a room that is dimly lit by several candles that offer a warm, comforting glow. In front of you is a large oak door. Notice how solid this door feels and see a large brass handle on the door. Turn the handle and open the door, then walk through and ensure that the door is closed behind you. Stand for a while and look around you, turn around and ensure the door is closed behind you. Walk forward and note that you are in a beautiful mountainous area. There are trees surrounding you and plants of all shapes and sizes. You can hear the birds singing and observe that the flowers in the garden are some of the most spectacular colors you can see. Look beyond and see that a path is leading to the beginning of a majestic mountain. There is a spirit animal waiting for you to accompany you on your journey.

The animal can be anything you wish or the first thing you see subjectively. Notice that your spirit animal friend is guarding many bags of worries and fears that exist from your lower self. These fears and worries are what you have been carrying for a very long time. Walk toward your friend and show him some love; you are grateful to the spirit that he is there for you.

Bags are everywhere, and you have to carry them with you spiritually just as you have done all your life. Notice these bags are so heavy they almost buckle you, but you have to carry them. It's not about strength, it's about your inner chains of bondage that you have created and have kept you prisoner for so many years.

You are beginning your journey and you realize what you have done to yourself. Those bags you are carrying are so heavy and your heart has been so full of sadness, but you can't get rid of them yet. Your spirit friend cannot help you either and can only comfort you as you walk along your path of despair that you created. You are tired, your bags are heavy, your body cries for rest and peace, and you nearly collapse under the weight, but your spirit friend urges you on. Not long now, and things will get easier. But you are starting to climb the path higher and higher and your burden is heavy. Your spirit friend cannot allow you to drop your baggage, for you must see it through and carry them farther up the mountain path.

Don't worry, it won't be long now, your friend tells you. Just when you feel there is no end in sight, you notice the path begins to wind along a single track on the ridge of the mountain. Something is different. As you look over, you realize that you have come so far and have gone so high, but as you look over the side, you notice there is no bottom, there is no ground; there is only a vast nothing. You turn to look at your spirit animal companion and note that it has gone, yet in its place stands an older man. He is wise and has beautiful long white hair and a beard. He smiles and introduces himself to you. He is a spirit person who has come to show you that you have the power to change. He asks you to drop your bags and separate them into a line. As you do this, notice they are all now marked with words. One bag is marked "fears," one is marked "worries," one "anger," one "sorrow," one "suffering," and the last is "abuse." Your spirit guide asks you to throw each individual bag over the edge and to let them go so you may be renewed. He asks you to think of each one. He asks that you show it love and say a blessing, telling each that you have no use for these emotions and negativity in your life on the earth plane.

Picking up the bag of fear, you begin to visualize all the fears that have existed in your life and that stop you from progressing along your spiritual path. You note how heavy it has been—your fear of taking leaps of faith, your fear of what others think, and all your fears of failure are in this bag. Now you are given the command to throw it over the side while blessing it for serving its purpose. How much lighter you feel inside excites you, and the bag has gone over and fallen out of sight, but wait! When it drops out of sight, you can see that beautiful white doves have started to fly from where your bag had fallen, and they fly off peacefully in the distance.

Smiling, you take the second bag of worries. As you hold it, you begin to see all those thought forms and the visions of your worries—the worry that you are not good enough or the worry that you do not have enough, the worries of how others perceive you and the worries that you will fail at anything you do. Again, you throw this bag over the side, and as it disappears from sight you see that more doves have been released and again fly off peacefully in the distance. Now you feel happier and know that you are lighter in spirit.

Your body rises slightly from the ground and you are almost floating, yet inside, your self still has a little way to go. Knowing what to do next, you take the third bag marked anger. You see how your anger has affected others and how you have wasted so much energy being consumed by your emotional anger, knowing that you had a simple choice not to get angry. You feel that you do not need this anymore, for it is an energy that consumes and destroys. Once more you throw the bag over and become free and happier; you have risen so much now and are not limited to the physical form. You are floating in midair.

Taking two bags, one in each hand, of sorrow and suffering, you awaken to the negativity that has surrounded you. You see how your actions, speech, and thoughts may have caused suffering to others and as a consequence caused much sorrow in the hearts of others. You also see how you have suffered at the hands of others and offer a blessing that your prayers may open their hearts. Throwing both bags over the side, they immediately morph into millions of flower petals, and they fall all over. You know that energy has now been transmuted and you feel light—light and airy. You are happy and joyful and know only one exercise remains.

QUESTION

What are these bags that I am carrying?
The bags represent all your problems or your blockages and the suffering that you have created in this world. You are laden with the bags because you carry them with you spiritually, and these are the blockages that manifest in you physically. When you release these bags, you will be releasing all your fears and worries.

Your spirit friend now picks up your last bag and hands it to you. He knows this is the most important bag that you need to get rid of. Inside, it carries all the lifetimes of abuse that you may have suffered and dished out on all levels. No matter what you have gone through, this is the most important bag that you need to discard. He tells you that when this bag of abuse is gone, you will no longer suffer from it. You have to say a prayer of forgiveness and not only forgive those who may have hurt you but also forgive yourself. This is the hardest thing for you to do. With one last heave, you throw the bag of abuse and let it drop into the nothingness below. Expecting to see the most wonderful crowd of doves flying up and away, your spirit friend smiles. In an instant, you hear the majestic cry of an eagle, rising up from the nothingness. He flies up and near you and almost bows a majestic wave toward you.

The magnificent eagle now flies away in the distance and you know that all is well. You have achieved so much and are now lighter than ever. As you turn to thank your spirit friend, you notice that he has gone. No one is there, yet you feel amazingly light and no longer have the burdens of life that you carried with you. It is now time, as a new being, to begin your journey back down the mountainside. Beginning to walk slowly, you are immediately joined by the very same eagle that you released. This eagle is the spirit of universal love and flies slowly beside you. You both enjoy the beauty and the majesty of universal harmony, and you realize this is the dawning of a new era, the dawning of a new you.

Going down the mountainside, you feel rejuvenated, and soon you come to the end of your path. It is now time to say your farewell to your spirit companion and know that you are always loved and protected by universal love. You see the doorway in front of you and you walk toward it. Turn and take one last look at the mountain behind you and see how far you have traveled and what you have achieved. Enter through the door and ensure it is closed behind you. Begin to become aware of your material surroundings, begin to witness your breath once more, and find yourself back in your room once more.

This is a meditation practice that helps individuals release any harbored negativity. Many individuals have experienced tremendous changes after carrying out the meditation, once a week for a few weeks. The meditation was divinely inspired and given in such a way that it achieves many objectives in one guided meditation. This meditation not only helps you to heal from negativity and past life scars, it helps to raise your vibration and develop your spiritual awareness and gifts. Those in the spirit have to be recognized as coauthors of this meditation.

Psychosis and Consciousness

Psychosis is considered an abnormal condition of the mind, but there is a great deal of misunderstanding of the condition. There is a very fine line between psychosis and conscious experience on a higher level. Scientists claim those who hear things or see visions are psychotic or have an abnormal condition of the mind, and that those who suffer from psychosis are not in touch with reality. How can this be, when no one really has proof or evidence in the material world of what the mind actually is or where it belongs?

Now to play the devil's advocate. What do you consider reality? Are humans just part of a holographic experience and game of the gods? And if indeed what you see is illusion, then what you see cannot be reality. This begs the question then: Who suffers from psychosis? Are those whom science considers under the veil of psychosis really under the veil, or are the so-called normal people the ones who are really suffering from psychosis? It then leaves a very gray area as to what the levels of conscious experience are to one who is supposed to be of abnormal mind. Yes, of course there are individuals who have psychological imbalances due to abnormal brain function, yet another hypothesis exists that involves spirit intervention of a negative persuasion. The gray areas are very thin, as is the veil. Psychics and mediums are often called crazy and psychotic because they appear to have gifts that are considered abnormal within the fields of scientific exploration. However, there is more to reality than meets the eye. Again, psychosis is therefore an illusion or false perception born of man's ignorance.

ALERT

Psychosis is a pretty gray area, for it suggests that mental imbalances exist through seeing visions and hearing voices. This is the mainstay for the professional medium, yet mediums are considered to be sane individuals with no mental imbalances and special spiritual gifts. You must understand that a misunderstanding does exist, and be careful never to judge.

People experiencing psychosis are supposed to have hallucinations or beliefs that are not in keeping with normal dogmatic belief systems. A person suffering from psychosis will apparently show personality changes and have thoughts that are external from his own personality.

These perceptions and/or conditions are those that evidential mediums and trance mediums portray and experience on a regular basis by reaching higher levels of consciousness, in everyday experience. Yet mediums are not considered mad or mentally ill. Now, these levels of consciousness and psychosis are what you want to try to achieve under controlled conditions to heal from past life traumas. There is a case to be made for past life trauma causing mental disorders in the material realm. Perhaps medical science should blend with quantum science and utilize the skills of the spirit to tackle cases that may have a past life cause.

CHAPTER 9

Regression Methods of the Pros

If you know anything about past lives, regression, or perhaps have read other works, you will more than likely only have learned of one methodology for approaching the subject. It may surprise you to realize there are far more methods for achieving the same goal. In this chapter, you will be introduced to these methods so that you can learn from the professionals who do it on a daily basis. The only difference in these methods is that they are normally carried out by seasoned professionals, but these methods will give you an idea of other ways that you could investigate at a later date. You could also employ the methodologies on a smaller scale for yourself as long as you take the appropriate protective measures.

Hypnotic Suggestion

This is by far the most widely accepted form of hypnotism. It is by suggestion that the therapist will be able to take you to altered states of consciousness where you will be able to access those memories that are attributed to your previous incarnations. A wise man once said that everything is about suggestion—life is about suggestion and individuals act on hidden suggestions. Some scientists also coin the phrase differently, but the basis of it all is suggestion but on a mass consciousness scale.

Consider an example of mass suggestion and how this may work in the business world. For instance, if you look at the diet industry, you can deduce that everything about this is about suggestion to the individual but from a mass consciousness angle. The suggestion is that you are unhealthy if you are overweight, and the industry leaders solidify this suggestive process by stimulating you visually and through suggestive phrases. These suggestions will act upon your conscious mind and may invoke negative discourse within the feelings of the self. This discourse causes you to search out ways of changing yourself for various reasons. Very often these reasons are not born of health worries but are more of an aesthetic need to follow the pack. This is a form of social injustice that is caused by suggestion alone. Suggestion is not just prevalent in the diet industry. If you look around you, there are suggestions everywhere that make you think if you have this product or that material item, it will enhance your life in some dramatic way.

Applying Suggestion to Hypnotherapy

To the hypnotherapist, the suggestive phrases are what will allow the entranced individual to change her patterns of negative behavior. This is done by a simple process of retraining the conscious mind when the sitter is in a deeply relaxed state. The mind is open to suggestion when in a relaxed state, and this is when the mind will accept the patterns of suggestion that will change the negative patterns of behavior.

So, how does this work when looking into your past incarnations? It is this same process, and the suggestive phrases will not only take you into another conscious state but will allow you to access your memory banks of past lives. You will be taken to the appropriate juncture in time and given the suggestion that you view this time once more only from a detached state.

The hypnotherapist will then offer suggestions that will help you to heal from any trauma that you may have experienced in a past life.

Mediumship

Mediumship is the ability of an individual with certain divine gifts to communicate with discarnate entities from the world of spirit. Mediumship has existed in some form or another for thousands of years and is becoming even more prevalent in the modern world. Today, mediums are used for wide and varied tasks, and not just to provide evidence of life after death. There are various forms of mediumship, including mental mediumship, direct voice, physical mediumship, healing, and trance mediumship, which has some parallels to past life methodologies. The trance condition is what one would expect to enter in order to experience one's past life memories. However, there are some differences in the trance condition from a medium's perspective in that the medium will step aside and allow a spirit communicator to use the medium's faculties to communicate with those in the physical world. Mediumship also has a place in being able to help those heal from past life conditions. The spirit communicators can often pass on vital information that pertains to conditions that the individual may be harboring due to any past life trauma.

How Mediumship Works and Aids in the Past Life Experience

This is a hypothesis only, as there is no scientific proof for how the mechanics of mediumship actually work. The only evidence comes from validated information that has been gained from a discarnate intelligence, such as guides and loved ones on the other side of life. Mediumship is the blending of the medium's mind faculties and the discarnate communicator's faculties. The medium has to raise her vibration enough so that the meeting of minds can happen while the discarnate presence reduces its spiritual vibration to match that which is requested by the physical world. This is not an easy process and has its inherent difficulties on both sides. The medium can get in the way and the message will be distorted, as the medium's own beliefs and experiences can cloud the issue. The medium also has to be in a good mental state in order to ensure the message is not tarnished or tainted in any way. The guide can only communicate within the medium's sphere of experience and uses symbols and words to convey messages that the medium may understand. This understanding has to be vibrationally matched between the discarnate and the medium. This is the very basic idea of how communication occurs between a medium and a discarnate being.

The medium will then be able to convey messages or view possible information that is given by the discarnate as to the sitter's blockages that may have resulted from past life trauma. Often, the discarnate being will be able to see the paths that one can take to heal from the trauma or condition that has caused the blockages in the sitter's life. It must be noted that predictions will never be made at this point by the discarnate, as too many factors could cause change, and the reality of free will has to play its role in soul growth.

Regression Therapy

Regression therapists are a little different than normal hypnotherapists because they specialize in past life regression therapy. This is the only field they study—they have no need to become trained hypnotherapists who will alleviate negative behavior patterns, such as smoking cessation and weight loss. They will be more inclined to help the individual in a therapeutic manner by helping them to heal from past life issues and trauma. The regression therapist perfects the art of taking the individual to the appropriate level of trance and will have the right model to initiate a past life memory. Some hypnotherapists claim to be able to do past life therapy but do not understand the mechanics of it; they claim it is the same as any suggestion exercise, which it is not.

QUESTION

How do I find and select a reputable regression therapist?
You should search and identify a good regression expert by the successes that he or she has. Look for verifiable evidence based within their cases. If you can confirm evidence, you'll know you have found a qualified therapist.

A therapy session may also induce certain emotions, and these emotions can be upsetting. The therapist will be trained in some counseling techniques, which will be needed should the session prove to be upsetting for the patient.

Psychomanteum

The psychomanteum was also known as the oracle of the dead and was originally invented by the ancient Greeks. This was a room where individuals would come and sit in the dark and mirror-gaze in order to communicate with loved ones on the other side of life, or learn from the world of the spirit. The room would normally have a brass cauldron or reflective surface that would be elevated so the sitter could not see her own reflection. The idea was that individuals who had crossed to the spirit world could be seen and could communicate with their loved ones. Very often other visions and images could also be seen. This is perhaps closely associated with vision quests of the shamans. This practice had to be done in complete darkness, this being considered the optimum conditions for being able to witness the visions.

In Jeffrey Wands' book, *The Psychic in You*, he recounts Dr. Raymond Moody's interest in replicating the near-death experience. Moody had claimed that ancient reports suggested a great deal of success in seeing and communicating with loved ones. He also recounted a story of a woman who not only saw her husband, who had been killed tragically in a battle, but was able to communicate with him. Archaeologists have also unearthed these rooms in ancient buildings in western Greece.

The psychomanteum was initially created with a visual goal in mind, but it soon became evident that communication on another level was entirely possible. Moody knew that if he could replicate this idea, he could help alleviate the suffering of those who had lost loved ones. Moody consulted with many experts in the field of the paranormal to ensure there would be no danger in using this form of communication. It was agreed that no dangers were known at that time, and the only caveat was to ensure one's state of mind before attempting to mirror-gaze.

Moody's psychomanteum was constructed as follows, and you may wish to replicate this, but ensure that you are not alone and you are of sound mind. There was a 4- to 5-foot mirror positioned at the end of a darkened room. The mirror was elevated 4 feet above the floor, and a comfortable chair was positioned about 4 to 5 feet away from the mirror. A small low-watt lamp was in the darkened room to be used during the process. The idea was that one would gaze into the mirror at an angle in the darkened room and allow the communication from the world of spirit to take place.

ALERT

If you are going to attempt any form of mirror gazing, you must be assured that you are in a positive state of mind and are not suffering from any form of mental imbalance. This is one caveat that Raymond Moody had to ensure before anyone was allowed to sit in his psychomanteum.

It became clear through Dr. Moody's experimentation that one could indeed communicate and replicate the near-death experience. Many individuals were given comfort and evidence to be validated in this world from the next, beyond the veil of material perception. To this day, the psychomanteum is still used in homes and in research laboratories to replicate these experiences.

It is suggested that communicating through the psychomanteum can replicate similar results that a medium would give and could help in the past life experience. So if you have constructed a psychomanteum in an appropriate area, you could entrance yourself to watch a past life from a detached point of view with the idea of learning from the experience. The first step that you should take is to ensure that you have the right intention in your mind and what you would like to achieve by entering that state. Again, you must take the appropriate protective measures, and do not enter the psychomanteum with any expectations. Sit back on the chair and relax yourself, take several deep breaths, and ensure that your body is getting into the relaxed state. Now, wait and see what happens. You may have loved ones come forward, or you may have a guide come forward and offer information that may be blocking you. You should also see visions of your past incarnations in the psychomanteum, and you may register these for further investigations.

Scrying

Scrying is very similar in nature to using the psychomanteum. The differences are that you can scry at any time of the day or night, and all you need is a quiet area and a reflective surface. When talking about scrying, the first thing that normally jumps to mind is the image of an old gypsy sitting with a crystal ball. A word of caution: The problem with scrying is that you have no control of what you are going to see. Some individuals have claimed they have seen grotesque figures that have undoubtedly been released through their own fears. The scrying method involves a process of getting yourself ready and letting your mind go to receive whatever should come in visual form. Scrying is dangerous if not used with the highest intent and with protection. This is why it is important to take the appropriate protective measures. If this is done correctly, there is no reason why you would not have some success in viewing your past incarnations clairvoyantly. For a more in-depth look at scrying, see Chapter 14.

The Gifts of the Psyche

In the book, you have read about certain spiritual gifts and yet you have not delved into what these gifts are and how they may be used. There is a valid reason for keeping this from you until now. It was so that you could fully understand the mechanics of how things work, and so you could have an appreciation of the benefits before you were thrown into the psychic side of things. If you learned all about the psychic gifts at the beginning of the book, you may have been put off as it may sound so out of the perception of what the norm is supposed to be. If you are a skeptic by nature, it will be harder to swallow.

There are several gifts of the spirit that are endowed to the individual in varying degrees. Each gift will be discussed to give you an overview of the power and how you may appreciate the workings in your sphere of experience.

Clairvoyance

Clairvoyance is the gift of spiritual sight, and it comes from the French words *clair*, meaning "clear," and *voyant*, meaning "seeing." Clairvoyance has been used in some form or another for thousands of years. Individuals who use the gift are known as clairvoyants, seers, visionaries, and psychics. Clairvoyance is broken down into two areas of sight: objective clairvoyance and subjective clairvoyance. Objective clairvoyance is the ability to perceive visions with the physical eyes. Subjective clairvoyance is the ability to perceive inwardly with what is known as your third eye.

A psychic medium utilizes the gift of clairvoyance daily in his work schedule while giving readings. However, you do not have to be a professional psychic medium to utilize the gift of clairvoyance. You often use clairvoyance of some form, though it may be out of your field of understanding and—pardon the pun—perception. For instance, imagine that you are talking with your friend and she asks what you were wearing when you went out on Saturday night. You immediately respond by visually seeing what you were wearing and describe it exactly. This is the beginning of understanding your innate clairvoyance. If you were asked to describe a favorite scene, such as a tropical beach, the chances are that you would view the scene in your mind before explaining it. This is simply a form of clairvoyance that everyone can do; it is not a special gift held only by gifted individuals. Professionals have a stronger ability in this field, and coupled with the natural ability they are endowed with, they set themselves apart from what is perceived as the norm. Natural psychic ability such as clairvoyance can be developed, but only to the extent the individual is supposed to use it. Clairvoyance is a natural innate gift that you can use to enhance your life in many ways, and it is a simple case of understanding symbolism.

Information is given using symbols that you would understand and are within your realm of experience. These are accessed from your subconscious memory banks. This is how you may perceive information when you begin to look back at your past lives. You will see clairvoyant visions and symbols that will help you to remember issues or events that have existed in some form or another in your past incarnations. You may even witness individuals with whom you were involved on some soul level. Look at an example of how your clairvoyant vision may help you to understand what is causing a particular fear.

Assume that you have a fear of driving, and while you are engaged in the process of looking back into your past life, you see that you were involved in an accident that may have killed you. Perhaps you were run over by a horse and cart hundreds of years ago. The essence would be the fact that you have a fear of transport, and as evolution progresses, the horse and cart become the car, and so you carry the fear with you into your present incarnation. So you see that your clairvoyant nature can in fact open the doorway to the healing process.

QUESTION

Is the clairvoyant third eye similar to the third eye mentioned in Hinduism and Buddhism?
The third eye is the spiritual eye that all people have, and it has been talked about in many religions, including Hinduism, Buddhism, Taoism, and even Mormonism. Common to all of these is that the third eye, or spiritual eye, is situated in the forehead area, in front of the pineal gland, and is the gateway to other (higher) forms of consciousness.

Clairaudience

The faculty of clairaudience is the gift of "clear hearing," and it is often developed at the same time as clairvoyance. Again, it is broken into the two areas of perception: subjective and objective. Some individuals hear objectively, which is with the physical ears and as though the sounds were coming from an external source. This is normally only confined to natural mediums and will never usually surface during a past life experience. The individual who is going through a past life regression will hear words and sayings from discarnate beings as though it were an inner dialogue from the mind. This can often sound muffled and will not be something that you would normally think of. Andrew Jackson Davis says in *A Guide to Mediumship and Psychical Enfoldment* (E. H. Wallis):

> *When spirits speak to us they address our interior and spiritual sense of hearing, and when we behold spirits we exercise the internal principle of perception or seeing. It not infrequently occurs that an individual thinks his outward senses addressed when, like Saul, he hears a voice pronouncing his name, apparently, from the depths of the air;*

and when spirits have been seen, the beholder is apt to believe that the vision was confined or addressed to the outward sense of seeing, so distinct and self-evident is a real manifestation of spiritual presence . . . To the healthy and discriminating mind there is no confounding of a substantial vision of supermundane personages and scenery with the dreamy hallucinations of the disturbed intellect. When the interior senses of the mind distinctly see a spirit, or hear its serene, rich, friendly tones, it is impossible for the thus favored individual to be mistaken. If, however, as it sometimes happens, we get only an imperfect glimpse of some guardian spirit who seeks our recognition and welfare—and if we cannot be absolutely certain and honest in our convictions of that angel presence, and have not a perfect assurance that the vision was no illusion—then it is wisdom to keep our understandings open to the reception of more substantial evidence, to the end that the mind may not be conducted into regions of uncertain hypothesis and imagination.

This form of inner dialogue is what you will hear and use when you investigate your past lives. Look at an example of how this may manifest in your realm of perception. When you read quietly to yourself, you experience this same form of inner clairaudience. Now, if you imagine that you are in the meditative or trance state and you begin to see a field and a working farm that seems to have existed in another past existence, you may also see a person working in the field and will immediately wonder who this person is. Immediately in manifesting the question as a thought form, you may hear a name that comes at you without having to make a conscious attempt at getting it. This is you using your gift of clairaudience.

If you have certain past life blockages that hinder your progression in this life and are viewing your past life under the trance state, you may hear information that will give you answers to the questions you seek. For instance, if you saw a person and heard the word "abuse," this would be a good indication that you suffered at the hands of this individual. This is important, and you must understand that you may have to go into the meditative or trance state several times to gain information that will aid your healing.

This will happen in various steps, and soon you would have to take the next step of performing more exercises to gain insight into what you have to do in order to begin the healing process. If you went into the next stage and witnessed a similar scene with the same characters and you perhaps heard the word "forgiveness," you would have your answer. Obviously this process can take a long time, but it can be healing and the beginning of a happier life for you and your loved ones.

Clairsentience

Clairsentience is the gift of feeling, and this is quite a rare gift to have. Mothers often show signs of this gift if their children suddenly become ill and the mother feels this same sensation within the physical body. It is also especially prevalent between twin siblings. Mediums will often feel how someone may have passed to the spirit.

As an example, the author once had a gentleman come for a reading to his home office, and as the reading began, the medium felt a tremendous sharp pain in his side and immediately felt that he had trouble breathing. Clairvoyantly the medium then saw the image of a pointed blade. He knew that the man's loved one had been violently stabbed in the lungs and this was the cause of his death. This example is somewhat extreme, but it does give a clear indication of how clairsentience works.

A Clairsentience Example

It's a dark night and you are watching yourself in another existence. The rain is heavy and you see a man sitting, sad and emotional, by himself. Suddenly your vision changes and you see a gravestone. Almost immediately you experience choking and feel a rope being put around your neck. You will know from your vision that you passed in that life by either hanging yourself or being hanged. Of course, it would be too difficult to carry on with that visual experience, and this would be the right opportunity to come away and go further at another juncture. You can see how this feeling that you would get within your realm of physical experience would give you much needed information that would help you in your quest to heal from past life trauma.

ALERT

Forgiveness is perhaps one of the major blocks to everything in life. Not learning to forgive can cause physical, emotional, and mental illness. However, forgiveness is not such an easy thing to do, and takes a great deal of enlightenment. The first thing you have to do is forgive yourself before you can forgive others.

Clairalience

Clairalience is the gift of smelling. Spirits are able to enhance the molecules and atoms that can replicate the smells that would be able to cause the appropriate link to manifest to your past life. You may wonder how that would fit into investigating your past lives. Imagine if, when you were under your trance condition, you smelled a terrible sulfur smell or the smell of burning. You may find that any conditions you currently suffer from in this life may have passed to this life from a past life trauma. The smells that arrive in your trance condition may help to acknowledge the issues that cause you the problems in your present incarnation.

Clairgustence (Tasting)

This may sound like a weird thing, but you can be assured that the ability to taste spiritually will open many avenues of understanding. Again, there is an energy manipulation here by those in the spirit, and they are able to place those tastes in the realm of your physical experience. Perhaps you choked in a past life, and you have a deep fear of fish. Perhaps the taste, emotion, and vision of eating fish in this present life will help you to understand your issues. Imagine if you had been poisoned in a past life and you had that taste placed in your sphere of experience. This would give you the evidence that you require to move forward.

Using Your Psychic Gifts

All of these gifts can be used either singularly or at the same time. It is quite possible for the spirit individuals who may be working with you to offer the information to you in a similar fashion to the way they communicate with mediums. You may get symbols, tastes, words, and an inner knowing.

All of these work as one unit, like the mind, body, and soul as one, and not a separate body of consciousness. You can use these spiritual gifts much like a jigsaw puzzle, and anything you experience will be another piece of the puzzle. Eventually, you should have a full picture of what your past life was, which will explain any issues that may cause blockages now in your present existence.

CHAPTER 10

Take a Walk on the Wild Side: Exploring Your Own Past Life Incarnations

Now it's time to take the journey and view elements of your past incarnations. Read on to discover the requisite steps you need to take to initiate your own past life experience. Here you will enter the realm of your subconscious to learn from the past and take a wild walk on the other side of your mind.

Beginning the Journey

The journey that you take now is dependent on the expectations that you harbor. In Chapter 4, you learned how to recognize your expectations, but now it's time to put that knowledge to use. Imagine that your mind is a castle full of various rooms that hold information about your past incarnations. In order to enter this inner sanctum and begin your investigations, you will have to go on a journey within the confines of your mind. This journey will take you into a relaxed state of being and allow you to enter an altered state of consciousness. You will then be able to enter each individual room that you are drawn to, to realize your past incarnations.

FACT

It is a common misconception that people cannot visualize. This misconception will slow your progress; you will not make progress if you do not believe you are able to visualize. The truth is that you can visualize, and you probably do it every day without thinking. If you really wanted a new car and you saw one at your local dealer, you would be excited to describe the car in detail to your friend. You would not be able to do this had you not been able to retrieve the image from your mind to describe it.

Within each room are the answers to your questions. This is where you can review your past lives safely from a detached point of view. Each room takes you to a different timeline and contains the reality of that timeline within it.

Exercise: Your First Regression

Find a calm and relaxing place to sit. Ensure your chair is comfortable and that you are not slouched in any way. If you prefer, you may choose to lie on a mat on the floor with your head elevated slightly on a soft pillow. The preference for this exercise is a comfortable chair, as you may be inclined to fall asleep when you are lying down. Ensure that you have suitable clothing that is loose fitting and comfortable and will not restrict you in any way or cut into your skin. Place your hands lightly on your knees and close your eyes.

ALERT

The importance of wearing loose-fitting clothing is paramount and will be conducive to the success of any meditative experience you undertake. If your clothing is tight fitting and restrictive in any way, you will not be able to calm your mind enough to reach an altered state, as your conscious experience would be aware of the restriction.

Begin by taking a deep breath in through your nose and out through your mouth. As you breathe in, know that you are breathing purifying energy, and as you breathe out, tell each of your body parts to relax one stage at a time. Start at the feet and in each breath tell each body part to relax. Release your fears and worries as you exhale; move to your legs, then your arms, and so on. As you begin to move through your physical body, you will note that you are beginning to feel relaxed and sleepy. This is the point where you may begin to fear, and as your fear of not being in control takes hold, you may come out of your relaxed state far too quickly. There is nothing to fear, and it may help you to reiterate this to yourself over and over a few times. Repeat something like the following statement, which includes your relaxation affirmation too:

There is nothing to fear and safety surrounds me; within the safety my body is relaxed, comfortable, and in no stress. The divine authority within allows the full expression of my spiritual self in safety and harmony. The safer I feel, the deeper I move into the trance state.

Find yourself at the bottom of a golden escalator and see that it goes up toward a golden gate that is situated at the entrance of a golden castle in the sky. Take one deep, relaxing, cleansing breath and step onto the escalator. The step you take will move gently up toward the golden gate, and as you become more and more elevated, you will be getting more and more relaxed; your troubles and fears will leave you. You are comfortable and in a complete state of relaxation. Soon you will reach the golden gate; notice how beautiful it is, how radiant the color is, and how the energy exuding from it touches you. Take hold of the handle on the gate and feel the ethereal energy run through your body, cleansing every part; it's like surging electricity, but pure and cleansing at the same time. Open the gate and walk through. You will now find yourself standing on a golden drawbridge, and beyond you is the entrance to the castle, which stands majestically before you. Inside of this majestic building are those answers you seek. Now you must have the courage to move forward and investigate the castle. This is indeed an exciting journey!

ALERT

Fear is a great barrier to success, and the way to overcome it is through the use of your affirmations. The words that are created in your affirmation have a commanding effect over your mind. It is like re-training your subconscious mind to accept these commands and respond in a kinder way by releasing your fears. The secret to ensuring that the affirmation works is to believe it.

Walk slowly through the gate and find yourself in a courtyard where the sun is shining through from the sky above. Notice that castle walls surround you on all sides, and looking toward the sky above, you can see the four turrets on each corner. Around each of the walls are various doors that will lead to a small stone spiral staircase, and on each of the doors is a particular date (such as 1847), which leads to that time period. You must choose one of these doors with the years on the front to go through and explore further. Which will you choose to explore? Is there a particular date that you are drawn to?

QUESTION

What do the dates on each door correspond to?
Each date that you see upon the door represents a time period. You should only choose the door that feels right with you. You will feel which one is right as the excitement builds within you when you see the corresponding date upon the door.

Great! You have chosen your door and now find yourself at the bottom of a spiral staircase. You must begin to walk up the stairs toward another door—can you see it? It is a strong oak door with a golden handle, and again the door has a date upon it—and also a name. This name is who you were within that time. Remember this name, for it will be an important piece of information for you in your search for answers. Open the door and walk in; you are now in the place that you lived, and beyond the room is another door that leads to the outside environment, which you lived in.

What do you notice? Who are the people there? Are there any familiar smells? What are the sounds that you hear? Take in all the information that you need at that moment in time. Register this in your mind. Now you can ask to be shown information that you need, such as: What happened in this lifetime that has caused the blockages in my present incarnation? Immediately, you will be shown or transported to witness the event or the cause that co-created your present incarnation. (Note that there is nothing to fear at this time and you are perfectly safe; you are viewing this from a detached point of view and will not be emotionally attached in any way.)

QUESTION

Will I really be the person whose name I see etched upon the door? Only you will know this, and it will come as a spiritual awareness that only you will recognize. It will be like an etheric cord has been attached and filled you with the energy of recognition.

After you have taken as much information as possible, you will turn around and walk out of the room. You'll know the experience has enlightened you considerably. You will feel that you have gained much knowledge, and know that you can return at any time to further this knowledge. Walk out of the door and down the spiral staircase once more. Soon you will reach the bottom of the staircase and will be faced with the door to the courtyard. As you walk out into the courtyard and back to the gate, you will feel the beautiful sunshine beating down on you, bringing an air of calm and warmth around you.

You will soon find yourself at the top of the escalator that brought you to the castle gates. Just before you step onto the escalator to go back to your own reality, you may wish to take one look back at your golden castle. Now, step onto the escalator and feel the movement gently taking you back to your own awareness. As you move down toward the bottom, you will begin to become aware of your breathing once more, and you will become aware of the gentle movements of your body. You may even notice that your eyes are beginning to move, and with the awareness of your breath you will find yourself back in your comfortable seat.

ALERT

During your journey, you may at this time decide to walk through another doorway in the castle if you feel you are up to it, but if not, you can make your way back out of the courtyard and know that you can return to investigate the other doors and other incarnations any time you choose. Walk once more through the drawbridge, and as you walk, contemplate what you have just learned.

You have finished this exercise. How well do you think you did? You're not done yet, though. This is when you have to take your notes and contemplate what you have just learned. You will see the importance of the journal in the next section, but if you have a notepad and paper, write down what you saw or what you heard. How did you feel, and how do you think it relates to your present circumstances? Well done! Go back and do it all again to learn more, but do not do this any more than two times in a row or you may overload yourself. Perhaps stretch this out over a few weeks, maybe once a week for a month or so.

Keeping a Journal

Your journal will be one of the most important records that you can have in your life. It's indispensable as you embark on your spiritual journey to keep track of all your thoughts, feelings, and experiences within its pages. The journal also acts as a measurement tool that will denote your progress and level of spiritual growth. Do not see it as a notebook for jotting down the odd thought but more of a tool on the path to spiritual progression. It is important to utilize your journal as much as possible, for this will help you to analyze information that you receive and write down, which may appertain to particular events or occurrences in your past incarnations.

ESSENTIAL

Your journal should become your new best friend; it will be the yardstick that will measure your successes, your failures, and your greatest achievements. It can show you, through your own awareness, what patterns are emerging and where your weaknesses lie. Do not go anywhere without your journal, and have it near you even while you sleep.

Adding to Your Spiritual Arsenal

Your journal should be cherished and should become part of your spiritual arsenal. It is important to ensure that your journal is on hand whenever you take part in any of the spiritual exercises within this book. For instance, if you had some success with the previous exercise, it would make sense to write down everything that you can about your experience. As you progress along the path, you will notice that patterns in your journal begin to emerge. These patterns may be congruent to your soul growth and may show hidden information that may give you answers to the questions you may have in the present moment.

Just a word to the wise: Don't select an ordinary notebook, as you may be more inclined not to treat it with the respect it deserves. You may wish to have a journal made for you, or you could search the Internet to find one that you are drawn to. Your journal should be something special; it should speak volumes to you.

Making Changes in Your Life

After completing your first regression exercise, you have gleaned much information regarding your past incarnations. Now it is time to make changes in your life so that you can co-create the life that is your birthright, not the one that may be governed by other peoples' perceptions.

ALERT

Most people's lives seem to be dictated by what others say is the right thing, or that their way is the right way. How many people do you see who follow what the rest of the country is doing because that is what they are told is correct? This is all about perception, and what some may perceive will not be what fits you. It is important to follow your intuition and your heart. You do not have to be a sheep!

It is no use having all the intelligence and information at your fingertips—life is about action. In order to co-create your life and to heal from your present blockages, you have to do the work yourself. This book is your guide, and it can only give you the tools that you need in order to progress you in your present incarnation.

Imagine you have just taken your car to the garage to be fixed. When you arrive, you find that no mechanic is there to help you, but inside are all the tools that you need to fix your car. You can know what all the tools are, and you may have all the knowledge on how to use them, but if you do not actually take any action or attempt to use the tools, your car will remain in a state of disrepair. This analogy is exactly what your life may be like; only you can make the decision to change, and only you can take the action now.

Abusive Patterns

Many individuals who have suffered abuse in this lifetime may also have suffered abuse in a past incarnation. The reason that they continue to suffer from this is because they continually carry out the same patterns in life, which keep them in that cycle of abuse—like a circle with no beginning and no end. The only way that you can make the requisite changes is to create a new circle yourself. Of course, you have to have the belief that you can do this. Follow the simple belief process of manifestation: perceive—believe—conceive. These three stages are the secret ingredients to manifestation, and along with the correct emotion, you can achieve anything and create your new circle as long as you take action.

ESSENTIAL

Perceive, believe, and conceive. This is the secret to manifestation; there is no way that you can manifest something if you do not adjoin the emotion and the belief together as one spiritual energy. When this recipe is followed, it almost feels like a magical awakening.

You will find that when you take action, your life will run smoothly, and all you need are the tools, which you have been given in this book. What you must remember is that although you have all the tools, you are the only one who can change you for the better. Life is all about choice, and you are the only one who can make that choice by using your gift of free will.

Relaxation Techniques

There are a myriad of relaxation methods that you can use, and these exist in all walks of life. In fact, it is big business, and the alternative therapy business that offers so much healing and relaxation is worth millions—if not billions—each year. You would think that relaxing is the easiest thing in the world to do. The truth is that it is easy, yet within the ease, difficulty is concealed. It seems that for something so easy, most individuals find it difficult to achieve. Consider the act of meditation. When you first start it, you may find that it is difficult. Your mind and reality keep you from entering that relaxing state. When you listen to music, it can take you to a state of relaxation, but only so far because, again, your mind becomes alert depending on the rhythm of the music.

But what of your emotions and your fears? These are the elements that keep you away from that relaxation that you crave. If you are worried or nervous, you will stop yourself from relaxing as your lower self revels in those issues that are the cause of your emotional point of attraction. It is a simple spiritual law of cause and effect. The cause is the trigger to your negative emotions, and the effect is the fact that you cannot relax or that you cannot find that inner peace. What you must remember is that you have that inner power that you can call upon to defeat anything that may be hindering you and causing your present circumstances.

It's All in the Breath

What is the secret then? Ask yourself this question over and over, and notice what comes to the forefront of your mind before you find the answer. It really is simple—without it you could not live, and you would not have any existence in which you could experience the now, the present, and the inner worlds. Have you guessed it or recognized what the secret is? Everything is in the breath, and within the breath is the secret to life and the inner worlds. Breath is the secret to meet the you that is the *real you*, the one who exists on all levels and has experienced the many lives that have been the cause of your incarnation now.

ESSENTIAL

The secret of life is in the breath, for everything exists this way. Without it, you would die, and to harness its power brings peace, tranquility, answers, direction, and inner cleansing. The breath has been discussed and practiced in all ancient civilizations, yet its power is often overlooked in the modern day.

To get a deep appreciation for the breath or for breathing properly, you need to understand that the simple act of breathing is what fuels you. It's what keeps you alive, yet very often most individuals take this for granted. You breathe in air each day and do not see that you are indeed living the miracle that is life itself. You only need to refer to scripture to see how important breath is. It was noted in the beginning of the Bible that God breathed life into man, which was how that indomitable spirit became animated within human creation. So the secret to relaxation is to learn to become aware of the breath, even before you start to learn how to breathe deeply. Deep breathing is a skill in itself and is not that easy to keep going properly—but it most certainly is the key to relaxation. The following breath awareness exercise will allow you to become more in tune with your body and mind as one working unit. To be able to understand anything on a much deeper level requires awareness, and this awareness is the inner knowing of yourself— not just a case of registering your external environment by physical senses and perception.

Exercise: Breath Awareness

Choose a suitable place that you can lie down in relative comfort and ensure that no external distractions exist—remain in complete silence. You may wish to choose your own bed; this is where you will spend almost half of your life, so it would seem a suitable choice where you can contemplate in comfort and safety.

Lie on your bed, and when you have reached an appropriate level of comfort, cross your hands gently on your abdomen. Now close your eyes and begin to take your first breath. As you inhale, you should begin to notice how the air is drawn in by your physical attributes of your body, and become aware of how it really feels. Keep your mouth closed at this point, and only inhale through your nose. You will notice the air you inhale feels almost cold and refreshing; this feeling is clean and comforting as well as life giving. You should also notice that you are able to feel the air rushing through your nasal cavity, almost purifying as it goes. Now exhale and take another breath inward, and this time become aware of how your chest rises and falls with each inhale and exhale. Feel the weight of your hands and notice the air coming in, how it animates the physical movement of your hands up and down, gently without restriction.

ALERT

Do not force the air in through your nose or mouth, as this will also take you out of your relaxing state of being. You should ensure that you breathe in a deep but gentle way to ensure that you get the maximum effect and that you stay in your relaxed state.

Take one more in-breath, but this time you may open your mouth to experience the inflow of the breath. Repeat the same process, and notice how your physical body feels as you draw the air in through your mouth. How does it feel when you fill your lungs with fresh air? Can you imagine how cleansing the air is as it enters your body and purifies as it goes? Do you feel the freshness of the air? You will also feel your hands moving up and down just the same as before, unrestricted and with ease.

You should now have an awareness of your breath, and this beginning awareness will be added to your subconscious so that you become more in tune with the breath each time. It won't seem like something you don't think of and take for granted, and you will come to a recognition of its inherent power the more you carry out the exercise. At this point you will be able to move forward and learn to relax using this breath awareness. In the following passages, other exercises are offered with the use of breath awareness to enjoy the ultimate relaxation. You may wish to test this by taking your heart rate and making notes of how you feel physically and mentally.

Walking Relaxation

This is an exercise that is very relaxing, but of course many of you who are not used to taking exercise will find this a chore—only do as much as you can do. You can be assured that if you do this exercise correctly, you will not exert yourself at all. What you have to do is choose an area where you can do a short walk—preferably a circular walk that will start and end at the place you started. The importance here is that you walk slowly and mindfully, and this should be in an area of natural beauty away from the hustle and bustle of life. As you walk slowly, you will continue the breathing awareness exercise, but do this as you walk. Take your deep breaths and become aware of your breathing as you walk. Perhaps you will want to breathe in deeply with each step. At this moment you can allow your mind to wander off; you will become amazed at the insights that you have during the relaxation. You can find answers to problems, and you could even possibly cast your mind to a previous incarnation that you know about. You are in natural beauty—a miracle of the great spirit.

Bath Relaxation

When most people think about relaxation, they almost always include having a nice warming and comforting bubble bath. The truth is that even when in the bath, your mind will constantly keep going over the problems that have caused you anguish and stress during the day. Just like before, the awareness of the breath is most important, and this is the key to relaxing in the bath; actually, it is the key to relaxation. What you must be aware of is that you do not fall asleep, as there is a danger of drowning. When you are in the state that keeps you relaxed, you can once again allow your mind to drift off and ask to be shown in your mind any issues that may be blocking your progress in life. Also, if you are experiencing an issue and cannot find an explanation or a solution, you will find that you can access your higher awareness when you are in this relaxing state in your bath.

Music Relaxation

It is said that "music soothes the savage beast," which does have some truth in it, but it really does depend on the type of music. Imagine if you had heavy rock music playing while you are trying to meditate or relax. This type of music is certainly not conducive to relaxation because of the intensity of the vibrations. These vibrations are too strong and cause mental fluctuations within your brain waves, which in turn react in a physical and emotional way. There are times when the music can make you overjoyed, and other times where the vibrations can evoke such emotion that it can literally give you goose bumps. So you can see how music can have an effect on you in mind and body. It would then seem appropriate to suggest that if you are musically minded, you would react positively to the right music with the right ambiance in order to promote a deep relaxation within the mind and body. Of course, many people may not necessarily react the same way to the type of music that would have an effect on you. The constant, however, is this—music that will promote relaxation will be quiet and melodious music and not the type that is rapturous in rhythm.

Choose the music that you are drawn to, and ensure this piece of music is calming and relaxing. Once again, lie on your back in the bedroom and ensure that you are not disturbed in any way. Remain in the dark. Go back to the breath awareness exercise and carry this out once more but with the music playing lightly in the background. This is an effective method of promoting relaxation, and this time it is quite all right to fall asleep.

Relaxation with Your Pet

It may seem strange to add an exercise that involves animals, but animals have been used to promote good health, to offer comfort, and to soothe anger and upset for a very long time. The use of animals in alternative therapy is certainly evident, even within hospitals today, and so you can use your pets to promote relaxation.

ESSENTIAL

Pets such as house cats, rabbits, and dogs have been used in many healing methods in the modern world. If you consider how an animal such as a guide dog can bring happiness, comfort, and ease a lonely heart, surely it is easy to see the benefits of other animals at easing negative emotion and promoting relaxation.

If you have a pet that you are drawn to, such as your cat or dog, sit with your animal on your lap and allow it to settle. Again, do the same breath awareness exercise, but this time as you breathe in stroke your pet with your in-breath and your out-breath. Soon you will find that you are deeply relaxed, and your mind can once again wander to the inner workings of your soul to retrieve information. As a side effect, you should also see positive signs in your pet as you become more relaxed; so too will your favorite cat or dog. These animals are used because they are most conducive to the promotion of relaxation. Spiders, snakes, and other creepy crawlies will not have the same effect.

CHAPTER 11

Accessing Dream State Lives

In this book, you have learned a little about your dreams and your past incarnations with regard to your dreams. In this chapter you will expand your awareness of your past life dreams by learning how you can recognize your dream states and what is real and what is not. In this way you can learn to analyze what is truly from a higher authority or the product of an overactive imagination.

Past Lives and Dreams

In the last chapter you learned how to access your past life incarnations, but now you are going to go one stage further. After becoming aware of your past incarnations, it's now time to activate your dream state. When you activate your dream state, you go one stage further because you are entering a deeper altered state where the senses are heightened. No one can really explain how this happens, and as far as science is concerned, it is a question that remains unanswered. When you sleep, your inquiring mind will already have been activated during your research phase. In your sleep, your dreams may have some hidden meaning that is being brought forward from your subconscious.

Edgar Cayce gave readings that enlightened the nature of dreams. He stated that dreams are often given for your benefit, and that you experience many different levels of awareness when you are in the dream state. In this state you can access information that relates to your life on all levels.

Dreams therefore can help you to diagnose issues that may be related to these incarnations, such as health issues, any negative events that you may have partaken in, and the decisions that ultimately led to blockages in your present incarnation.

QUESTION

What do my dreams contain?
Your dreams often contain a great deal of information on your life in the present and can often give you a window through which to view the past. Cayce maintained that nothing happens on a large scale in your present existence that has not already arisen previously in your dream state.

Once you have gained some insight into your situation or your life, you as the dreamer can decide how you will act upon this information in your waking state. It could be that you need to change careers or that you may have to have a new perspective in life that will change many elements. You may have an anger issue that was highlighted in your dream. Then you can take the appropriate measures to rectify the anger. You have to be the one to take action; you are responsible for all your actions.

Types of Dreams

In trying to break down the types of dreams that you may have, keep it simple. There is no need to delve into scientific protocols for this; the easier it is for you to understand, the more rapid your progress will be. There are only a few types of dreams that you need to learn about. These are prophetic, intelligent, and medical dreams. Many people claim that there are more areas of dream research, but you will make progress if you just keep it simple.

Prophetic Dreams

These dreams are not the kind that you would take much notice of when it comes to past lives. However, you should be aware that your past incarnations have helped to create your present circumstances. Would it not seem natural that the flow of those circumstances could cause other events to be predetermined at a future point in time? With dreams of a prophetic nature you can work your way from the effect back to the cause. This is quite a difficult method to teach, and only you will be able to become aware of the intricacies and nature of the dream. Suppose you have a recurring dream that you were in a train, and the train was always coming off the rails. This could mean many things, but it would be safe to assume that your subconscious is pointing you in the direction of the path you are currently on. Write this down in your journal and look at your present circumstances to identify if there are any patterns. Ask yourself what you may be able to change in your life in order that you do not go wrong anymore, and see what comes up in your next dream. You may then experience the same dream, and the train could remain on the rails. This would obviously tell you that you are on the right track, so to speak.

Intelligent Dreams

These types of dreams are the ones that will enlighten you and give you information that pertains to your past incarnations and the issues that may have created your present circumstances. These dreams will be in depth and will include a great deal of imagery that you will have to put together, rather like a jigsaw puzzle. Therefore, it will be difficult to provide a solid example here because everyone's imagery will be different.

However, that is not to say that you cannot learn how to read this type of dream. What you must do is ensure that you take down as much detail as possible—that means remembering as much as you can, which is not as easy as it sounds. Dreams are not easy to remember when you wake up simply because of the spiritual vibration of the dream itself. Before you panic, there is some preparation that you can do to remember your dreams, which you will learn in the next few sections. As you become aware that you have had this type of dream, you will wake temporarily from your sleep because of the emotional effect of the dream. This is when your journal—which should be by your bedside and ready at any time—will come in use.

Medical Dreams

Medical dreams are those dreams that potentially will evoke the most emotions. They can show you how you may have passed in your previous life and what medical conditions you may have brought with you into your present existence.

ALERT

Do not force the air in through your nose or mouth, as this will also take you out of your relaxing state of being. You should ensure that you breathe in a deep but gentle way to ensure that you get the maximum effect and that you stay in your relaxed state.

Say you were injured on the battlefield in a past incarnation, and in this life you suffer in the same area that you sustained your injuries. You may also suffer from a rare disease, and the disease may have been manifested from your past karmic ties. Obviously, if you can identify these issues and deal with them, there is a high probability that you will heal from any disease or health-related concerns that you may have. Fear of diseases and injuries could also be attributable to past life circumstances, and these types of dreams will give you the answers that you seek.

Why Can't I Remember?

Before this question is answered, you must come to the realization that you are a spirit in human form and not a human in spirit form. This statement is incredibly powerful and is a spiritual truth as to the reality of existence. This means that you are a material substance that clothes the real you, which is in essence the etheric counterpart. Your body is the covering of what is known in spiritual circles as the perispirit. As was mentioned previously, everything in life, either animate or inanimate, consists of atoms that vibrate and bind together under certain conditions. When the conditions are present, then it is perceived by the material senses. You are also made of these atoms and are nothing more than energy under superconscious direction.

QUESTION

What is the etheric?
The etheric is the matter that makes up the spiritual reality that surrounds and is part of you. Humans are essentially made of this etheric matter, and this is the real you. The etheric is also matter that creates much of what the spirit world is. If you look at everything around you, in reality it is an illusion that cloaks the real matter.

As a spiritual being, you vibrate at a different rate than your physical counterpart does. So what does this mean when it comes to your dream state? What actually happens each night when you sleep? This may seem like a "way out there" statement, but you leave your physical body and you visit the world of spirit where you learn and prepare for your entry into your next phase of life. This means that your perispirit leaves your physical vehicle and goes back to its real home where you will learn lessons, spend time with loved ones, and prepare for your next life. While you are in the spirit world, you can also learn about your past incarnations and the karma that has beset you, and what you must do to repay the debt. This all happens on such a light vibration that when you come back to the physical realm, you have to reduce your vibration to become animated once again in the physical vehicle. It is at this point that you will forget your lessons and your visit to the realm of the spirit. This is why you cannot remember your dreams.

However, it should be noted that your soul never forgets anything at all; that should give you some comfort.

Are There Answers in Dreams?

Yes, just as with past life regression, there are answers to your life's problems in your dreams. However, not all dreams will be spiritual in nature, and some can be just sheer nonsense, perhaps manifested from a chemical imbalance due to certain foods that you may have consumed. A dream could also relate to your point of emotional balance. There is a clear distinction between these dreams. If the elements of the dreams follow some form or pattern that activates some inner awareness, you can be assured that you have discerned the dream as being from your higher self or from what you may have learned in the world of spirit. If the dream makes no sense and invokes no deep knowing or spiritual response from your inner awareness, you can be assured this dream means nothing.

Stuck-in-the-Past Dreams

What if you were continually having the same dream and found yourself in the same time period over and over again? What do you think this would suggest to you? It could mean that you have unresolved issues from the past incarnation that you are dreaming about. Again, this is an awareness issue; you need to become aware of the fact that you may have unresolved issues. The content of the dream will be what will point you in the direction of the event that causes you to constantly return to that time in your dream state.

The spirit world will cause you to continually have the same dream until you take the appropriate action. Remember that to change anything in your life you must have the awareness of the cause and the effect. Once this awareness has been reached, nothing will change until you take action. Therefore, if you do not want to be stuck in the past, you must take the appropriate measures to ensure that you rectify any mistakes you have made.

Controlling the Outcome of Your Dreams

Can you control the outcome of your dreams? The simple answer to this question is no! You cannot control dreams yourself, because most of the time it will be the spirit part of you, or even other discarnate beings, that will be communicating with you in this particular dream state. The information can be accessed memories, or it could be loved ones who are trying to impart information—perhaps even a guide. The truth remains that when you are in the dream state, you are not able to control the outcome, and if you do try to intercept anything, you will find yourself coming out of the dream state rather quickly. It is important then that you enter this state with no expectations, fully aware that you will only be taking part in the dream from a detached perspective.

CHAPTER 12

Astral Travel

In this chapter you will learn about astral travel and how this unique skill can help you in your search for answers from your past incarnations. In the following sections, Camilla Persson, an expert and advisor to the ASSMPI (American Society for Standards in Mediumship and Psychical Investigation), has included her professional perspective to ensure that you are receiving the best information this book can offer. Camilla Persson is also an author of books on astral travel and soul journeying. Much of what is contained in this chapter has been gleaned from Camilla's many years of experience.

Astral Travel Defined

Astral travel is also known as astral projection. This is the ability to travel outside of your own physical body by thought projection. This involves getting into an altered state of consciousness and using the spiritual body, or the perispirit, as the vehicle for this form of travel.

QUESTION

What is the perispirit?
The perispirit is the etheric counterpart of the physical body. It replicates your physical body in every way. It is interesting because the perispirit is not subject to disease or irregularity; if you lost a limb in this life, that does not follow in the next life or with the perispirit.

During the process of astral projection, the conscious part of the mind leaves the material plane by raising the vibration enough to exit from the crown chakra, which is the spiritual gateway to the astral from the material. This means that you are consciously aware of what you see, hear, and feel in the realm of the spirit, and you are continually attached to the material plane by a silver etheric cord. This cord is not restricted in any way and is what keeps your connection to the material world. When you pass into the world of spirit, your etheric cord will sever, and you will no longer be connected to the material plane of expression. As there is no conception of time or space in the spirit world, it would seem evident that you could visit your past incarnations if you were allowed to do so.

An interesting fact to note is that with the information that has been gathered from individuals who have taken part in astral travel, either self-induced or naturally, they have all returned with reports of seeing the silver cord.

Common Myths about Astral Travel

There are many myths when it comes to astral travel, but for the most part, these myths are merely the result of fear and ignorance. Fear may be from the consequence of individuals not understanding what actually happens during the process of astral travel. Fear may have been created in your own mind because you are frightened of anything happening that you cannot control. In the following sections, several myths are described so you will have a basic understanding and can allay any fears that you may have.

ALERT

One of the most important things that you should ensure when astral projecting is to be comfortable, and that means for your physical body that you have left behind. The reason is because there is a tendency for your body to become cold when your spiritual body is off on its travels.

Myth: "You can die while having an astral projection."

Comment: This myth is based on misunderstanding what you are. You are eternal energy; therefore, you cannot die and cannot be destroyed, which should empower you. Anyone who has ever studied physics has learned that energy is a constant in motion and cannot end; its expression just changes into another form. Moreover, you must go back to your physical body and physical reality—your time has not ended yet. Besides, research, surveys, and the content in related literature shows that there are no dangers with astral projections at all.

Myth: "You can get stuck out there."

Comment: This is a common fear among inexperienced explorers, but, no, you cannot get stuck on an astral plane, and nothing can happen to your physical body. These are irrational fears from the ego and brain based on false notions that you have something to worry about. Again, nothing bad can happen in the astral that will affect your physical body. One suggestion that explains this is due to spiritual law, and the fact that the cord that is connected between the energy body and the physical body only snaps when the death of the physical body is about to occur.

Myth: "You need to be a clean living person without any burdens or habits."

Comment: No, but you will probably start to improve your life and fitness as a consequence of your astral explorations when you progress in spirituality, which is inevitable. (Astral travel does attract to you the experiences that replicate your vibration, which is why those on drugs rarely have good experiences.) This used to be an immediate effect of the insight that you are more than your body and there are more planes of existence than the physical. Often you will return from your journey with a heightened awareness of the soul, and psychic abilities will normally manifest.

Myth: "You can lose the concept of reality and become psychologically imbalanced."

Comment: The reality is that you become wiser through this exceptional adventure as you learn about the realities of the spirit. The spirit world is a rich tapestry of reality, and you will find that you are spirit in human form. This will empower you and show that you have an innate spiritual power that can help you get through anything in life. The spirit world is just as real as your own reality—only better.

Myth: "You will become tired or drained from astral projections."

Comment: Given that you handle your inner journeys with some sort of balance, you won't be tired; in fact, these travels will instead give energy and vitalization.

Can Anyone Do It?

The question cannot be really answered in its entirety because it comes down to a simple case of choice. The question then should be proposed in another way, such as: Do you want to travel to another dimension? Within this question is the carrot that may dangle in front of you. As a youngster, you most probably had an imagination that took you to alternate realities. Therefore, the chance to return to this alternate reality but in the real sense of the word is too much to pass by. In essence then, the truth is that, yes, anyone can travel, though has to be a personal choice.

Everyone is doing it already without any knowledge. Every night. The soul never sleeps; you're just unaware that you are visiting other dimensions during the night. But to do conscious projections in real time and have the ability to remember them, you need to work on it, as with anything in life.

How to Travel

There is only one way to travel, and following are several facets of that method for your study and participation.

Eliminate the Fears

Keep in mind that the law of attraction governs everything. Try to get rid of fears of the unseen realms. Fear could attract energies that will create an astral projection that may result in a negative experience. It's better to desire and have a strong positive attraction. That will also serve your outside body if you want to reach higher planes. You have no benefits from fear in this state.

Lie Down and Keep the Body Still

You cannot stand or sit if you want to leave your body. You must place your body on a bed or sofa with the intention that your body will go to sleep but not your awareness. The body should be kept as still as possible, and the spine must be perfectly straight and still, which enables ease of travel of spiritual energies through the chakras. When the physical body is still, the etheric body starts to move.

Learn to Deep Breathe

Try different breathing techniques in order to reach altered state of consciousness. If you remember from the previous chapters, it was discussed how important the breath is to life itself. It is through the breath that you will reach the alternate states.

Give Yourself Suggestions/Affirmations

Suggestions like "I am satisfied and have no fears" or "I am soon out of body and I can see with my psychic eye" will trigger your hidden know-how. Create your own affirmations that will suit your desire.

Deepen the Entrancement

Learn how to open up each of the seven chakras, the energy vortex going through the spine. Use your mind to spin each chakra and raise the bodily energy. Start at the bottom of your spine and go from tail to skull. Pay attention to what happens inside of your body. Notice that, when you increase the speed, your body will naturally become vibrant. At this stage, when the body is becoming vibrant, you increase the potential for the projection of the astral body or etheric body. When the speed is very high, you will leave the physical plane and enter into a new one, one that matches the speed of your astral body.

ESSENTIAL

The chakras are very important when it comes to astral projection. Chakras are spinning energy centers that influence your well-being. Without control of your chakras and understanding the energy associated with them, you will not be able to project your body outside of yourself. You will therefore be stuck in the same physical reality that you are trying to leave. For more on chakras, see *The Everything*® *Guide to Chakra Healing*.

Be Purposeful

It can take quite a while to induce the deep trance state and the energy work that is needed for astral projection. You should persevere and stay with the program; some things are worth waiting for. You should be able to stay in the deep trance condition for at least one hour if possible. The out-of-body mode is a very deep state of mind that is close to the sleeping state. But it's not an unconscious state like sleep, it's the opposite—you are awake, but in a new way.

Exercise: Traveling to Another Time and Realm

This exercise is kindly given by Camilla Persson, who is on the board of the ASSMPI (American Society for Standards in Mediumship and Psychical Investigation). Camilla is a resident expert in out-of-body exploration and an author of many works on the subject. She currently resides and teaches in Sweden and is a member of the Swiss SPR.

Exploring other times and space through inner journeys demands an open mind, right intentions, and a strong will. Back in history there was a secret code of prerequisites for astral travelers, only for the initiate. It said:

- To know
- To desire
- To have faith
- To be silent

To be able to achieve real astral journeys, you must raise your bodily vibration. By doing this you achieve the state that is the catalyst to your leaving through your crown chakra. This will automatically give you an altered state of consciousness and allow you to reach other planes of existence, such as astral planes and the higher realms of the spirit world. It is called an "inner" journey, but in fact those worlds are not more "inner" than the physical one; it just appears to be like that. These experiences will give you another insight and a different overview.

The key to astral journeys is relaxation and concentration, but both at the same time. You might realize that relaxation and increased focus in mind are in conflict, as you often fall asleep when you get very relaxed. This, however, will decrease after some training and become a natural state for you, where you don't lose consciousness but instead learn about your hidden resources. When you are ready, you can try to deepen the muscular relaxation as much as possible and, at the same time, increase your awareness. The goal is to achieve a state where your body will sleep but not your mind. You are making a change within yourself with the result of losing earth consciousness. It will be replaced by spiritual awareness, which is a superconscious state of mind.

Self-Induced Practice: Traveling to Another Time and Realm

This is a short exercise that you can try. Do not think that you will be able to achieve success instantly, because it takes some time and practice to induce astral travel effectively. Please note that the time indication is just a suggestion.

Step One, Approximately Twenty Minutes: Muscular and Mental Relaxation

Lie down on a bed or sofa. Take a deep breath and relax thoroughly. Allow only a happy mental and emotional state when entering spiritual exercises. Drop all your daytime problems and focus on nothing. Try to be calm in mind, and if you have any fears for the exercise and the unknown, please deal with that before doing this exercise. To keep alert, place all your attention, all your consciousness, a bit outside your forehead, just in the third eye, right between the eyebrows, but 4 inches outside your face. Try to hold your spinal cord straight and avoid moving your body. Walk through the body and press the muscles by physical action with your conscious mind, then relax the muscles each in turn and from top to toe.

Allow yourself to relax more and more. If there is any emotional disturbance in your mind, just ignore the thoughts, watch them drift away, and don't get attached to them. Your thought pattern will slow down for now, and the only thing you should focus on is to get thoroughly relaxed without falling asleep.

ESSENTIAL

The importance of relaxation is paramount. If you cannot relax yourself effectively enough, then your attempts to master the altered state that you seek will be futile. You will find that the more you try to force the issue, the further you will get from your goals.

Use a breathing technique to mesmerize yourself and help spirit guides to link to you, but don't drop your consciousness. Remember, your only intention is to deliberately project yourself into a past time and reality.

Step Two, Approximately Thirty Minutes: Linking to Your Inner Light Guide

When you are totally relaxed, try formulating a wish to your inner light guide and ask to see a glimpse of a past life. When you telepathically (in your mind) communicate with your guide's lines, it will respond in such a way as you are capable to receive. Try to eliminate all other thoughts and ideas and just focus on your wish to explore another time. Be patient and wait for the opportunity. Be aware that you may not be allowed to view this because of the level of your own soul growth. All you can do is ask, and if it is in alignment with your highest good, it will happen.

It's important to understand that some people will immediately be given an ecstatic conscious experience of another time and place that will astound them for months or even years, while others will have less magnificence and perhaps think it was only a daydream or a fantasy. If that is the case, try to be patient. Keep in mind that there are many ways to perform inner journeys, and some of them are just mind travels not using the astral body. Try not to have any preconceived ideas about how the journey will take place. The answers to your prayers will come; the delivery from spirit is given when spirit thinks the time is appropriate. It's a true gift from spirit to enlighten you, and it could be on top of whatever you experienced in your life.

Step Three, Approximately Ten Minutes: Content Analysis

Write down your experience and what it meant to you. Repeat the exercise a couple of days later and see if something has changed. Enjoy!

What Can You Learn from Astral Travel?

The benefits and advantages of astral travel and out-of-body experiences are countless as you reach the deepest, most profound aspects of yourself. You leave the physical realm, entering another energy system, the so-called astral dimensions, and the spirit world. This experience will definitely bring you a whole new perspective on life. Your intention to learn can open up wondrous possibilities, and in the words of the Nazarene, "all answers are within."

Who was or is the Nazarene?
Who do you think this is in reference to? It is, in fact, Jesus Christ, who was a normal man born with the strongest facet of divinity that is known today. There is a great deal of controversy surrounding Jesus, and millions worship him in the modern world. Jesus was the greatest expression of divine authority that incarnated and was the greatest medium who ever walked the earth.

In general, astral travel and out-of-body experiences give you answers to a number of existential questions, such as "What am I?" and "Where did I come from?" These journeys will primarily teach you on a subjective basis; you get to know yourself better and learn about the mind, but you will also find out about spiritual laws and how the universal consciousness works on a higher level.

The spiritual laws are the divine laws of nature that govern all that dictates life, creation, and the results of actions. The laws are immutable and perfect in expression and operation. They give no quarter and no one can escape them; these are the laws that show that miracles are natural and not an expression of unusual supernormal means.

Revisiting the Law of Attraction

The law of attraction is among the first things you'll learn in the out-of-body state. This means that you will attract to you what you vibrate at, so if you are vibrating at a high level, you will attract those experiences that replicate that level. If you are vibrating at a low level, then, similarly, you will attract those experiences that vibrate at that level. This is an immutable law that cannot change; it is perfect in operation. This immutable law exists within the spiritual and even within the physical plane that you live on. But in the heavenly realms of bright light, this law takes on a new context, for darkness cannot exist in the higher levels of the spirit world. Those worlds of pure love and joy, which are also a target for astral voyagers, are the expression of divine authority.

As the law of attraction is essential for your life in the physical plane, you have to become more aware of your thought processes. Therefore, you should only allow positive thoughts to attract positive experiences. In the astral dimension you will also study how the matter correlates to the mind. Another thing you can study in the astral dimension is how easily you get distracted and influenced by the subtle variances in vibrations. If you ever wonder why things take such time to manifest or why you feel sidetracked, you will understand it's because you allow yourself to be disoriented, unfocused, and easily distracted. You see things much clearer here, and you can learn from it and bring it back to your ordinary consciousness and time sphere. Through astral journeys you can improve your psychic character, which will help you in your daily life. You will get wiser as the things you learn on the astral planes are connected.

What Am I?

This is a question that burdens the greatest thinkers in life. In the spirit you will find many different states and conditions of consciousness, and these are possible for you to explore. In some inner journeys you'll find that your ego and personal characteristics are lost. Instead, you feel that you are part of the universal consciousness; you are aware of the higher intelligence and infinite love. This experience is tremendous when it comes to understanding life on a much higher level. Other journeys show you the lower frequencies where you still have an ego and are attracted to lower influences. These states remind you of your common, earthly consciousness. In literature this is called lower astral realms, where the space is habituated of minds that are far from perfect.

In further journeys you'll find yourself so changed that you can no longer identify yourself as a person. Instead, you might say that you just explored a higher consciousness, totally free from every thought, emotion, and impression of a negative sort. You had the sensation of existing in a much more positive state in a realm and in a consciousness without fear and disharmony. Many people say that this was real, similar to a feeling of being carried back home.

Where Did I Come From?

This question can be answered in many ways, and inner journeys are a perfect way to explore where you come from, not only involving the spirit world, but the actual life before the one you have now. This is how you can view your past incarnations.

Visiting Past Life Through Astral Travel (Camilla's Case Study)

One of Camilla's course participants is absolutely sure she was shown a past life via the out-of-body state. She is totally convinced she was brought back in time and could recognize the surroundings, house, people, as well as time period. She has done some research afterward, even visiting the place, which made her absolutely convinced she really was experiencing a past life. She says this journey didn't have the character of a hypnotic regression to a past life that she has also experienced. This past-life journey was much more than that; she was really there, she states.

But she is not the only one who has experienced this type of exploration; it's often mentioned by astral travelers as one of the things you can do while outside the body. As it's possible to explore a past incarnation, you can also try to move in the opposite direction—to the future. Astral journeys are all about self-exploration, transformation, and stretching the borders, and there are no limits to what you can do, other than the limits you yourself put up.

ALERT

Visiting a past life during an actual out-of-body experience can be such a validating experience because of how real it seems. This is like having a conscious experience in a dream state with all the conscious faculties at your disposal.

Visiting a past life through astral projection or regression seems to have many psychological benefits and positive effects. Understanding the past might give you the opportunity to understand who you are today and resolve problems that affect you. This is another answer to the question, "Where did I come from?" You came from the light, as well as you are the light. This could empirically be studied through those extravagant inner journeys called astral travel, soul travel, ESP projection, or out-of-body experience.

CHAPTER 13

Spirit Guides, Angels, and Regression

In this chapter you will learn about the role of your guides and your angels and the important role they play in your ability to travel back in time. You will learn that you have a spiritual ability to communicate with your celestial friends and how they may let you know they are around. You will also take part in exercises to meet these friends, and they will take you on your soul journey to your past incarnations.

Spirit Guides and Angels

In order to make your learning easier, angels and guides will be discussed together as they are both guides in the same sense of the word. The difference between the guide and the angel is that one has incarnated and one has not.

QUESTION

What is the difference between a guide and an angel?
A spirit guide is a discarnate entity that has incarnated on the earth plane. It has evolved and become very spiritual, and returns to give you guidance and aid in your soul development. An angel is a celestial being who has never incarnated upon the earth plane and exists to serve God and humanity.

What this means is that the guide has walked upon the earth and the angel has not. The reasoning is simple. The angel is a celestial being that is of pure divinity and is a messenger from the creator. An angel's vibration is so high that it has no desire to incarnate on earth. Angels know of nothing bad; they are pure in spirit and are the closest to God. The angels were created to serve the creator and to be of service to humanity; they are neither male nor female and only have purity of spirit. A guide is one who has already lived upon the earth plane and led a spiritually enlightened existence on earth and progressed further within the spirit realm.

These are your guides that will take you on your inner journey to witness and learn from the past. You cannot just expect that you will meet them and then all your answers will be revealed; you have to be sure that you are able to discern them.

ESSENTIAL

You must ensure that when you make the acquaintance of your guide or your angel that you use the power of discernment. You have to distinguish between reality and imagination, real communication and not the musings of a wandering spirit that remains tied to the earth plane.

This means that you have the requisite proof that a guide or angel will give you to prove who they are. After all, mediums look for evidence, and so should you. At this point in your journey, you are going to become your own medium at a lower level than a professional medium; there will be an element of spirit communication. Here you will learn basic communication skills that will enable you to create the link that will take you from the material to the spiritual and learn from your past lives. You will have to develop a relationship with your guides and your angels. This means that you will not be able to meet them and go straight into learning about your past lives, which is more of a long-term goal. Take your time and progress slowly but surely.

Types of Guides

So far you have done an excellent job, and you have probably gleaned a lot from other exercises. Now it is time for you to get acquainted with your spirit guide. At this point in your training, you can consider this as a gift from the world of spirit—to be introduced to your lifetime aide—the spirit who has been with you for a long time, guiding you gently with love and compassion. Notice that similarities exist with the meditative experience; this will ensure this process is etched in your subconscious mind. The differences exist when you are to meet your spirit guide. Before you get to the exercise, consider who guides may be and why.

QUESTION

Can my guide be someone of normal origin?
Yes, of course, but this all depends on the soul growth of the individual entity. The individual would have to have evolved to a high level in order to become a guide. The job of a guide is very important and carries with it much responsibility. So as long as the spirit person was evolved and took the requisite responsibility, he or she can be your guide.

What Kinds of Guides Exist?

Spirit guides are normally from some kind of ancient indigenous culture that existed before you incarnated on this earth plane. So why is your guide not Old Joe who lived during the war, or Sarah who was a cleaner down the street? The answer is simple, and although these types of guides also exist because of their spiritual understanding and growth, your guide will most probably take the aforementioned accepted form.

This accepted form of being is normally a person from an ancient indigenous tribe such as the Native Americans or the Tibetan monks. Perhaps even a seer or a spiritually enriched individual could be your guide, but he will have to have existed long before you were here. Most spiritualists will claim that the guide they have is some amazing Native American chief or famous warrior, but it could easily be a normal person; it's just what makes you comfortable and how evolved the guide actually is.

ESSENTIAL

There is a very good reason that guides are normally from indigenous tribes and similar cultures. This is because many of those individuals did not subscribe to dogma and creed and were therefore very close to the natural order of the universe and natural law.

The reason these are accepted is because these indigenous individuals led a very spiritual existence and were not bound by material concerns. They were more in tune with the world of spirit and followed no creed or dogma. That is why these individuals are chosen to become guides. They were so in tune with nature that it was a natural transition to the world of spirit. These guides have gone through many tests and naturally communicated with the world of spirit when they existed on the earth plane. When they got to the spirit world, they found it easy to carry out the tasks that were given to them.

The truth is that everyone has a guide whose job it is to help the person on her journey through her lifetime; very often they go unnoticed. This is a great shame, because your guide wants a closer relationship with you. The guide wants you to recognize him and his vibration so he can help you with your spiritual growth in this lifetime. This, of course, can mean they help you to visit past incarnations if you are stuck with issues in this lifetime. Do not deny the existence of your guide, for he does not deny you and wishes to develop a closer relationship with you.

QUESTION

Do all people have guides?
Everyone is assigned an angel and a guide. Your angel has been with you since you have existed; however, your guides often change with the type of guidance and work that you are assigned to do. Very often many individuals never notice the communication from their spirit friends, and they remain oblivious. Your spirit friends love you and are constantly trying to awaken you to their presence.

Exercise: Meeting Your Guide

Get yourself ready and wear suitable loose-fitting clothing. Find yourself a quiet spot where you will not be disturbed, and, if you wish, select some gentle music to play in the background. It is preferable not to play any music so that your spirit friend can learn to communicate with you through mingling with your energy emanations or auric field. Music will distract your mind patterns and may cause you to miss the gentle changes in the energy surrounding you.

ALERT

It is important to realize that your spirit friend only comes on a vibration of love and compassion; therefore, if your intention matches that, you need have no fear whatsoever of attracting the wrong being. At first glimpse you may be shocked or become a little fearful, and that will bring you out of your meditative state. Do not worry—just take several deep breaths and enter this state once more, and your spirit friend will come and join you again, providing the energy is still strong enough to hold the vibration.

Find a comfortable chair to sit in, but make sure that you are erect enough that you can keep your spine and torso relatively straight. Sit in the chair and begin to take deep breaths, in through your nose and out through your mouth. As you breathe in, visualize white purifying smoke coming into your body. See the white smoke coming down from the heavens above and enter through your head. Witness as the purifying smoke runs all through your body, picking up all the negative vibrations and negative energies that may be blocking your path. When you have felt the smoke has been all around your physical body picking up the negative energies, take the smoke, which will now be gray in color and heavy with all the blockages that have been inside you. Visualize the now-gray smoke leaving on your out-breath and being sent back into the atmosphere to be transmuted. You are feeling much lighter and cleaner. Now visualize a beautiful white ball of light before you. It is the most amazing light that you have seen, yet it does not blind you. Walk toward the light and enter it; feel its radiance surround you, and know this bubble of white light is always around you.

ESSENTIAL

Remember that you are protected at all times when entering the white light; ensure that you do not let any doubt creep into your mind. Remember the intention and manifestation motto: First you must perceive, then you must believe, and only then will you conceive. This statement is a secret of the universe. It is important that you do not let any thoughts of failure or fantasy enter your mind.

Imagine that you are now walking along a beautiful winding path through an enchanted forest. Feel the sunshine on your face and witness the beauty and majesty that Mother Nature has to offer. You are totally safe here and the animals have no fear of you; see them dance and play in this glorious place. As you walk along the path, you hear the gentle trickling of a stream in the distance. The sound brings you comfort, and you decide to walk toward the stream. At the edge of a stream is a large seat that is carved into a tree, and you decide to walk toward it and sit down for a while. The sounds of the birds chirping and the animals that are around are very comforting. The sun shines through the trees and cascades all over the area.

Shimmering sparkles of light cover the water, and you are totally safe and relaxed.

Sit here for a while and enjoy the area and all that the universe has to offer. Allow your thoughts to drift away and make note of anything that comes to you. Now get up and continue along your path. You are already at one in this spirit land that you have visited and are totally safe. As you walk along your forest path, you will start to see in the distance the glow of a small fire. This fire is in a clearing in the forest, and as you draw closer toward the area you will note that you are feeling more comfortable and a gentle heat caresses your spiritual body. The forest animals are following you, for they know what is about to occur and they are excited in antici-pation of the meeting that is about to take place. As you draw closer, you will note that someone is waiting for you. This is your spirit guide and can be a male or female. Do not be afraid, and feel the love that exudes from them. Take a note of who this person is; notice what this person is wear-ing, and be excited at the prospect of developing a relationship with this spirit being. This person comes to you with a pure heart and has always loved you. The spirit being makes no judgment of you and is excited that you have finally spiritually awoken. Your guide will want to make you com-fortable, and she asks you to sit by the fire with her to converse and talk. Notice everything the guide says and how the guide gestures toward you. Notice how you feel with this first meeting, and enjoy your time with your new friend.

After you have been there for a while, start to realize that you have learned a great deal and that the wise counsel of your spirit friend has allayed any suffering that you may have experienced before. You now have met your guide, and she will offer you wisdom and guidance, and promises you a sign that you will receive soon. Get up from your seat by the fire and look around the area once more. Walk along the forest path and note that your friend is becoming faint in the distance. As you walk along, you know that you have had a wonderful time in the universal garden, and know that you can revisit at any time. At the end of the path is another white light, a kind of doorway. Go toward this doorway and walk through. You now find yourself back in the room that you were in, and now you should become aware of your body in your chair and your breath. Slowly open your eyes and take one last deep breath. You are now recharged and lighter in energy.

Signs from Your Guide

You must have proof from your guide that it is really he or she who exists and is your spiritual companion. This allays any fear of being duped by some unscrupulous spirit or being played with by a grounded entity looking for fun and frolics. You need to be aware of the singular way in which the guide communicates with you. Most individuals are forever waiting for some amazing epiphany or a full-form materialization of a spirit being that will prove its worth and that the spirit being is who it claims to be. This is not the case, just a product of fantasy, for your guide will communicate with you in a more subtle way—unless you have a very strong gift of clairvoyance.

QUESTION

What is clairvoyance?
Clairvoyance is the gift of spiritual sight, which is how psychics are able to clearly see images that they can impart as information. Everyone has this gift, and it may be developed to some degree. The seat of clairvoyance is what is known as the third eye.

These signs can be so subtle that you may miss them. The truth is that the world of spirit sends signs nearly every day on the continuance of life, their compassion and forgiveness, as well as their love for us. The tragedy of it all is that most people are still asleep, and some miss these wonderful opportunities to commune and learn from those that have gone before. Therefore, the communication may be by way of a name that you hear several times, such as the name given to you in your meditation. Someone may give you a picture of your guide or something to do with the guide or the guide's culture right out of the blue. Your guide may have given you prior notice of something that would occur. Someone else could give you a message that relates to your guide, or you may even hear music that has something to do with your guide. The truth is your guide will communicate in many ways, and you should not just accept one form of proof. It is essential that you receive at least three forms of consecutive proof; then you will know it is safe to work with your guide.

The Role of Angels

The angelic spheres exist on a higher level than guides and are the purest facet of divinity that you could imagine. The angels exist to serve the Great Spirit and to be of service to humanity.

The word "angel" comes from the Greek word *angelos*, which is translated to mean "messenger." However, there are references to the angelic spheres long before the Greek language was derived. For instance, *El*, from the ancient Aramaic language, means "being of light." Therefore, "angel" (el) is the being of light that vibrates at the purest and highest vibration that is closest with the creating force vibration. The angels were created by the Great Spirit, which you would understand as God or the creating force of the universe. These angels were created in order to serve the Great Spirit, and as a consequence they serve humanity as best they can due to the fact that humans are also created with a smaller divine essence of the creating force that pervades the universe.

Angels have varying levels of responsibility. This means that each sphere has a particular job, similar to the various departments of a company. These spheres are often referred to as the heavenly choirs. They allow you to gain a greater understanding and connection to the higher realms. They know only love and nothing else; the ability to perceive anything apart from love is nonexistent. They can be called on in your time of need and are always wishing to awaken you to their presence.

Angels are a higher vibration and have a pure divine consciousness. They do not have karma or harbor low vibrations, and they do not suffer from negative emotions that are connected to the earth realm or the lower spiritual planes.

Angels are known as God's messengers and, if needed, can walk with you more closely, drawing near to guide you and assist you with your life's lessons or to help you in spiritual growth. You have heard of a guardian angel; this angel is your own personal protector that is looking over you at all times—since your incarnation in this life and in previous lives.

Angel Hierarchy

Dionysius the Areopagite wrote extensively about the angel hierarchy, which is often referred to as "the Nine Choirs." This breakdown was extensively detailed in his writings dating to the sixth century. It was noted throughout history that these choirs of angels performed specific duties according to their own particular vibration and development. However, before the works of Dionysius, another book, called the *Book of Enoch* or *Raziel*, was said to have come directly from the heavenly realms. These books exist today, but like the Bible, are only a version of the original.

What is the *Book of Enoch*?
The *Book of Enoch* is an ancient writing that came from the Jewish belief system. It was said to have come from Enoch, who was related to Noah. It is also believed that this book was given by an angel of the Seraphim.

There are three spheres, and within each sphere are three levels, which make a total of nine—this explains the nine choirs. The first level, which is at the highest level of the astral plane, is collectively concerned with the universe and the manifestations of divinity within it. The angels within this sphere work on pure divine thought alone and have the closest relationship with God (or whatever you believe to be the creating force of the universe). The angels of the first sphere are the Seraphim, the Cherubim, and the Thrones. The angels of the second sphere are the Dominions, Powers, and Virtues. The angels of the third and final sphere are the Principalities, Archangels, and Angels. All of these different spheres have different responsibilities to the divine and are charged with working with humanity in some way. The angels that are assigned to humans are guardian angels, and these are the ones that can often manifest physically in material form when there is a dire need to do so. They carry your thoughts and your prayers to the divine, and though they usually cannot interfere with your life lessons, they can intervene if they are averting some danger that would cause you to turn away from your mission on the earth plane. These angels exist as your closest companions and often work hand in hand with your spirit guide.

Exercise: Meeting Your Angel

It is now time to meet your assigned guardian angel, and this is done through the meditative process. There will be major similarities in the meditation with a few changes added so that you can meet your angel on a higher vibration. Then, just as before, you will ask for the signs that your angel is around you.

Find a calm and relaxing place to sit. Ensure your chair is comfortable and that you are not slouched in any way. If you prefer, you may choose to lie on a mat on the floor with your head elevated slightly on a soft pillow. The preference for this exercise is a comfortable chair, as you may be inclined to fall asleep when you are lying down. Ensure that you have suitable clothing that is loose fitting, comfortable, and will not restrict you in any way or cut into your skin. Place your hands lightly on your knees and close your eyes.

Begin by taking a deep breath in through your nose and out through your mouth. As you breathe in, know that you are breathing purifying energy, and as you breathe out, tell each of your body parts to relax. Start at the feet, and in each breath tell each body part to relax. Move to your legs, then your arms, and so on. As you begin to move through your physical body, you will note that you are beginning to feel relaxed and sleepy. This is the point where you may begin to fear, and as your fear of not being in control takes hold, you may come out of your relaxed state far too quickly. There is nothing to fear, and it may help you to reiterate this to yourself over and over a few times. Repeat something like the following statement, which includes your relaxation affirmation too:

There is nothing to fear and safety surrounds me. Within the safety my body is relaxed, comfortable, and in no stress. The divine authority within allows the full expression of my spiritual self in safety and harmony. The safer I feel, the deeper I move into the trance state.

Find yourself at the bottom of a golden escalator. See that it goes up toward a golden gate that lies at the entrance to a golden castle in the sky. Take one deep, relaxing, cleansing breath, and step onto the escalator— have no fear. The step you take will move gently up toward the golden gate, and as you become more and more elevated, you will be getting more and more relaxed. You are comfortable and in a complete state of relaxation.

Soon you will reach the golden gate. Notice how beautiful it is, how radiant the color and energy exuding from it is. Take hold of the handle on the gate and feel the ethereal energy run through your body, cleansing every part; it's like surging electricity, but pure and cleansing. Open the gate and walk through. You will now find yourself standing on a golden drawbridge, and beyond you is the entrance to the castle, which stands majestically before you. Inside are those answers that you seek. Now you must have the courage to move forward and investigate the castle.

Walk slowly through the gate and find yourself in a courtyard where the sun is shining through from the sky above. Look toward the middle of the courtyard, and there you will see a beautiful angel who is beckoning for you to walk toward her. You will hear the angel give you her name as you get closer. Feel the embrace of the angel's love surround you entirely. There is no need to speak, for the angel knows your every thought and desire. Notice the lightness in the angel's vibration and see the intensity of the color that surrounds the angel. This color can also give you an idea of who the angel is and from which level she originates.

Ask in your mind for the angel to give you confirmation that you will be sent a clear sign on the earth plane that you met your angel. Now spend some time in the company of your celestial guardian. When you are happy (and you will know when the time comes to leave this place), ask your guardian angel to take you home. Feel the angel wrap you in her heavenly wings; feel the love and compassion that surrounds you. For a moment you will experience a light feeling as everything begins to dematerialize, and you begin to see it all disappear as if you are moving away. You will soon feel your body become heavy once more, and you will become aware of your body. You can feel yourself in your chair, and soon you will become aware of your breathing. You are now in your own room, and your angel has brought you home. You can now believe that you have a closer relationship with your angel, and you can learn to communicate with your angel at any time.

Signs from Your Angel

Just as before, you must get the requisite proof from your angel that she is who she says she is. Therefore, you must be aware of how those angels communicate with you. Very often, angels will send you subtle signs that they are around, and they will utilize your physical senses in many ways.

One well-known way that an angel will communicate with you is by leaving little white feathers for you to notice. There is a little bit of conjecture and misunderstanding here, for people who are on a spiritual path become so desperate for signs that they take a feather anywhere as a sign from an angel. Scientifically, those odds are stacked in the favor of a normal explainable occurrence.

>> CASE STUDY: ANDREA

I gave a reading to a woman named Andrea. During the reading, her grandmother came through with a message for her father, who was rather skeptical, and mentioned some personal information to allay his skepticism. Andrea's grandmother then told her to tell her father that he would receive a sign from an angel that would give him a clear indication as to his path. The author then received a letter a few days after the reading, sent from her father. He wrote that he woke up the very next day after she had told him of the message. He woke up with a white feather on his lip. You may think that could have come from the bed covers or pillows, but he had no feather down pillows or covers as his wife was allergic. The only explanation was that this was animated by spiritual means.

ALERT

Please be aware that you should have a rational skepticism when it comes to receiving white feathers as signs from your angels. It will definitely be a sign if there is no other rational explanation as to how you may have received the feather under the certain circumstances that surround the event. Yes, an angel can use birds, but the situation will have paranormal undertones.

Other Ways to Recognize Your Angel

When you are looking for signs, like feathers, you must ensure that there are no other normal explanations, and make rational investigations before you accept it. Another way in which your angel could make herself known is by something, such as a name or word that you have been given, standing out either in a book or on another object that is out of your normal sphere of experience. You could also hear music that is classical or spiritual in nature but has no rational explanation for where it is coming from. You may hear the sounds of bells ringing without any explanation. Again, signs can be similar to that which you would expect from your guide. There are so many that another book could be written on signs alone.

Past Life Requests

Your angels and your guides can help you with your past life requests. Assume that you have now created and developed a close relationship with your guide and your assigned guardian angel. You can request that they help you to investigate or bring you evidence of your past incarnations. They could even bring you evidence of what it is that is blocking you from your progress in this life. Both of these beings will bring to you the knowledge of what you need in ways that are similar to how they proved their connection to you. However, as they do not have to prove themselves to you anymore, they will bring you what you require in a not-so-subtle way.

Joe's Story

Joe was an average American, a family man with children, and he worked in the financial industry in New York. Joe had many fears that he could find no scientific or rational explanation for, and so he turned to the universe for answers. Joe had heard of past lives and was an acutely spiritual man who had a relationship with angels and guides for many years. This was primarily due to his grandmother, who was blessed with spiritual gifts and had taught him to listen to his intuition.

When Joe was in a bookstore, he was sitting in a comfy chair looking at a science fiction novel. Just as he was sitting there, a book fell from the third shelf above him onto the floor and landed at his feet, which was unusual, as the book had to land at an angle. Joe put the book back on the shelf and sat down again. No sooner had he sat, then the book once more fell to the floor and landed in the same position. Again, Joe just ignored this, thinking that something must be wrong with the shelf. He put the book back again, and as he sat down, it happened once more.

Something was different this time, because as he went to pick up the book, he noticed the title and the picture on it. He felt an amazing surge of energy and recognized that it must be from a guide or an angel. The book was about the American Civil War, and Joe had a keen interest in this area. He had always collected memorabilia and wondered what it might have been like to be living in this time. Joe bought the book and took it home with him. The more he read, the stronger his inner recognition of being there became. Joe decided to get this tested and went to a regression expert. He found that he was in fact one of the historical figures described in the book and that his fears were attributable to the way he suffered in that time. What was astonishing was that the marks where he was shot and killed in his life as a Civil War soldier had carried into his present incarnation.

This is an amazing story, and it shows you how your guides and angels can manipulate events to make sure you wake up and notice them. Joe received the information he needed, and that information came in the form of a book. That book initiated a domino effect that led him to past life regression.

Exercise: Listening for Your Spirit Guide

This exercise is one that will use your natural ability to hear spiritually. You are going to learn how to hear your spirit guide and your angel, but not instantly, as there has to be a measure in place to ensure that you do not create it through your own imagination. The protocols for this exercise will be scientific in nature and will involve you writing down three questions that you want answered. One of these questions must pertain to your past life, and the others must be simple in nature, such as the name of your guide, or perhaps where your guide was incarnated on earth. You can ask your angel to give you a gift or to tell you something that you need to know. The exercise will be primarily based on you learning to hear.

What you need to do is write down the three questions that you would like answered. You should do this a week before you sit down to meditate, or even longer. This is so you allow the intent to formulate in the spirit, and so you are not wholly set on getting the answers right away, as that could be formulated out of your desires. When you eventually come to sit again, this should be after you have continued your daily spiritual practices. It will be like any other meditative experience. It does not follow that you will get the answers exactly a week after. The truth is that the answers could come at any time, within days, weeks, or within the month. You will hear these when you are not expecting it, when your angel or guide is ready to give you the answers clearly by using your natural clairaudience.

CHAPTER 14

Scrying

In this chapter you will learn what it means to scry, a useful tool to add to your arsenal. When you think about scrying, you may immediately conjure images of an old fortune-teller sitting in her darkened room, staring into an inanimate crystalline object that is spherical in nature. There is some truth in this imagery; however, there is also a great deal of misdirection, supposition, and irrelevance. Scrying, when used properly, can help you gain insight into your past lives. There are dangers, which you will learn about in the following sections. Consider this verse from W. B. Yeats: "Gaze no more in the bitter glass, the demons with their subtle guile, Lift up before us when they pass, for there a fatal image grows."

What Is Scrying?

First of all, before you can really understand scrying, you have to understand the mechanics of the art of scrying. The gift of clairvoyance is the primary spiritual faculty that you will use. That is how you will perceive the images: using clairvoyant means. As mentioned previously, clairvoyance comes from the French words meaning "clear sight" or "clear seeing." It is this gift of being able to see clearly that you will use when scrying.

QUESTION

Can everyone use clairvoyance?
Many egotistical mediums and psychics would love to tell you that you can't, that it is a gift only for the specially endowed. The truth is that every being on the planet can use the gift of clairvoyance, but it varies according to ability. It can be developed to a certain degree, and it is true that some are endowed with a greater ability. However, you probably utilize it every day. Imagine if someone asked you to describe what you were wearing yesterday. As you recall the image in your mind's eye and describe it to the one who is questioning you, this is clairvoyance, albeit at a small level. Everyone uses it daily and never notices it. If you learned to notice it more, you would see how easy it really is.

Think back to your childhood. Is there a particular time or an event that you saw scrying without knowing it? You may be shocked, but Walt Disney captured this mystical art in one of his most famous productions, *Snow White and the Seven Dwarfs*. There is a part in the animated film when the evil witch uses a mirror to view the present and the future. This is the idea behind scrying. Another well-known movie in which scrying was used was in *The Lord of the Rings: The Fellowship of the Ring*. Galadriel scries in a bowl of water (the Mirror of Galadriel). She then sees the visions of the enemy and what would happen if the Fellowship were to fail on their quest to destroy the Ring of Power.

The History of Scrying

Scrying dates back thousands of years, and it was prevalent in ancient civilizations such as the Aztecs and Incas. These ancient civilizations used the art of scrying as a link to the spirit world. The seers of these civilizations used the art of scrying to prophesy events, possible problems, or successes for groups and individuals. Many objects were used for scrying, including water, mirrors, crystals, and oil. Probably the most extreme object that was used for scrying was the blood the Aztec priests used. The blood would be placed in a receptacle such as a plate or cup, and the priests would then stare into the blood to gain insights. The visions that were received were considered to come from only a few sources; this would obviously be dependent on intention and belief. It was asserted that all information came from either God or a religious deity, members of the world of spirit, Satan (or whoever their culture personified as evil), the psychic, and the subconscious mind.

ESSENTIAL

Divination comes from the Latin term *divinare*, which means "to forsee," and is related to deities that are divine in nature. Divining is the ability to answer a question by supernatural means using divining tools. These tools are integral to the diviner and relate to culture and beliefs such as scrying, Tarot cards, rods, crystal, runes, and many more. Diviners proceed by reading signs, events, or omens through contact with those in the spirit world.

Scrying and Religion

Religious cultures have also used the ancient forms of scrying and divination. One religion actually is founded on what was gained in this way. This religion is known as the Church of Jesus Christ of Latter-Day Saints (Mormonism) and was founded by Joseph Smith. The information that was presented to Smith came from images that were supposedly shown in the seer stones. These stones belonging to Smith were found when he was helping to dig out a neighbor's well, and one stone in particular took his eye. Joseph used these stones while he was digging for treasure, and soon enough, his thoughts turned to religion. The method that he used was to place the stones in his hat, and then he would bury his face in the hat and recount the reflections that he saw. The truth is that Joseph was using clairvoyant means to gain information, and this information then became the Book of Mormon.

ALERT

Religion is a man-made thing and is open to interpretation. No prophet ever came to earth in order to teach religion. Each historic prophet came to teach the three fundamental lessons of love, forgiveness, and compassion.

Seers in History

The most famous seer known for scrying was Nostradamus. Supposedly he used a bowl, and the water in the bowl would provide him with the visions he became so famous for. However, the facts surrounding his life are widely disputed, and Nostradamus reportedly used other methods to get into an altered state, such as meditation, hallucinogenic compounds, and divination tools. He claimed that through his study of astrology he gained information of a celestial persuasion.

There is a little-known Scottish seer you may not have heard of, known as the Brahan Seer. Alexander Mackenzie has done a great deal of research and asserts the following in his book *The Prophecies of the Brahan Seer*:

Kenneth Mackenzie, also known as Coinneach Odhar or the Brahan Seer, was a legendary Scottish clairvoyant. Tradition dates his birth to the early seventeenth century in Uig, on the island of Lewis. This is the northernmost island of the Outer Hebrides, a chain of islands to the west of Scotland's northern coast. Legend has it that he came into his talent after napping on a fairy hill and finding a small stone in his coat, which allowed him to view the future. Predictably, legend has it that he was eventually burned to death as a sorcerer by being immersed in a barrel of burning tar. Before his death he forespoke the doom of the noble Mackenzie family who had him executed: the last male heir of this line would be deaf. In the nineteenth century this came true, as the last of the Mackenzies lost his hearing in his youth.

He is inevitably compared with Nostradamus. However, unlike Nostradamus, many of the predictions attributed to the Brahan Seer are very straightforward and literal, instead of being cloaked in word games, riddles, and allegory. For instance, a typical prediction is that a specific church roof would collapse when a magpie made a nest in it for three years running. There are predictions of the birth of a two-headed calf, a boulder falling over, and the plaintive death of a French expatriate in the Isles, mourned by a local woman. Other reputed predictions were of "a chariot without horse or bridle," and "fiery chariot[s]" which could be interpreted as a premonition of railroads or automobiles, and "hills strewn with ribbons," which sound like power lines, but this is about as futuristic as he gets. Unlike Nostradamus, none of his predictions are about geopolitics, global war, or the distant future.

It is interesting to read the extract, for you can deduce that the Brahan Seer tapped into his skills of clairvoyance by using a stone to scry the future. For the most part, all seers in some way utilize these tools. Even the use of Tarot cards is a method of scrying, and scrying is used in daily life in many ways without knowledge. It can happen when performing normal tasks, such as looking at a map or staring into a crowd to find someone or something; the answer can come as an internal flash of inspiration.

ALERT

Aleister Crowley was known as "the most wicked man in the world," though this would seem to have been a title he gave himself. No matter what individuals thought of Crowley, he was deeply intelligent and an expert in the occult. He was the only man to scry thirty Ethers of Enochian Magick.

Scrying is also a fundamental skill used in magic and within its rituals. The best-known Old English magician, Merlin, adopted scrying as a method of predicting and contacting the unseen realms. Another well-known scryer, though perhaps more known for his macabre personality and dark magic, was the infamous Aleister Crowley. He was the only human ever in history to scry all thirty levels of what is known as the Ethers, derived from Enochian Magick. This form of magick is very questionable and involves rituals to command spirits. This is wrong! You do not have the authority to command a spirit to your will, only the divine creator has this authority.

Types of Scrying

Scrying is simply attempting to contact the spirit world with the aid of an object, usually something shiny. There are many methods of scrying—probably hundreds if not thousands of versions. Following are descriptions of some of the main methods. This book describes only the basic ways of scrying. There are other ways used by occult practices that will not be discussed.

ESSENTIAL

Within all the versions of scrying is the truth that it can be either dark or white in nature. You have a choice as to which version to use.

Mirror Gazing

Mirror gazing is perhaps the best-known form of scrying. There are countless tales of mirror gazing, as well as many myths. For example, in Victorian England, it was thought that a young lady should hold a mirror in front of her and walk backward up the stairs in the dark. It was believed that she would see her future husband, though there was a macabre side to it, too. If she saw a vision of a skull, it was suggested this would be the foretelling of her pending death or that of a loved one.

Another tale involves the story of a young mother whose baby was stolen from her. She was so stricken with grief that she committed suicide. Her name was Bloody Mary, though the "Bloody" was added to her name after the event occurred. It has been suggested that Mary was in fact Queen Mary I (known later as Bloody Mary), who suffered from severe miscarriages. The legend eventually turned into a spirit game of sorts. It was said that one should stand before a mirror in the dark and repeat the name "Bloody Mary" three times. This physical invocation would then force the spirit of the young woman to appear. Other invocations are associated with this story, such as chanting the name thirteen times with a lighted candle at midnight, which will purportedly allow you to speak to someone who has deceased, chanting her name one hundred times, or chanting her name while spinning around or rubbing your eyes.

Another spirit game attached to the Bloody Mary story was designed to be a test of courage. In this variation, it was said that if Bloody Mary was summoned, she would either kill or haunt forever the person who summoned her.

These legends suggest that divination is possible—both good and bad—and that some of the questioners died mysteriously after carrying out these silly games.

Crystals

Another method of scrying is through the use of crystals and shiny crystalline objects. This was especially prevalent in ancient cultures that recognized the high vibrations of these rocks and minerals.

ESSENTIAL

As everything consists of energy in motion, this energy has a frequency that vibrates at a certain resonance. It is true that each crystal has inherent energy vibrations, and these frequencies work in many different waves within the material realm.

The Aztecs and Egyptians were renowned for using obsidian, which is also used as the wizards' stone or witches' stone in some indigenous cultures. An interesting point is that alchemist John Dee used obsidian and a small crystal ball to communicate with other worlds and to receive images of the past, present, and future. The theory behind this form of crystallomancy was to put the practicing individual into an altered state of consciousness to make a connection with those in the spirit world. The crystal ball and wax tablets used by Dee are on display at the British Museum in London.

What is crystallomancy?
Crystallomancy is another name for scrying with a crystal ball. Also known as crystal gazing, this form of divination is used not only to predict the future and tell fortunes but to analyze a client's character and help with whatever concerns a client may have.

Psychomanteum

As mentioned in Chapter 9, the psychomanteum is a room where individuals would sit in the dark and mirror-gaze in order to communicate with loved ones on the other side or to learn from the world of the spirit. The idea was that individuals who had crossed to the spirit world could be seen and could communicate with their loved ones. Very often other visions and images could also be seen. This practice had to be done in complete darkness, considered the optimum condition for being able to witness visions. Psychologist Raymond Moody claimed that ancient reports suggested a great deal of success in seeing and communicating with loved ones.

Oil

Another substance that was used for the art of scrying is oil, prevalent with the high priests in Egypt and in some areas of Persia. The seer would pour the oil into a suitable receptacle and let it settle. He would then stare at the oil, which would eventually put him into a trance state, and he would note what visions he saw. This was mainly used to give information to the gentry of the time. There do not seem to be any cases of the lower classes discussing this. The ancient Greeks also used this method. Of course, this method could also be used with water, as was often the case in ancient Egypt.

Candle

This method dates back for many years and is especially prevalent in the modern world. People are encouraged to stare at the candle to invoke angels or to enter an altered state of consciousness. There are a plethora of New Age books that support this method of scrying. It is suggested that by staring into this candle, you enter a sphere of birth and death where you are reborn and have access to the realm of the spirit through celestial guidance.

Learning How to Scry

There are no hidden secrets in learning how to scry, and it is not as mystical as it may seem. As with previously discussed methods, it follows the same routine and is just another tool to activate your clairvoyant potential. However, there are a few pitfalls that you may discover, and this must be taken into consideration. There are obviously dangers that exist, which are similar to any of the dangers discussed before, including the dangers of obsession, psychic attack, and mental imbalance. However, these dangers are purely born of fear and come from your own self-loathing and inner fears that you have created. Therefore, it is good to practice the following regime of preparation before scrying.

Preparing Properly

You should perform this preparatory regime before you carry out any type of scrying. It is of paramount importance that you cleanse yourself and the area that is to be used before any scrying is attempted. This involves a period of prayer, fasting, and cleansing of the area and the physical body. The following techniques are from the book on the dangers of psychic development, *Dark Waters—Navigating the Dangers of Psychic and Mediumship Development*. First of all, you should prepare yourself by eating less food in general while concentrating on more high-vibrational foods (good organic produce that has not been tainted by chemicals or animals that have been reared in the best and most humane conditions).

What are high-vibrational foods?
High-vibrational foods are foods that have been treated with care and have come from nature in a natural way. For instance, there is a great deal of difference between eating the egg of a chicken that has been reared in a caring way and fed naturally compared to the egg of a chicken that has been locked in a compound, unable to move. Imagine the vibration of each of these animals and their inner emotions—this vibration is carried through the food to you.

Follow this cleansing routine for a period of at least a week before you attempt to scry. Then you should cleanse your body. A salt bath is preferred, but there are many ways to cleanse your body. In ancient Greece and in Persia, oil and smoke were used, and incense is still used in Asia.

Salt baths are an excellent way to cleanse your auric field; the salt acts by absorbing all negative energy from your auric field. Ensure that when you make a salt bath, you only put in two tablespoons of natural salt crystals. Too much salt in your bath can be dangerous. (Have you ever looked at dried fruit? It has very little shape and no moisture within it—so it looks rather wrinkled.)

Once you have done this, you will want to cleanse your area, and that should involve sprinkling salt in doorways and other entrances to negate the entry of negative spirits. The Native American Indians employed the use of the sacred sage to cleanse the area, and this method is still prevalent today, but it is not restricted to this indigenous culture. Many professional psychics, mediums, and healers employ this technique with much success. The sage ceremony is used to drive out negative spirits to cleanse and purify areas and auric fields. Traditionally, white sage is used with cedar, normally in a wand formation, and wafted with a white feather. To begin a sage ceremony, it is important that your mind and body energies are aligned and have the purest of intentions. You must light the sage and put this in an abalone shell or hold it in your hand. Start from the farthest eastern part of your home

and wave a white feather over the smoke that is created. Traditionally, it is said that you should start at all four directions. This is said to bring in the winged beings (the angelic realm) to help purify. As the smoke permeates through the atmosphere, it binds the negative energies and spirits and carries them up through the atmosphere to be transmuted to positive energy. It is important that you also open windows and entrances, in order to create a space through which the smoke can escape and carry the spirits away. Clear all areas and walk slowly, ensuring the smoke is abundant to cleanse and purify.
(Taken from *Dark Waters*)

Setting the Intention

Now it's time to move onto the next phase, which is setting your intention and praying that the information that you receive is for the highest good. To set your intention, you should write or say your own affirmation. This will ensure that you attract the right information and the right spirit toward you. As mentioned before, in order to manifest, you must perceive, believe, and conceive.

It is really important that you cleanse your mind of all impurities. To do this, you may have to begin a process of meditation and prayer over a period of time. This is essential, because as you scry, you will be activating deeper elements of the subconscious mind, and your fears could also be released during the process. There is no guarantee that you will receive any information that reveals a past life existence during your first attempt. Nevertheless, with practice you will receive this information, but only when your mind, body, and soul are purified. Going through the process of preparation will also release the innate gifts that you have. Some are more adept than others, but all people have the same innate gifts, just at varying degrees of power. With the case of scrying skills, some individuals are more susceptible to the perception and communication of spirits and psychic energy. The mirror seems to act as a powerful conduit, but it is not restricted to only good things—it can reflect your innermost fears, and you can conjure frightening experiences from this. This can act as a gateway to emotion and fear, and that is why you must prepare adequately.

Exercise: Scrying

Some of these elements will be similar in nature to what you have read before, with subtle changes that will allow you to attempt your first basic scrying exercise. You must understand that the information you will receive will almost ultimately be clairvoyant in nature, and this is concurrent with the intent that is set in place. Choose a large enough mirror that you feel comfortable with and that you can sit in front of on a suitable table. Ensure that when you deal with this type of exercise that you do it in pure darkness.

Why Is Paranormal Research Conducted in Darkness?

This is a question that has perplexed everyone involved in the field of psychical research. Kai Muegge, of the ASSMPI and the Felix Group, offers the following explanation:

> *I believe it is righteous for you to say that you do not get persuading evidence in the dark, that for you light is needed. I know a lot of people, including me, that have been present at séances in which supernormal proof was given—either survival evidence or phenomenological evidence—in darkness. If people see self-consistent movement of ectoplasm in good red light, materialized hands waving in good red light, or columns of ectoplasm building up in the séance room, the proof has worked—for them! Because let us be aware that proof is always a personal thing. The moon landing was well documented, even though many think it was a hoax. So to find conditions that we can term as "proof" giving for all will be very hard to achieve. Furthermore, as far as I know, darkness is a certain condition that is deeply connected with this part of Western trance-work culture. We know so many reasons, beginning with the observer effect, overpsychological or mental effects, and ending at several biological effects (photosynthesis), which seek darkness. Then there are the philosophical implications regarding the occult—the whole word comes from the term "darkness," and there are many guides that tell that darkness sets the human mind into the special condition that makes it receivable for the "unseen." Furthermore, controls have claimed that what happens in the dark cannot be completely understood by our cognitive system. Because our awareness is built this way, it fills in the gaps when perceiving unknown matters.*

Here the danger develops, when sitters see things that are not actually there . . .

That is because our mind is completely built for the range of perceiving three-dimensional space-time. Moreover, the entities claim that the final proof won't be given to us easily and that doubt, like the process called cognitive dissonance, is permanently holding us in a reflective thinking process. This shall broaden our thinking processes and involve others to take part in the awareness process!

Consider also that babies in the womb are in complete darkness until it is their time to be incarnated upon the earth. Then they arrive in the light. Scientific experiments are done in dark conditions too, and photos are normally developed in dark conditions. Consider too that everything that germinates or grows is done in these conditions. It should therefore not be something to fear but to be embraced.

Find a comfortable chair to sit in, but make sure that you are erect enough that you can keep your spine and torso relatively straight. Sit in the chair and begin to take deep breaths in through your nose and out through your mouth. As you breathe in, visualize white purifying smoke coming into your body. See the white smoke coming down from the heavens above and entering through your head. Witness as the purifying smoke runs all through your body, picking up all negative vibrations and negative energies that may be blocking your path. When you have felt the smoke has been all around your physical body picking up the negative energies, take the smoke, which will now be gray in color and heavy with all the blockages that have been inside you. Visualize the now-gray smoke leaving on your out-breath and being sent back into the atmosphere to be transmuted. You are feeling much lighter and cleaner. Now visualize a beautiful white ball of light before you. It is the most amazing light that you have seen, yet it does not blind you. Walk toward the light and enter it; feel its radiance surround you and know this bubble of white light is always around you, and that you are totally protected. In your darkened condition, look into the mirror and begin to take deep breaths in as you gaze. Tell yourself that you are relaxed and open to any images pertaining to your past incarnations that may come forward. While you do this, you may feel strange sensations in your physical body—this is nothing to worry about and is just a measure of your altered state. Continue to breathe deeply, and soon you will perceive images. There is also a high possibility that you could induce an out-of-body experience from this state or that you could go into a deeper form of trance. This is when your experience will be expanded tenfold.

ESSENTIAL

Do not be afraid of the dark. Fear is a misrepresented emotion that evokes a negative response. Know within yourself that you can become master of your emotions. You came from darkness to the light; this is just like regressing back to spirit. Go boldly and know that you are protected.

There is a danger that you will expect to see visions in the mirror, and while this can happen as an objective reality, it would depend on the limits of your own mediumistic potential and power. The likelihood is that you will receive this information in a subjective clairvoyant manner. This means that you will perceive the images in your mind's eye. You will see pictures, and scenes may play back in your mind. Furthermore, you must consider that some of what you are perceiving can be released from deep-seated emotion.

The Dangers of Scrying

There are dangers with scrying that are similar to other dangers discussed in this book. As was mentioned, the state of your mind is what will dictate what you perceive. Remember the spiritual law that like attracts like. This is the same law that will dictate what you attract while you scry. So the real danger lies in what you create; if you are of a weakened state of mind and emotionally unstable, you can attract those spirits of a similar disposition. Scrying is very similar to using the Ouija board, and so the dangers are parallel to that. You may inadvertently open a portal to the astral world, and, dependent on your preparation, your state of mind and your purity will be the deciding factors in what you attract.

Like any exercise that you undertake, you have to have a period of time to cool down and return to normal. This is true with scrying, and you must ensure that if you open yourself up, you must take the time to close yourself down. The intent of this is to ensure that any portal you may have opened will also be closed. Imagine if you left the door to your home open for all to enter. Would you leave your spiritual door open? No, you must ensure these are closed.

Recording Your Findings

It is important to record all of the information that you perceive, no matter how silly you think it is. You will inevitably receive contrasting information, some from the conscious mind and some from the subconscious mind. This is the difficulty that most will come up against—being able to discern what information comes from what part of the mind. The information will fit together like a kind of puzzle; this takes time and patience to learn. Also, you must be aware that information can be given from a spiritual being who resides in the other planes, and the information that is given will show its level of intelligence.

Edward Kelley

One of the most famous scryers of the sixteenth century was Edward Kelley. He was an alchemist and would frequently scry using crystals and other objects. It was claimed that he could frequently see, hear, and feel the touch of spirits, and this would be an objective perception—outside of his crystal or mirror. Before he sat, he would see these same spirits; soon they became his guides. It was these spirits who would act out what he needed to know, or they would tell him what the images he perceived meant. You probably won't experience anything like Edward Kelley. Kelley was obviously a natural-born medium and had extremely well-developed gifts that helped him to perceive the realities of the spirit world objectively.

Using Your Spirit Guides

You can, if you wish, ask your own spirit guides to be the facilitators when you scry. It would also be prudent to ask them for the appropriate measures of protection to surround you when you scry. Your guides can also play a very important role when it comes to recording your findings. There is a chance that you will find it difficult to remember lots of detail due to the whole atmosphere that surrounds you and the emotional information you may perceive. If you ask your guides or angels to help you to remember, they will play or send these mental images to your conscious once again, so you can record them in your journal.

CHAPTER 15

Automatic Writing

If you don't have natural mediumistic tendencies, you should seek an appropriately trained medium to help you with this process. This is one process that you do not want to dabble in without the right protection and knowledge, for if you do and forget to ask for protection, you could cause yourself some issues on a psychological level. Nevertheless, when done properly, automatic writing can produce wonderful results, and many spiritual classics have come about this way. In this chapter, you will learn to use a form of automatic writing that is not fully induced in an altered state but more on an inspirational level, and you will call upon your guide to help you.

The Mechanics of Automatic Writing

Automatic writing is a mediumistic state where you become the medium. You allow the spirit entity to take control of your physical and psychic faculties. The spirit has to overshadow you and will then utilize your psychic faculties and express its thoughts by having you write them down under its control and influence. This should not be considered a form of possession, for your spirit and body are not taken over—you have just allowed temporary use of your consciousness.

ALERT

Please be aware there are dangers in automatic writing if you don't take the appropriate measures. One thing that you must believe is that you will not be possessed when taking part in automatic writing—you are only allowing the spirit to overshadow you within your aura. Under the appropriately controlled conditions, no danger will befall you.

Some magnificent works have been transmitted through the process of automatic writing, such as *Spirit Teachings* by William Stainton Moses, as well as elements of other scriptural writings. In the past, mediumistic individuals received these messages through the automatic writing process by using an Ouija board and a planchette, although this is not recommended for the untrained individual whatsoever. Misuse of the board or not understanding how the board works can create a portal through which uninvited spirit beings can operate. This is done through the intent alone.

FACT

The Ouija board was originally invented as a parlor game. It is a tool that was widely used in Victorian England to communicate with the world of spirit. To some it was an oracle; however, it must be noted that the board merely facilitated the energy of the intent from the inquirer. The board itself is not dangerous; it is the intent to communicate on a spirit level that attracts the spirits of varying vibrations. Using the board indiscriminately without due care and attention is very dangerous indeed.

Well-known mediums have explained their feelings of control under this trancelike condition. Medium W. T. Stead explains:

I hold my pen in the ordinary way, but when the writing is beginning I do not rest my wrist or arm upon the paper, so as to avoid the friction and to give the influence, whatever it may be, more complete control of the pen. At first the pen is apt to wander into mere scrawling, but after a time it writes legibly. Unlike many automatic writers who write as well blindfolded as when they read what they write as they are writing it, I can never write so well as when I see the words as they come.

The statement from this medium gives you an understanding of how your own mind may get in the way, and so it is better to deprive your senses by way of blindfolding yourself. Of course, what you write in this condition on the first occasion may seem somewhat illegible at first, but as with anything, practice makes perfect.

Just another word of caution: Some individuals have been known to write what is considered impressionable, which is purely passive in essence. This is perhaps the best way for you to work, as the information will be coming from deep within, like a hidden and forgotten memory. The only thing that you have to understand is that at first you may have your own desires, and the products of imagination may get in the way. But soon enough, a pattern will emerge that shows you what you have written does indeed form some basis of fact. Some mediums who are excellent at this process can carry out other tasks while doing automatic writing, such as reading or watching television or listening to the radio. The reason this will happen is because the medium's faculties are under the control of the influencing spirit person or communicator.

The Dangers of Automatic Writing

One danger that does exist is that when you begin and you start to see some results, in your excitement you may want continue to write and therefore want to do this on a regular basis. You could mix up your needs with your desires, and you could also be fed wrong information from a wandering soul who sees an opportunity to have a little fun. This will be primarily the result of your being an undeveloped channel for communication. The best way to proceed is to set the intent to work on an inspirational level, other than fully immersing yourself in automatic writing in a full trance condition.

In *A Guide to Mediumship and Psychical Unfoldment* by E. W. and M. H. Wallis, the authors state the following:

> *The communications that are received by the various forms of passive, impressionable, automatic, and inspirational writing must not be regarded as valuable merely because of the conditions under which they were obtained, nor because of their spirit origin, real or supposed. Under all circumstances receive with the utmost reserve and caution long-winded communications from notable characters who claim to be "Napoleon Bonaparte," "Lord Bacon," "Socrates," or other great personages; for, in the majority of cases, the value of the communication is exactly the reverse of the importance of the name.*

ALERT

Be aware of receiving communication from one who claims high standing or stature. Untrained people often exude an aura of desperation to communicate, and a wandering spirit will see this. The spirit will identify the desire to communicate with some wise and well-known figure and will come forward as this person. Soon enough, though, the level of communication will show as being poor and lacking evidence.

This highlights one of the danger areas of any form of spirit communication. Many grounded wandering spirits will identify the desire and excitement within the medium. When this excitement to communicate has been noticed, the wandering soul is able to begin communications of a supposedly high nature, claiming to be someone of high personage. The spirit knows that you will respond to this through pure desperation and excitement, and this can be the beginning of many other issues.

Getting Out of the Way

One of the common beginner's mistakes is getting in the way of your attempts to carry out this form of communication. This is due to your innate desire and excitement at delving into the unknown. Though you will often do this with some form of deep expectation, this expectation will work in conjunction with your ego and will often cause you to create what you desire within your own mind. The trick is to give your conscious mind something to occupy it and have the intent that you will allow your subconscious mind to rise to the top and release the information needed for you at this time.

FACT

> Spiritualism, with its belief that spirits of the dead have the ability to communicate with the living, was a popular religion in the early twentieth century. Two famous names associated with Spiritualism at this time were Harry Houdini and Arthur Conan Doyle. Doyle thought Houdini showed promise as a medium when Houdini, in his first attempt at automatic writing, wrote the name of a Spiritualist friend of Doyle's who had just died. Houdini, though, disavowed that he had ever been taken over by a spirit and even spelled out in a notarized deposition that "no one will claim that the spirit of Sir Arthur Conan Doyle's friend Ellis Powell guided my hand."

So how is this done? A good trick is to read something entertaining or to watch something on your television that is light in content—something that you do not need to concentrate on. By taking part in another subject, you will allow your conscious mind to remain active on that subject. This is when your subconscious can release the information to you that may arrive in your conscious thoughts as an idea or as forms of words or images. It is then that you should write these down in your journal. The key to getting yourself out of the way is to simply occupy the physical. You can do this even as you walk in a beautiful area. As you walk you can hold your journal and a pen and allow your mind to drift off as you enjoy the scenery.

Preparing Yourself for Automatic Writing

There is a good reason for taking some preparatory time before you attempt to delve into the realm of automatic writing. This is so you can get the right information by having your vibration raised enough that you attract the right help from the right discarnate spirit. This ensures that when the spirit makes contact with you, the right level of spirit will give you the correct information you need. If you remember from Chapter 13, spirit guides and angels are beings that could help you after you have made their acquaintance and developed a closer relationship.

ALERT

To be on the safe side, it would be prudent to set your intention to allow only your guide or your angel to overshadow you. At this point in the proceedings, you should be well acquainted with your spirit guide and your guardian angel. You should have gotten to know their vibration and the signals that show they are near.

These beings could be the very ones that will help you with the task of automatic writing, so it would seem prudent to set the intent to have your guide and your angel overshadow you and help you achieve the level of information that you seek. You have heard the saying "don't rush in where angels fear to tread." If you were a soldier or someone in law enforcement, you would not rush into any situation without preparing yourself or gathering intelligence to give you an advantage. An athlete has to prepare her body by training it to become supple and strong enough to withstand the rigors of competition. The athlete will also have to ensure that she is ingesting the right nutritious foods so her body can cope with the demands of the training. No athlete in her right mind would take the chance of not preparing for fear of failure. This is the same with any spiritual endeavor that you will take. Everything in life is about preparation, and there is no difference here between the material and the spiritual.

Let It Flow

What happens when you see a door in front of you and push it open? You push the door away from your body. This simple example shows that if you push something, you are completing the act of moving the object away from you. Anything that you push, whether spiritually or physically, will be moved farther away from you. Have you ever thought about how sometimes you want something desperately, but it seems to get farther and farther away from you? This is because you are pushing too hard to receive something. You see, all real law is natural law and perfect in its application and operation. What should happen is you should allow this energy to flow toward you in a natural manner. Imagine that you are standing at the bottom of a beautiful waterfall. The water flows to you naturally. If something were to impede the water, it will find another route around. Just as the water in the waterfall flows downward in a natural manner, your thought stream comes to your consciousness from your subconscious mind.

ESSENTIAL

Imagine that your flow of thoughts comes to you as gently as a flowing stream. This visualization coupled with your inner intent will help to create the flow that you require. Then, thoughts of your past incarnations and released memories will flow to you as naturally as the stream itself.

The subconscious mind is the waterfall, and when the conditions are correct, the information will flow toward you naturally and unimpeded. This is what is meant by letting it all flow, as the words and the images that you require will naturally come into your awareness when you are clam and relaxed.

When you sit down to carry out your automatic writing exercise, you want to just let your subconscious mind release the inner knowledge toward you—just like that waterfall.

Exercise: Write Your Life

Sit down at a table or on a comfortable chair if you have one. Ensure that you have a pencil/pen and notebook or your journal ready. Play some light music in the background or watch something very easygoing on television, like your favorite sitcom. Again, you want to start by taking in nice long, deep breaths, and as you breathe in, imagine you are breathing in the pure energy of the white light in through your head. Take the white light from your head and slowly pass it through all the parts of your body, ensuring that as it passes, you become more relaxed, cleansed, and know that you are safe. As you exhale with each breath, release any fears and any worries that may be bonding you to the material plane.

When you have completed this task and you have relaxed your mind and body, ask that your guide or guardian angel draw close to you to help you with this task for your highest good. At this point you may feel a surge of energy as your celestial friend or your guide will draw close to you, or you may feel heat and loving warmth as you are surrounded by love and compassion. Ask the spirit to help release the information or enlighten you to the steps that are needed so that you can heal from any of your past incarnations and make your present incarnation free from the blockages that hinder you.

Let your conscious mind enjoy the sitcom or the music. Sooner or later, images and words will come into your awareness rather naturally, and you should notice them as they arise in your mind. Write them down. Do not concern yourself with content; keep writing, no matter how silly it sounds or how silly your images may seem. You will be able to analyze the content later for some pattern that exists.

This exercise may take some practice, because inevitably in your desperation and excitement you may not be able to calm yourself first time around. After each session, look at what you have written and identify any pattern that emerges, such as the images corresponding to words or events in some kind of chronological order.

Avoiding the Dangers of Automatic Writing

The following is a story from *Dark Waters*:

A client named Martha contacted me a few years ago and stated that she had done a terrible thing. She was a developing medium but had been rather carried away and let her ego run riot. She was a member of the Spiritualist organization in the UK and implored me not to tell anyone of her problem. She thought she knew more than her teachers knew and loved the idea of automatic writing and channeling. She began to meditate, and when she was ready, she would invite spirits to draw close and communicate through her by controlling her hand to write messages from the spirit world. For the first few months, the messages were good-natured and she believed they came from her grandmother. But over time, the messages took a sinister undertone, until one day the words on the paper were evil in nature and claimed that it was demonical—in fact, she said it was the devil. I then made contact with the spirit world and my own guide enlightened me to the fact this case was merely a mischievous spirit that had attached himself to Martha. Martha was doing the automatic writing without protection and had attracted the mischievous spirit who wanted to have some fun at her expense. The good news was that it would be easy to get rid of the uninvited guest. It was not evil, but the spirit was masking as evil in order to scare her. The spirit was easier to deal with after that.

As with anything in life, there is a great need to have balance. If the scales are weighted heavily on one side, then you will feel the effects of that burden much easier in a heavy vibration. If you overindulge in the wrong foods, you will become overweight and as a consequence will manifest other physical ailments. If you consume too much alcohol, or if you take narcotic substances, you will cause damage to your body and mind. The same is true with spiritual practices, especially in the areas of mediumship. If you overindulge, you can cause irreparable damage to your mind and body. Think of it this way: As everything that exists is energy in motion, mediumship is a form of tapping and using energy. If used incorrectly, it could have detrimental effects to yourself physically and mentally. This happens if you become too obsessed with the ability and constantly use it without balance or consideration. Sooner or later, if you have a leak in your pipes and you do not repair it, the leak will get bigger and the flow will be constant with no way to stop it. You must take an active part in controlling this leak and not putting the hole under so much pressure that it bursts.

With the extended constant use of the psychic faculties without any balance, dangers exist on all levels of mind and body. There are dangers to the overall health and condition of the body, from nervous disorders to physical manifestation of disease, which is brought about by depleting the life force with the inordinate use of your spiritual faculties. Using up the stores of nature's life force within you can cause you to age prematurely; it can cause nervous and intramuscular weakness and destroy your vigor of mind. This vigor is further depleted if a wandering spirit is subjugating you. It is for this reason that you should try to remain as healthy as possible by having natural balance in your life and not persistently pursuing the gifts of the spirit. You must get adequate exercise and nutrition, and have a healthy awareness of what is good for your mind and body. This is another reason why it is better to build a relationship with your guide and your angel before you embark on something much deeper in your quest for enlightenment of your past lives.

Words Are Powerful

This chapter takes you to another exciting part of your journey, but it is wise to mention how powerful words can be. The words that you say or believe can either be uplifting or can cut like the blade of a warrior. Words have caused disagreements that have led to wars and the indiscriminate loss of innocent life. Primarily through ignorance and lack of understanding does the materially driven human being often choose the wrong words that inevitably lead to conflict. Your choice of words can have a dramatic effect on your state of mind and can put your body into a catatonic condition—just by choosing a string of suggestive words that act upon the mental condition of the subject.

Words indeed are powerful, and with this in mind, it is wise to choose your words carefully. Choosing your words with love and compassion will raise your vibration so that you need have no fear of attracting the wrong intention from those spirits that have gone before you. The simple choice of words that you express can bring comfort and joy to those who may be lost and who need to be awakened to the beauty of the soul. As Gandhi once said, "Be the change you wish to see in the world."

CHAPTER 16

The Hall of Records

Assume that you are adept at traveling to the spirit world and the inner realms of your mind. What you are going to do now is visit and learn about the hall of records. This may sound like something from a science fiction novel, but you can be assured that the hall exists. The hall is commonly referred to as the akashic records, and it's where the history and sum total of all the knowledge of everything that is part of creation exists. It is said that the hall existed even before time began, which is a hard concept to grasp. The very idea that creation was recorded before creation may be unbelievable; however, it does sound like it could have been a plan in motion.

Ancient Sources of Knowledge

The akashic records are the blueprint of all reality, which is at the foot of creation itself. *Akasha* is a word that comes from the ancient Sanskrit word that means "sky" or "space," and this is understood as the space within the spirit world. So in a way the records are the answers to life and the universe and everything that is contained therein. Many spiritually gifted individuals have visited this great hall to gain information.

ESSENTIAL

No one really knows why anything is recorded in the great hall. All of your soul's information is recorded in order that you may see and analyze your personal development. Perhaps there is a higher divine reasoning behind it, but you will never know until you pass.

History asserts that the truth of the akashic records was passed down and accessed by the ancient and lost civilizations, such as the Native North Americans, Incas, Tibetans, Druids, Mayans, and also the ancient civilization of Atlantis. It is considered that each civilization knew the secret knowledge that was passed from seer and sage, and that accessing these records was a fundamental part of their culture. It is believed that everything that exists and all soul information is recorded in a great book known as the *Book of Life*, which is held in the hall of records. They also believed that certain attunements could grant you access to this book and that you would be able to access all soul information including that of your past incarnations. Nostradamus, the great mystic and seer, claimed to have access to the hall of records from knowledge gained from these ancient cultures. Other well-known mediums and sages have also made this very same claim. Individuals such as Manly P. Hall, Charles Leadbeter, Annie Besant, Alice Baily, Dion Fortune, and the famous Edgar Cayce all claimed to access the records regularly.

Edgar Cayce said:

Upon time and space is written the thoughts, the deeds, the activities of an entity—as in relationships to its environs, its hereditary influence; as directed—or judgment drawn by or according to what the entity's ideal is. Hence, as it has been oft called, the record is God's book of remembrance; and each entity, each soul—as the activities of a single day of an entity in the material world—either makes same good or bad or indifferent, depending upon the entity's application of self towards that which is the ideal manner for the use of time, opportunity and the expression of that for which each soul enters a material manifestation. The interpretation then as drawn here is with the desire and hope that, in opening this for the entity, the experience may be one of helpfulness and hopefulness." (Edgar Cayce Reading 1650–1)

Edgar Cayce clearly shows what he perceives as the Akasha; he alludes to its use and where it may be. Of course, it is open to interpretation, and many individuals have interpreted his readings in different ways. However, what you need to consider is the parallel relationship to what others have seen and claimed in their own interpretations. Most of the interpretations are similar in nature, so there must be some truth due to the nature of these comparisons.

QUESTION

What is the *Book of Life*?
The *Book of Life* is a mystical record of all souls and of all creation. Probably the most famous detail about the akashic records was given by Edgar Cayce, who was known as the "Sleeping Prophet." It was said that he gained much of his information from visiting the hall of records every time he conducted a reading.

Location of the Hall

So, where is the hall? No one really knows, but in one of Edgar Cayce's readings he intimated where his soul traveled in order to access the records. As far as modern mediums and mystics are concerned, they think the akashic records exist within the vibration of an etheric plane. In essence, there is no particular place, so it is more like a particular vibration that you can access only when your own vibration is capable of reaching that particular level. Some cannot reach the Akasha because they do not have the right soul growth or cannot achieve that particular vibration. Ordinarily, a guide or an angel would become the intermediary. However, Cayce did intimate where and which levels he traveled through in the following statement:

I see myself as a tiny dot out of my physical body, which lies inert before me. I find myself oppressed by darkness and there is a feeling of terrific loneliness. Suddenly, I am conscious of a white beam of light. As this tiny dot, I move upward following the light, knowing that I must follow it or be lost.

As I move along this path of light I gradually become conscious of various levels upon which there is movement. Upon the first levels there are vague, horrible shapes, grotesque forms such as one sees in nightmares. Passing on, there begin to appear on either side misshapen forms of human beings with some part of the body magnified. Again there is change and I become conscious of gray-hooded forms moving downward. Gradually, these become lighter in color. Then the direction changes and these forms move upward and the color of the robes grows rapidly lighter. Next, there begin to appear on either side vague outlines of houses, walls, trees, etc., but everything is motionless. As I pass on, there is more light and movement in what appear to be normal cities and towns. With the growth of movement I become conscious of sounds, at first indistinct rumblings, then music, laughter, and singing of birds. There is more and more light, the colors become very beautiful, and there is the sound of wonderful music. The houses are left behind, ahead there is only a blending of sound and color. Quite suddenly I come upon a hall of records. It is a hall without walls, without ceiling, but I am conscious of seeing an old man who hands me a large book, a record of the individual for whom I seek information.
(Edgar Cayce Reading 294–19)

What Is in the Hall?

The first thing you should know is that just like any library in the material world, there has to be someone who keeps the records and who is of the highest order. Therefore, there is an angel and a spirit team that look after the *Book of Life*, or as is understood, the hall of records.

The akashic records chronicle all the events and all thoughts and deeds that are etched in all of consciousness. Within this are the details and conscious responses of every life form that exists. It's like a supercomputer, albeit one that records the details of every soul and everything the Great Spirit created. The information is then archived, to be viewed at a later date. One has to rely on the information that has been brought back by many seers and sages to comprehend what may be in the hall, but you'll never know the full truth until you go there yourself.

Accessing the Hall of Records

Anyone has the ability to access the akashic records; in essence, every human being has the innate qualities that could help him to access the records and essentially become the medium. This requires the individual to be awakened and to enter into an altered state to access the akashic records. Of course, the techniques themselves are accessible enough that you can achieve that state on your own, but you should take some time to acquaint yourself and choose what works for you. The techniques associated with entering an altered state have been discussed in previous chapters and are useful for entering the hall of records. There are other methods that you can use to prepare yourself for this task, from yogic exercises to spiritually based martial arts, but meditation, mindfulness, and prayer are by far the best ways to prepare yourself. For more on accessing the hall of records, see the exercise at the end of this chapter.

ALERT

Many gifted individuals in history have accessed the hall of records to gain unprecedented access to information they would otherwise not be able to access under normal circumstances. They had to learn skills in order to do this. If you follow the advice given in this book, you will be able to follow in their footsteps.

Famous Patrons of the Hall of Records

Consider the others who were able to access this area of the spirit world. As was already mentioned, Edgar Cayce, the "Sleeping Prophet," had unrestricted access, but there were others as well. Jane Roberts was the deep trance medium for a spirit being known as Seth. In the recordings and transcripts of the séances, Seth claimed the universe is made up of consciousness and ideas that form thought. He also asserted that "direct cognition" was the way that one would access such information. Helena Blavatsky was a Russian mystic and seer who eventually moved to live and work in the United States. She was the founder of the Theosophical Society. Helena asserts that the akashic records were far more than just a static account of information that could be accessed by a psychic or one with developed gifts of the soul. She maintained these records were almost a consciousness of their own that had a stimulating effect on the present. She dictates:

Akasha is one of the cosmic principles and is a plastic matter, creative in its physical nature, immutable in its higher principles. It is the quintessence of all possible forms of energy, material, psychic, or spiritual; and contains within itself the germs of universal creation, which sprout forth under the impulse of the Divine Spirit.

Rudolf Steiner, who was an Austrian philosopher and founder of the Anthroposophical Society, also showed remarkable ability in this field. He was able to perceive information and intelligences beyond that of the physical plane. He claimed to have direct access to the realm of the "Spirit World," which to him was as objective in nature as the physical. He states:

Man can penetrate to the eternal origins of the things which vanish with time. A man broadens his power of cognition in this way if he is no longer limited to external evidence where knowledge of the past is concerned. Then he can see in events what is not perceptible to the senses that part which time cannot destroy. He penetrates from transitory to non-transitory history. It is a fact that this history is written in other characters than is ordinary history. In gnosis and in theosophy it is called the "Akasha Chronicle" . . . To the uninitiated, who cannot yet convince himself of the reality of a separate spiritual world through his own expe-

rience, the initiate easily appears to be a visionary, if not something worse. The one who has acquired the ability to perceive in the spiritual world comes to know past events in their eternal character. They do not stand before him like the dead testimony of history, but appear in full life. In a certain sense, what has happened takes place before him.

Clearly, both of these modern individuals accessed much of what Edgar Cayce and other enlightened beings claimed. Surely the fact that most of these individuals brought forth evidence and teachings and different points in time suggests the reality of this other world. How much proof does one need to accept the possibility of life hereafter, or interdimensional life or life between lives? Perhaps the fear that subjugates people is what creates the blindfold upon which their lives are based.

What You Can Learn

What do you think you can learn? If everything that has ever been created, and all actions, thoughts, words, deeds, and conscious experience are recorded in the great hall, surely it would seem appropriate to respond by saying that you can learn absolutely anything. In the modern day that is certainly the belief; however, the spirit world asserts that you can only learn what your soul growth has achieved.

ESSENTIAL

Everything exists on a vibration, and in the etheric each level is about vibration. You raise your vibration by the way you live your life and how you develop your soul by your actions, thoughts, and deeds. As you learn the truth of life, which is in a similar vibration to the divine essence, your own vibration will begin to elevate. Like a trickle, it is sure to become a flowing stream.

There are things that many are not entitled to know yet because it is out of the realm and scope of apprehension. You must therefore evolve and develop enough that you earn the knowledge that you seek. It cannot be given to you on a plate; you must take action and evolve enough to earn the ability to find the answers you seek. In the Bible, Christ asserted that everything is within and that you can find the answer to anything by going within. This indeed is true, but it must be noted that what Jesus meant was that your soul holds the answers, and this is also dependent on the vibration that you have evolved to and have earned. It depends on the level of growth that you have achieved that will allow you to learn restricted information.

All manner of spiritual information may be learned if the individual has achieved the right level of spiritual growth. In this way the individual can then continue to grow spiritually even further to develop the soul qualities.

The Akashic Records and the Bible

The akashic records are alluded to in scriptural writings, and references occur in several places within the books of the Bible, both within the Old Testament and New Testament. A little-known fact is that the ancient Middle Eastern sect known as the Essenes, which Jesus the Nazarene actually was, held the Akasha in high regard as the book of God. History shows that many cultures, such as the Semitics, Babylonians, Hebrews, and other Eastern civilizations, accessed the Akasha in order to learn from it. Another little-known fact was that Moses's stone tablets, where the Ten Commandments were supposedly written, were given by God to Moses from the hall of records. Interestingly, Moses used spiritual gifts to perceive them.

The first reference in the Bible to the akashic records or the *Book of Life* is found in the book of Exodus 32:32:

> *And Moses returned unto the LORD, and said, Oh, this people have sinned a great sin, and have made them gods of gold. Yet now, if thou wilt forgive their sin—; and if not, blot me, I pray thee, out of thy book which thou hast written. And the LORD said unto Moses, Whosoever hath sinned against me, him will I blot out of my book. Therefore now go, lead the people unto the place of which I have spoken unto thee: behold, mine Angel shall go before thee: nevertheless in the day when I visit I will visit their sin upon them.*

From this Biblical statement, one can deduce that God had indeed spoken about his great book, now known as the akashic records. Later in the Old Testament there is another reference, in Psalm 139: "Your eyes saw my unformed body; all the days ordained for me were written in your book before one of them came to be."

Within the words of that psalm, David makes reference that God, in his infinite wisdom, recorded everything in the *Book of Life*. Moving onto Judgment Day, you can see that reference is made to the *Book of Life* within the final book of the Bible, in Revelation. It is referenced that God is supposed to have the names of all those who will be saved on Judgment Day, and these names will be etched in the *Book of Life*.

Intention Is the Key

Intention exists at the very foot of life, for without intent, nothing would be completed. Think about intention in the manner of your physical movement. Say you are sitting comfortably on your favorite sofa and you suddenly decide that you might like some tea. What has happened is that the thought process has just initiated a chain of events that will inevitably lead to you getting up and making your cup of tea. So anything that you set your intention on, you can invariably achieve when the right conditions are available. If you are sitting on a chair and decide to stand up and move into the kitchen, you will use your natural intention. First, the thought is conceived in your mind: that feeling of wanting to move from the chair to the kitchen. You will see this visually and then make the intent manifest to move. Then the electrical impulse will work throughout the central nervous system and you will feel the stimulation in your physical body via the kinetic movement of your muscular structure.

ESSENTIAL

You may not believe that you can be creative in your visualization, but if you can describe something, then you can be assured that you do have this skill available to you. It is easy to visualize; the difficulty is in holding the visualization. This will come with practice.

This is the same with any intent that you have in your life, day in and day out, and if you begin to understand the power of your natural intention, then you will be able to harness its power. It is your intent to carry out anything or do anything that is part of the energy that wills you forward in your quest.

Exercise: Past Life Theater

This exercise will help you access your past life records. This, of course, will take the same shape as a meditation, and again you will follow the same preparations as before.

Find a calm and relaxing place to sit. Ensure your chair is comfortable and that you are not slouched in any way. If you prefer, lie on a mat on the floor with your head elevated slightly; again, this will help with your breathing. Ensure that you have suitable clothing that is loose fitting and comfortable and will not restrict you in any way or cut into your skin. Place your hands lightly on your knees and close your eyes. Begin by taking a deep breath, in through your nose and out through your mouth. As you breathe in, know that you are breathing purifying energy, and as you breathe out, tell each of your body parts to relax. Start at the feet, and in each breath tell each body part to relax. Move to your legs, then your arms, and so on. As you begin to move through your physical body, you will note that you are beginning to feel relaxed and sleepy.

Come into your awareness now, and with every deep breath there will be a white mist that will surround you. This mist is a loving blanket, and you are totally safe in every way. You are now going into a deeper alternate state of consciousness. As the mist slowly clears you will find yourself seated in a beautiful white and very large, comfy armchair. The mist is still clearing, and as it dissipates it reveals to you a large cinema screen. As the final mist clears, you will notice that your loving guide is actually with you in another chair. Feel the love and the warmth of your guide, and as you sit there, your guide tells you that you can (if you wish) view your past lives or any issues that you have identified on the screen. Your guide also tells you that the information that is shown is accessed from the akashic records. When you have viewed the content that is shown on the screen, your guide will ask you if there is anything else that you wish to learn from the records. This is your choice; however, you must be aware that you may not get the answers you seek if your soul is not developed enough to receive them.

After you have sat with your guide and viewed all that you wish to see, say goodbye to your friend and relax again as the mist starts to come back. Soon the things that you saw around you will disappear into the distance, and again the mist will become thicker. It is not long before the mist will change, and when it does, you will find yourself in familiar surroundings. This is when you need to write all of your experiences in your journal, and notice if there are any patterns in what you have gleaned.

CHAPTER 17

Research and Validation

You are nearing the end of your journey, and if you look back to see what you have achieved, you should be absolutely amazed. You may have had glimpses into your past incarnations, and if you have developed yourself further on your spiritual path, you have envisioned the spirit world in all its glory and majesty. But all the information that you have received about your past incarnations should be validated in order for you to accept what you have been given as the reality and truth of your position in the present moment. This chapter is the culmination of all your experiences. Read on.

Healthy Skepticism

It is healthy to remain skeptical, but there must be some balance. Remember that balance is what allows you to experience and see both sides with love and compassion. When something is out of balance, it cannot stay there for long; soon enough an equilibrium has to be achieved. Many mediums have been known as skeptical mediums, which seems to go against the grain of what they do for a living. However, it should be noted this skepticism allows them to strive for the very best they can do for those in the world of spirit. It also helps them to research with an open and balanced mind.

ALERT

It is important that while you can have a skeptical nature, it will only be healthy if you have balance with it. You must expect your beliefs and your perceptions to be challenged. If you keep an open mind, you will learn the greatest lessons that life has to offer.

True Skeptics Versus Pseudoskeptics

There are two types of skeptics. Those who are considered "true skeptics" will test and analyze, but with an open mind. Then there are the "pseudoskeptics," who through their ignorance and lack of understanding refute everything and anything they fail to understand. These are the worst kind of skeptics because they hurt themselves with their ignorance and are so opposed to new ideas that they are almost radical in nature. Pseudoskeptics do not suspend judgment until they can analyze evidence from a balanced perspective. Instead, they will judge, and not from a rational state of being. Pseudoskeptics often act with parody and aggressiveness and try to convince others that what they believe is wrong or that it cannot be a good thing, and therefore the mediums and psychics must be actively spreading evil and duping the innocent.

A true skeptic objectively inquires and seeks evidence, challenging all sides, including his own beliefs. Healthy skeptics then are still truth seekers in the real sense of the word and will ask, test, analyze, and be open to challenging their own beliefs. Pseudoskeptics revel in ridicule and act like judge and jury. Furthermore, they treat science as an unquestioning basis of fact without further possibilities, which in itself is very linear in thought. You will normally find these individuals as staunch supporters of materialism and materialistic views. They will normally distort truth or possibility to suit their own means.

Balancing Belief and Skepticism

If there is a lack of balance in nature, then nature responds in whichever way necessary to rectify that balance. This can be something wondrous in nature, or it can be entirely disastrous, such as an earthquake or a tsunami. This is true with your own life as well. If you remain out of balance, you have to rectify this balance at some juncture. If that balance is not rectified, you can manifest illness and other malaise. To not have a healthy and balanced skepticism means that you are not open to the truth of your own existence. At some point this must be rectified, for who knows what the cost could be? After all, the universe is in a delicate state of spiritual balance itself, and none can escape its laws.

ALERT

While it is healthy to remain skeptical, you must be aware that you have to have a balanced skepticism, for in studying one note, you will miss the song; in studying one word, you will miss the book; in trying to understand one aspect of the present, you miss the universe, you miss the past, and you are blind to the future.

You should also consider that what was once considered fantasy and unrealistic became reality and truth within the material plane. In reality, what a skeptic sees is dependent on perception and understanding. For instance, what you are told is truth may in fact be illusion. Many years ago, the idea of a structure called an atom was refuted and was claimed to be utter fallacy and fantasy. The very idea that what you were seeing was completely illusionary in nature because the constituents of the atomic vibration were unknown, and any claims suggesting such were dismissed immediately. However, it is now known that an atom does exist and vibrates at a certain point and frequency. These atoms then bind and give us the illusion of solidity. You can assume if this possibility was refuted and then proven true, then surely all possibilities have the same chance, and pseudoskeptics are just playing with a gambling dice to be proven wrong in the final throw.

It is important that you have an open and healthy skeptical mind, which just means that you are a seeker of truth and that you are willing to have your old ideas, beliefs, and opinions challenged with new ones.

Recording Your Experiences

Previous chapters have detailed in depth how to record your experiences. Yes, it is easier said than done, but this is more important than you think. It's not so much about what you have written down or about the experience itself. It is more about the information that you have received, because with this information you can identify patterns and validate experiences. The trick to identifying these patterns is to listen to your innate intuition, for most of what you have recorded may not make any sense to anyone else. Only you will be able to make sense of what you have recorded, because as you read back what you have written, you will activate hidden emotions within you. With this in mind, you can then set out a plan of action to validate the information that you have.

You have your journal that you can record your findings in; however, there are other methods that you can employ. Read on to learn how you can make your investigations easier.

ALERT

It is important to record the time and date along with what you chronicle in your journal. This is for ease of reference and to be able to recognize patterns in time or patterns in your own spiritual growth. You can abbreviate to make things easier—just be sure to remember what your abbreviations mean!

What to Use

If you are not one to write down notes much and you forget to carry your journal with you, there is another way you can approach this. Portable recorders (digital or analog) are brilliant ways of recording your experiences, and you can often add more information than you would have originally written down. This is because when you begin to speak, your subconscious mind will release the information into your conscious experience; this is why you would be able to record a great deal more. Many cell phones and smartphones, including the iPhone and BlackBerry, have apps that you can download and use to record your experiences. Another way that you can record is to work with someone that you trust to take down notes for you as you speak. This will have to be someone who is on the same wavelength as you and whom you trust implicitly. You could use a computer to record your findings, but do this only for note taking, not while you are doing the exercise, as the energy will be affected.

Finding Reliable Evidence

When finding evidence, there are a few major rules that you should follow. The evidence that you are searching for has to be reliable, and that evidence should be easily verifiable. This is incredibly similar to the types of evidence that you would expect from a relatively good and accurate medium. You are looking for names. These names should have recognition or some form of relationship to you or any of your other family members. Areas that you recognize, including place names or street descriptions, are also very good measures of reality. These can be checked with some digging around. Work status and what you may have done is also a great indicator, for you may be able to trace the information regarding the work that you or a member you are attached to has done. Births and deaths are also an excellent indicator; these records are easily verifiable and you can match this information to other sources. The truth is that anything is valuable if it can lead to a source that can be checked.

There is a plethora of information available on the Internet, and you can trace information through many genealogy sites; perform a search using the term "genealogy," and a full list will be given. Most towns and cities have a library, and within the library are sections devoted to local history. Here you can find information that dates back considerably, even if the city has been changed. You must also remember that churches sometimes have the history of their members, including marriages, births, and deaths. Local councils or government, as well as historical societies, have these records as well.

ALERT

Anyone can create a past life out of her own desire and imagination. This is why it is imperative that you find reliable evidence. Only this evidence will be able to validate that what you have been given is true. Now this is very exciting, but just imagine what else this gives you: empowerment and knowledge of your own spiritual authority.

During your regression you may smell certain odors that could help you to join the pieces of information together. Other events that you may view may also give you a missing link. Do not discount anything, and realize that you can get valuable evidence in even the smallest of details.

Validating Your Experiences

Why do you think it is so important to validate your information? Imagine that you accepted anything that anyone told you as ultimate reality and truth. How do you think your life would eventually turn out? Perhaps you would be fed false information that could be harmful to your mind, body, and soul. This could be your nemesis. You should never accept anything as truth unless it is tried and tested for its validity. The great spirit guide Silver Birch said:

> In everything I say I am governed by the desire to be helpful, to bring some understanding, some knowledge, some truth and some wisdom into your lives. It is possible that the principles that we enunciate may be contrary to certain theological ideas of doctrines, dogmas and creeds on which you have been nurtured from childhood days. Our appeal is

directed to your reason. If there is anything we say or do that insults your intelligence or makes your reason revolt, do not accept it.

When you have tested the information that you have been given and you can validate it as truth, it will be something very empowering. This will help to break down barriers of false truths and beliefs, and it will show you that everything you go through is temporary in its nature. It will show you that there is another life, and that death itself is merely an illusion. It empowers you to overcome all the trials and tribulations that beset you.

Scientific Findings

It is very difficult to quantify the science of past life regression. It is not acceptable as modern science and is seen as something that is inscrutable and beyond scientific inquiry. Perhaps one day it will be accepted, just as hypnotherapy was, but for now it will have to stay in the realm of mysticism and New Age beliefs. However, the veil between the world of spirit and the material world is so thin, it often seems pointless to doubt. As far as science is concerned, past lives are about memory recall and may be a simple case of genetic memory. Researchers must adhere to scientific protocols, but future hypotheses could shed light and offer more clarity or proof. The key to past lives could be discovered through cryptomnesia, or when a forgotten memory returns. Therefore, further deliberation on this topic is necessary.

QUESTION

What is cryptomnesia?
Cryptomnesia is like a memory store; it is a forgotten memory that returns. Psychiatrist Carl C. Jung claims cryptomnesia is not only a normal mental process but a necessary one. He also claims that if one did not experience this phenomenon, the human mind would overload with random information.

There is a great deal of work that still has to be done as far as developing the process of past life regression. As far as understanding past lives, researchers and mediums are standing at the edge of a vast lake of uncertainty. As science progresses, so too does the desire to bring science and spirituality together. It is folly to think that science has all the answers, because before science, the questions were never asked—and these questions have given rise to science. Science does not hold all the answers; science and spirituality must mingle to form a new spiritual science.

CHAPTER 18

Stories from the Past

In this chapter you can read about other individuals' experiences with past lives and their regressions. The last story has been kindly reprinted with permission from Ian Lawton (spiritual counselor and regression expert). This case was revised and taken from Ian's own work. The other cases are in the clients' or the therapists' own words. These are printed with kind permission for your own study and enjoyment.

Case Histories from Jennifer Hillman

Jennifer Hillman studied and was certified as master hypnotherapist and NLP (neurolinguistics programming) practitioner in 2005 by Bennett Stellar University.

Jennifer's Story

I became interested in past life regression from my own experience with the process to locate and heal uncertainty, and questions about the connections with situations, patterns, and people whom I had met.

During this program, I met two people who had not met before this class. One, Roger Webb, was living in Phoenix, and the other, Susan Cook, was living in Portland, Oregon. Yet from the moment their eyes met, they felt an uncanny comfort that they could not explain. They decided to find out what the connection was during one of the practice sessions, under hypnosis during a past life regression. Each was placed in a hypnotic trance in separate areas, and the results were amazing.

I worked with Roger Webb, thirty-five, a business consultant, at the time married with four children. I placed Roger in a trance and asked him to go back to the time when he knew or had seen Sue Cook, forty-six. He went back to before the American Civil War to an oak tree and meeting a young Savannah (Sue). He was new in the neighborhood and they became fast friends. Neither had a good family or home life; the tree and the friendship became the sanctuary for both of them. The years moved along, and Savannah moved away for a few years. When her family returned to the area, she returned to the oak tree to find her old friend, John (Roger). The teenage years came and went with the two ending up marrying during the Civil War. It was their wedding night, and John was called into action, leaving his new bride. She would not see her husband again. John died on the battlefield, making a dying intention and vow to be with Savannah again.

Sue had the same exact story through her session with another person in the group. She came out of the trance in tears, reliving the moment of hearing of her husband's death. "I can remember one thing, carving our names in a tree with a heart . . . we found that exact tree and carving in a rock shop in Sedona," Sue said about it.

The outcome of this session was a deeper understanding of how two people had come together to heal the separation of past friends/lovers in this life. Now in this life, they remain close friends who are able to understand the power of love and the power of completing a vow to find each other, made over two hundred years before. The healing is complete and the vow has been kept, healing a premature ending to a relationship.

Christina's Story

Another client was Christina, who has had a rough life: She was abducted when she was a young teenager while walking along a river in Phoenix, Arizona. Something about this experience haunted her, and she wished to figure out why she didn't seem to get over something that happened so many years ago. It affected her relationships and personal well-being. Christina is a Christian Fundamentalist, so her belief system didn't believe in past lives, yet she was curious about the possibility. She became open-minded as I put her in a trance state and used a technique of NLP called Time Line Coaching. In this process, the client walks back on her timeline to the very moment that the situation that needs to be healed occurred. She walked back to the point in her childhood, along the river, and I asked to return to the original point or the point where this needed to be healed.

Christina talked while traveling backward in time. Soon she was past her actual birth year in this lifetime by around ten years. She stopped. She was amazed that she saw herself in a dance/party dress in the 1940s at a small bar in Hawaii.

She continued to travel back to 1737, to the Congo of Africa, as she walked along a river with her brother nearby. Soon she noticed that her brother had disappeared, and she was grabbed and chained by huge white men, and placed in a box on a ship heading for the Americas. She was a scared little girl who was separated from her brother, her family— off to another world. She was abused by the handlers and sold as a house slave in the Carolinas. She re-encountered her past life as being the same situation as in this lifetime. She was abducted and thrown in the back of a white van and later returned. The same feeling returned as she spoke about this African girl/slave as when she was on the river in Phoenix. We continued to work through the lifetime, bringing a sense of awareness of the past repeating, now healed. She still is working through a few things that have come up due to her remembering, through the releasing of the illusion in this lifetime.

That is something that happens with regression. It can be like Pandora's box in some ways, yet like the spiritual journey, you continue to go deeper within to release all the blocks that may be hindering your lessons in the ascension process. It is well worth the inner journey to heal those moments of time still clinging to you.

>> CASE STUDY: ANDREA'S STORY

I first had my interest in past life and life-between-lives regression sparked when a friend lent me *Journey of Souls* by Michael Newton. Though I was a little skeptical, I was nonetheless fascinated that so many people from different cultures and religions were all citing similar accounts of the spirit world. I had to experience it for myself. Before you have a life-between-lives session it is advisable to have a past life regression first, so that's what I did. The experiences I had felt very real. The most surprising things for me were that I was a male named Tom and the amazing feelings of love I felt for a lady whose name I gave as Agatha, but I knew that to me she was Aggie. The life was relatively unexciting. Aggie died before we had a chance to marry. Though I was at the cottage when she died, I stood back and let her sisters tend to her. I spent the rest of that life regretting that I hadn't comforted her and told her how I felt.

In this life I'd been very close to my grandmother. When I was eighteen she was diagnosed with cancer and died six months later. Throughout her illness I refused to accept that I might lose her and never told her how much I loved her. I could see similarities between this and that life as Tom. After my regression I went home and went to bed as usual. At 1 A.M. my mobile rang; it was my grandfather, he was incoherent, he'd had a severe stroke. I accompanied him in the ambulance, and as I sat by his bed in the hospital I held his hand and told him how much I love him. This is something that I wouldn't have done had it not been for my past life regression earlier that evening. Though (as Jock predicted) my grandfather made a full recovery, when his time does come I will know that I told him how much I love him.

After this experience I joined the Past Life Regression Academy and studied for my diploma. I have had some amazing results with clients, from curing arachnophobia to reuniting a mother and her daughter. I had one gentleman who felt that he was void of all emotion, and it was beautiful to be able to watch him shedding tears of joy while exclaiming, "I've never felt this happy" as his son was born in a past life. He took these feelings with him and due to identifying the son in that life as his current son, he was able to identify qualities in him that he'd never noticed. They now have a much deeper bond.

It isn't just a matter of a journey through the life, but the therapeutic work that is done while still in trance after the life. It is this part of the session that helps the mind to link the lessons and souls from the past life to the current, to understand and gain deeper insight into their situations, and to heal negative emotions or body memories. Whether it is a genuine past life or a metaphor created by the mind is not important. What matters is the therapeutic aspect and the amazingly powerful tool that it is in the way it enables people to tap into their inner resources and solve their issues, transforming their lives.

>> CASE STUDY: IAN'S STORY (PAST LIFE THERAPIST AND RENOWNED AUTHOR)

J is a young woman in her twenties who came to see me, suffering from severe lower back pain. This had incapacitated her for many years, preventing her from leading the active, sporting life she craved. Although this is her first regression experience, she soon drifts back in space and time to find herself walking along a Victorian street carrying a basket of fruit. As the scene unfolds she gradually becomes aware of a scuttling behind her and glances round nervously to see a filthy man in a black hat hiding behind a barrel. Without warning he rushes at her and stabs her in the side. She is fully back in the scene as she describes the cold look of triumph in his eyes, his bad teeth, and the stench of his breath. He takes pleasure in plunging the knife in deeper before pulling it out, casually taking a piece of fruit and giving her one last sneering look before running off up the street. She collapses to the pavement and, drifting in and out of consciousness, knows she is going to die.

We then established that earlier in that life she had lived on her brother's farm, and her assailant was a hired hand who had tried to rape her when she was in her teens. She fought him off by biting off his ear lobe. She was expelled from the farm when her brother believed his story over hers, and she spent the rest of her life eking out a living selling flowers. She had become pregnant by another street vendor, but, not content with having her thrown out of her home, the obsessed man had murdered her lover by pushing him into a cold river as she watched, only weeks before he took her life too.

I took her into the spirit realms where she was able to talk to the soul energies of the various characters in that life, particularly her murderer. After venting her anger we unsurprisingly established that his own tale was a sorry one, for he had been savagely beaten by his father and neglected by his mother. Nevertheless, his spirit guide indicated that he could have broken the mold but made some less-than-perfect choices, even though in his own way he loved her. Armed with this understanding, J's former personality was able to forgive him and heal herself. As we discussed what had happened afterward, J realized that the final twist of his knife had brought it right into contact with the vertebra that had been troubling her in her current life, and several weeks later she reported that all traces of her crippling pain had gone. This is typical of the kind of wonderful results that regression can achieve when used in a therapeutic context.

>> CASE STUDY: ANGELA'S STORY

Angela had a terrible fear of being under water, and this fear was preventing her from being comfortable enough in the water long enough for her to learn how to swim. Angela's fear did not come from this lifetime, as she has had no bad experiences with water and there was no rational explanation as to her distress. Angela was now eleven years old and wanted to learn to swim so she could join in with her friends who loved swimming. Eventually Angela's mother took her to see a hypnotherapist to try to locate her fear and heal it. The therapist said that sometimes people block out memories of trauma and completely forget about them, although the fear connected to the memory will stay with them. Angela was placed in a light trance and slowly taken back through her childhood to try to find the source of her fear. As this continued so far without locating any trauma, the therapist then asked Angela, who was now in a very relaxed state, to go to the time in her life that created her fear of water.

Straight away Angela became agitated as she gasped for breath and was calling for help. The therapist calmed her down and helped her to detach from feeling the memory by having her watch it happen instead of feeling it happen. Angela was then able to tell the story of why she was afraid of water. It was because she had actually drowned in a previous existence, and this trauma then carried over into her present life. Angela said that she was five years old and had gone to the lake with her sister and some other friends because it was a very hot summer's day. Angela remembers that her mother told her only to paddle in the water and not to go in any further. All the others were going further into the lake, and she didn't want to look like a baby so she ignored her mother's advice and went further in. Angela got into trouble and soon fell under the water. She remembers trying to find her way to the top but was gulping in water and soon she became confused. Suddenly she was out of the water and realized she could see her body floating face down. Angela had drowned. The therapist then helped Angela to let go of this memory by performing some healing work and explaining to her subconscious that this trauma did not belong to her current lifetime. Angela has now faced her fears and has already taken swimming lessons in her local pool. (Reprinted by kind permission of Joanne Brocas, author of *Psychic Children*)

The Case of Abby Swanson (from *Life Before Life*, Jim Tucker)

Abby Swanson, a young girl who lives in Ohio, was four years old when she began talking to her mother one night after having her bath. "Mommy, I used to give you baths when you were a baby," she said. "Oh really?" her mom replied. "Uh huh. You cried," Abby responded. "I did?" said her mom. "Yep," Abby said. "I was your grandma."

"And what was your name?" her mother asked her. She remembers her hair standing on end as Abby considered the question, tapping her mouth with her fingers.

"Lucy? . . . Ruthie? . . . Ruthie," she finally said. Since this was Abby's great-grandmother's name, her mother tried to ask her more questions, but Abby did not say anything else.

Abby's great-grandmother died in 1985, nine years before Abby was born. She had twenty grandchildren, and unlike most of the others, Abby's mother lived nearby and was close to her while growing up. They had some conflict when Abby's mother was a teenager but then got along well when she became an adult.

Abby's mother would occasionally mention Abby's great-grandparents to her children, but never by name, and she had not talked about them for at least six months before that night. In addition, Abby's grandmother lived on the West Coast and could not have been a source of information for Abby to learn about her great-grandmother. Later, her mother did check with Abby's grandmother to confirm that Abby's great-grandmother had in fact given her mother baths. Abby's grandmother also said that her mother cried a lot when she was given baths as a baby.

Abby's mother is certain that Abby had never heard her great-grandmother's name. In fact, when she asked her a few days later what the name was, Abby did not know. Whatever knowledge, or memory, was available to Abby that night was not available to her after that.

The Bloxham Tapes Abstract

One of the most celebrated cases of supposedly verifiable, past life recall involved the Welsh hypnotherapist Arnall Bloxham, about whose work Jeffrey Iverson produced a BBC documentary and book in the seventies. Bloxham's most responsive subject was given the pseudonym Jane Evans, and three of her supposed past lives are of particular interest. The most well-known personage is that of Rebecca, a persecuted Jewish woman in twelfth-century York, England. Rebecca's story has important weaknesses that are usually overlooked. Worse, although it is rarely reported, is that Jane's regression to the life of a Roman woman called Livonia in third-century Britain has been conclusively proved to stem from a historical novel. That would be the end of the matter were it not for a third life, that of Alison, a servant to the medieval French entrepreneur Jacques Coeur. Similar attempts to suggest a fictional source for this life have shown to be entirely inadequate. Indeed, it seems close to impossible that some of its obscure but eventually verified details could have been contained in any "normal" source to which Jane could have been exposed, however briefly. It would therefore appear that, overall, Jane's is a fascinating and mixed case that should hold some interest for believers and skeptics alike.

The following material is reprinted with permission from Ian Lawton, "The Bloxham Tapes Revisited," *www.ianlawton.com/plr1.htm.*

Background

When an acquaintance first suggested to BBC producer Jeffrey Iverson that he should visit the renowned hypnotherapist Arnall Bloxham in their shared hometown of Cardiff, he had little expectation of it coming to much. Bloxham was by then nearly eighty years of age, but for the past twenty years he had been regressing subjects back into previous lives and had tapes from sessions with more than four hundred subjects to prove it. Despite his initial skepticism, Iverson made a number of visits and spent many hours listening to the tapes, becoming increasingly intrigued. Like most people, he had accepted the misconception that people always claim to remember only famous and exciting lives, yet here he encountered regression after regression that was ordinary, humble, and often somewhat boring. Not only that, but many subjects used entirely different voices and words from their normal, conscious personality. But he also knew that the only way to satisfy his mounting curiosity would be to concentrate on cases containing detailed and obscure historical facts that might be verifiable. This he did, even bringing in the famous journalist and broadcaster Magnus Magnusson to assist in the investigation. The results were aired in 1976 in a BBC documentary entitled *The Bloxham Tapes*, accompanied by Iverson's book *More Lives Than One.* Between them they caused quite a stir.

The Case of Graham Huxtable

Iverson was intrigued by one of Bloxham's subjects, a mild-mannered Swansea man called Graham Huxtable who, when regressed, transformed into a coarse, illiterate gunner's mate in the English navy of the late eighteenth century. Using what appeared to be contemporary naval slang, he described how he was on board a ship called the *Aggie*, which was part of a fleet of ships involved in blockading the French just off Calais. Indeed, this case had come to the attention of two high-ranking naval officers, in the shape of no lesser personages than Lord Mountbatten and Prince Phillip, who had been sufficiently impressed that they helped to investigate it. Some partial names were given, but, coupled with incomplete contemporary naval records, the details were insufficient to prove exactly what ship the man had described. What is more, the trauma Graham had suffered when he apparently relived his leg being shot off in battle convinced both him and Bloxham not to attempt to elicit more details.

However, skeptics like Melvin Harris—a journalist, broadcaster, and indefatigable debunker of past lives whose 1986 book *Sorry, You've Been Duped* was republished in 2003 under the less confrontational title, *Investigating the Unexplained*—are not at all convinced by cases such as this. Researchers will attempt to trace the factual historical records for past-life cases in their attempts to verify them, and Harris showed that historical fiction is an even more likely source. In this instance he suggests that Graham provided no information that could not easily be found in the scores of historical novels and boy's adventure stories about life in the Royal Navy during that period. He also insists that naval records for the period are not incomplete and that, although there was one similarly named ship at the time called the *Agamemnon*, it had a massive sixty-four guns, double the size cited by Graham for the *Aggie*.

The Story of Jane

For Iverson, the case that seemed to hold out most promise was that of a local housewife, who he dubbed "Jane Evans" to protect her identity. She originally visited Bloxham in the late sixties after seeing a roadside poster about his health treatments, but she also proved to be an excellent regression subject. Over a number of sessions she explored what appeared to be six different previous lives, the earliest in Roman Britain in the late third century, the most recent as a nun in Maryland at the turn of the last. Iverson asked to meet her and by coincidence found out that they had both attended the same secondary school in Newport, although a few years apart. From this he was able to independently establish that the she had never studied history at an advanced level, and none of the relevant periods in any detail, and that neither of her parents had read much or showed any great interest in history when she was younger.

A Weak Case: Jane's Livonia Regression

Some of Jane's regressions provided little in the way of verifiable detail, but others appeared to be more promising. The earliest involved a woman called Livonia who lived in Roman Britain towards the end of the third century. She was married to Titus, a tutor to the boy Constantine who would go on to become known as "the Great" and whose father Constantius eventually became Caesar. Jane provided many details that were reasonably obscure yet known to be historically accurate, but in fact Constantius's whereabouts in the earliest years discussed in the regression, that is around A.D. 286, are unknown. She reported that he was in York and already acting as the Roman governor of Britain—a country that history does not link him to until a decade later, when he invaded to crush the independence movement of Allectus. So was she really a firsthand witness who could fill in the missing blanks of history, as Iverson suggests?

Unfortunately, it appears not, because Harris remembered a book by bestselling novelist Louis de Wohl that covers exactly this "missing" period. First published in 1947, it was called *The Living Wood*, and in it de Wohl effectively lays out a fictional narrative interspersed with known historical facts to tell a story that is in parts identical to Jane's recall of the life of Livonia, except that he has Constantius serving merely as a legate in Britain during the missing period. As Harris points out, the only major discrepancies in the fictional elements are that Livonia and Titus are extremely minor characters in the novel, but Jane's imagination appears to elevate them somewhat. In fact, Livonia is merely a lady-in-waiting in the book, but she has "pouting lips and smoldering eyes" and in Jane's story becomes much more identifiable with the lead character—Constantius's first wife Helena, who would go on to be canonized for supposedly discovering the "true cross." Meanwhile, Titus appears to be based not so much on his namesake, a briefly mentioned Roman soldier, but on the romantic lead, another fictional character called Hilary; because what happens to him—he is converted to Christianity by a woodcarver called Albanus, ordained by the Spanish Bishop Ossius, and then killed shortly afterwards as part of the persecution of Christians at the time—is exactly what happens to Titus in Jane's version.

Not only that, but in other places the correspondences in terms of names and actions are even more exact, and again what is most damning is that they relate to fictional rather than historical characters. For example, both stories have a military tutor to Constantine called Marcus Favonius Facilis, de Wohl's inspiration for whom came from the tomb of a Roman soldier at Colchester Castle that is known to date only to the first century. Moreover, both contain Roman deputies to the governor of Britain, called Curio and Valerius, but these were again made up by de Wohl. Meanwhile, the historian turned paranormal investigator Ian Wilson—whose 1981 book *Mind Out of Time* and the 1987 follow-up *The After Death Experience* are important, additional, skeptical sources—adds that in both stories everyone refers to Helena as "domina," and the Roman name for the modern town of St. Albans is shortened from Verulamium to Verulam.

An Inconclusive Case: Jane's Rebecca Regression

Despite the apparently foolproof explanation for this case, in fact, Jane's other regressions may not be as easily explained as Harris and Wilson suggest. The one that is most commonly referred to by supporters of reincarnation is that of a persecuted Jewish woman called Rebecca, again in York but this time in the late twelfth century. In outline she reported that she was married to a wealthy moneylender called Joseph, and they lived with their son and daughter in a large stone house in the north of the city. Iverson approached Barrie Dobson, professor of medieval history at York University, to help with the analysis of the more specific details of Jane's recall.

First, she reported that her fellow Jews were made to wear yellow circles over their hearts. History records that this identification was only enforced by papal decree in 1215, but Dobson suggested it would have been quite conceivable for this to have been a practice in York or even the whole of England several decades earlier. Second, she said that the Jews lent money to the king, Henry Plantagenet, to finance the war in Ireland, and that as a result he was well disposed towards their attempts to recover money in the courts—although they had to pay him a levy of "ten parts" of any such sums; this was certainly historically accurate. Third, she described how a priest came to York to recruit men for what would now be called the Third Crusade, and that both Jews and Muslims alike were regarded as "infidels," this hatred being stirred up by the pope himself. Moreover, she said the Jews of York were so worried by uprisings against their kinsmen in other cities that her husband had shifted much of his money to their uncle in Lincoln for safekeeping. Again, all this is perfectly feasible, because Dobson himself had documented the emerging ties between the Jews of York and Lincoln at the time. Fourth, she recalled that a young man called "Mabelise" had borrowed money from her husband, and that they had to take him to "the assizes" to recover it. This is pretty close to the name of a local noble recorded by chroniclers of the time, Richard Malebisse, who did indeed owe money to the Jews of York and led the subsequent uprising against them, in part to avoid paying his debts.

Fifth, she recounted how after Henry had died and his successor Richard had immediately left for the Crusades, her community felt they had lost their last protection and were getting ready to flee the city. She also gave the date as 1189 and said that Henry had protected them for thirty years, both of which are exactly correct. Sixth, she recounted how an elderly Jew called Isaac had been killed in the leadup to the riots in "Coney Street," and this too is recorded, although without the name. She further recalled that at about the same time their neighbor Benjamin's father had been murdered while on a visit to London. Apparently some months had passed, and then rioters broke into his house next door, and she heard the screams and smelled the smoke as they set fire to it. Again, these obscure details are confirmed as a wealthy resident of York called Benedict was one of thirty Jews killed in riots in London at the time of Richard's coronation, and Dobson himself records that it was the subsequent attack on this man's house, and the killing of his wife and children, that sparked the uprising.

As a denouement to all this, Jane reported, Rebecca and her family fled their own house and headed for the castle where they took refuge with all the other Jews. History confirms that this siege lasted for several days before those inside, realizing their position was hopeless, took each other's lives. But, according to Jane, on that first night they were only allowed "just inside the gates," and they could hear the mob screaming at them to come out and be killed—and asking if they had "crucified any little boys," a known accusation of the time. Then they started to ram the gates, and the terrified Jews resorted to killing their children to save them from their persecutors' clutches—another poignant and distressing fact confirmed by contemporary chroniclers. It seems that Rebecca's husband managed to bribe someone to get his family out, and they fled to a Christian church "just outside the big copper gate" where they tied up the priest and his clerk and then hid "down below in the cellars."

According to Jane's report, it seems they must have stayed in this cellar for several days, terrified for their lives and growing increasingly cold, tired, and hungry. In desperation, Rebecca's husband and son went off to find food, but while they were gone she heard rioters on horseback preparing to enter the church. The final, highly charged scenes of the regression see her praying in vain for her menfolk to return and save them, hearing the rioters entering the church and approaching their hiding place, then seeing her daughter being dragged away before she herself becomes, simply, "dark."

We can see that much of the information Jane came up with was relatively obscure and yet still factually correct. Dobson was apparently impressed by the accuracy of much of her recall and felt some of it would only have been known to professional historians. He did question one point, which was why she had referred to the modern name of "Coney Street" when in the Middle Ages it was marked on maps as Cuninga or King Street. But Iverson suggests that the more modern name, derived from the sale of rabbits, may have been in everyday use for some time before the change was noted on maps. Moreover, Dobson himself refuted another potential problem, which is Jane's reference to the "big copper gate." Although there was no gate actually made of copper, there was a street called Coppergate at the time, and it would have had a large gate at the end leading into the precincts of the castle. In addition, it's not relevant whether she said it as two words or just one.

Dobson also apparently identified St. Mary's, Castlegate, as the prime suspect for the church in which Rebecca and her family hid. It was close to Coppergate and in sight of the castle. But the problem was that, in common with all the churches of the area, it had no crypt or cellar. Then in late 1975 he wrote to Iverson with the news that is still, in many quarters, trumpeted as the pièce de resistance of this and indeed all reincarnation cases:

In September, during the renovation of the church, a workman certainly found something that seems to have been a crypt—very rare in York except for the Minster—under the chancel of that church. It was blocked up immediately and before the York archaeologists could investigate it

236

properly. But the workman who looked inside said he had seen round stone arches and vaults. Not much to go on, but if he was right this would point to a Norman or Romanesque period of building, i.e., before 1190 rather than after it.

The problem, however, is that it is rarely reported that over the next decade more was established about this supposed crypt. Harris corresponded with Dobson in 1986, and this time he revealed that "it now seems overwhelmingly most likely that the chamber . . . was not an early medieval crypt at all but a post-medieval charnel vault." This seems to have been based on the findings of a Royal Commission Survey in 1981 that it was "probably a later insertion." In fact, to Harris's delight, Dobson seems to have been put off the case completely by this revelation: "The evidence available is now revealed as so weak in this instance that it fails to support any thesis which suggests that Rebecca's regression contains within it genuine and direct memories of late twelfth-century York." But what about all the other elements of Jane's recall that had so impressed Dobson ten years previously, which had not changed at all? One cannot help but wonder whether an ambition to progress to the higher echelons of the academic field might not have had some influence on this apparent change of heart; after all, within another two years Dobson would take over the chair of medieval history at Cambridge.

But what of Rebecca hiding out in a crypt? Harris himself reports that originally Dobson identified three potential churches close to Coppergate, and St. Mary's was simply the most convenient for filming the documentary. So perhaps one of these others contains a crypt that has yet to be discovered. Or perhaps one of them had a rather different configuration in 1190, or there was even an entirely different building on one of the three sites or at another nearby site that has now been lost to time. One of these is surely not impossible.

Harris has only two other possible criticisms of this case. First of all, he repeats the obvious criticism of Jane's assertion that the Jews of York had to wear badges several decades before the formal papal decree, and he argues that the yellow circle was only used in Germany and France. But Dobson originally accepted this as a possibility and he was *the* expert, even if he decided to make an about-face later on. The other apparent problem is that Jane repeatedly referred to living in a "ghetto," a word only invented several centuries later. But regression subjects can use a mixture of modern and archaic language, nor does her use of the word necessarily infer, as Harris suggests, that this was the only area the Jews lived in. He makes great play of the fact that these passages were left out of the book and documentary, but in fact there may be nothing in this at all. Above all, it seems fair to say that he has done nothing but snipe around the edges without tackling the wealth of accurate and obscure facts that emerged during this regression.

Harris must have accepted that Jane was unlikely to have read any of the relatively obscure, nonfictional sources that might have played a part in her recall, nor does he come up with any possible fictional sources. However, Wilson does, reporting that three of his correspondents recalled having heard a radio play on the subject of the York massacre some time in the fifties, though none could remember the name, and he was unable to trace it. All in all, the facts these rebuttals are based on are about as convincing as the facts revealed in Jane's Livonia regression, which is why it seems fair to regard this case as inconclusive one way or the other.

An Unexplained Case: Jane's Alison Regression

Harris and Wilson separately managed to track Jane down, and both insist that she refused to speak to them, which on the face of it appears to be extremely damning in itself. But there must have been more to this than meets the eye, because another of her regressions is in a different category entirely. In this she found herself in mid-fifteenth-century France, acting as a servant to an important contemporary figure named Jacques Coeur. Iverson established that Jane had never studied the period in question in any detail, certainly not French history of the time, and she had only been to France once, to Paris for two days, whereas the town of Bourges on which this regression centers lies some 150 miles to the south.

Before you examine Jane's recall, you should acquaint yourself with a few known historical facts. Coeur was born in around 1395, in the middle of the Hundred Years' War with England. The son of a rich Bourges merchant, he began building up his own trading empire in his early thirties, and in time his massive fleet of ships would become pre-eminent in the import of all manner of goods from the eastern ports of the Mediterranean. As his wealth grew, so did his estates, his portfolio of debtors, and his influence in royal circles. In 1436, he was summoned to the recently reacquired Paris by Charles VII to become master of the mint, two years later he was made steward of the royal expenditure, and within another ten he had started lending the king himself money to finance his new thrust to oust the English from his northern territories. It was because of this that Coeur formed part of the royal procession that triumphantly entered the recaptured city of Rouen in 1449.

His service to his country was ill-rewarded, however. Many merchants whose profits had been squeezed by Coeur's monopolies were keen to see his downfall, as were those who owed him money—the king and many of his senior courtiers included. Meanwhile, the king's mistress, Agnes Sorel, whose huge influence and inordinate beauty caused much jealousy in royal circles, died suddenly a year later at the tender age of only twenty-eight. Unsurprisingly, a rumor soon spread that she had been poisoned, with the king's son Louis—who had been agitating against his father since his forced marriage to Margaret, daughter of James I of Scotland, in his early teens— the chief suspect. However, events took a rather different turn when, more than a year after Agnes's death, a courtier who owed Coeur money formally accused him of her murder. It seems everyone knew this was a ridiculous accusation, but the king showed his gratitude by having him arrested for this and other charges, financial and otherwise. His estates and stocks were seized and distributed to various royal favorites, including the men chosen to preside at his trial, while the king reserved a substantial portion of Coeur's money to finance further war efforts. After nearly two years of imprisonment he was finally convicted, but he escaped from prison in 1455, only to die a year later on the Greek island of Chios.

Jane's Recall

So what of Jane's story? The broad thrust is that her name was Alison, and she was found by Coeur in Alexandria. As a young servant girl she had been ill and effectively unwanted, but he took pity on her and brought her back to France, where she remained in his employ until he was taken into custody. Apparently he gave her a draft of poison at this point, and it seems reasonable that if she was of infidel Arab descent then, robbed of his protection in such a staunchly Christian country, death might have been the kindest option. This suggests she may have grown quite close to him by this time, and he certainly seems to have taken her into his confidence on many things about court life.

There is one unusual aspect of Jane's recall picked up on by Harris. When she was asked whether Coeur had ever been married, her response was "not that I know of." Yet history clearly shows that in his early twenties he married Macé de Lodepart, the daughter of a wealthy Bourges family, and that they had a number of children together. Harris reports that again he found an appropriate fictional source, this time *The Moneyman* by the renowned historical novelist Thomas Costain, first published in 1947 and republished in 1961. Moreover, Costain admits in his introduction that he deliberately omitted Coeur's family from his novel "because they played no real part in the events which brought his career to its climax." So at first sight Harris appears absolutely right to suggest that this cannot be mere coincidence, and Wilson again praises his sleuthing without adding to or questioning it. But, unlike with Livonia and *The Living Wood*, Harris says little more about Costain's novel except that "it is based on Coeur's life and provides almost all of the flourishes and authentic-sounding touches included in her past-life memory."

To anyone who takes the trouble to read the full five hundred pages of *The Moneyman*, this is something of a generalization at best and a downright misrepresentation at worst. It is a romantic tale in which many of the key characters apart from Coeur are entirely fictional, along with much of the narrative, and its main thrust involves Coeur supposedly attempting to find a successor for the ageing Agnes Sorel as the king's mistress. One of his associates chances upon a fictional teenage girl called Valerie, who had been fostered and then orphaned, and who also could pass as Agnes's double—in fact, she eventually turns out to be her illegitimate niece. Valerie is tutored for the part of royal mistress and easily wins the king's affections, but then she runs away with a fictional friend of Coeur's and marries him. This tale of a blond-haired, porcelain-skinned girl attempting to become the king's mistress bears no resemblance to Alison's life as a humble servant of Eastern extraction who remains in Coeur's mansion at Bourges. Indeed, the latter is hardly mentioned in Costain's novel, and there is no character on which Alison could be based.

Other Historical Facts
More important even than this, Jane came up with a significant number of historically accurate facts of varying degrees of obscurity, the majority of

which are not mentioned in *The Moneyman* at all. Nor did she repeat any of its many fictional "mistakes." All of which leaves Harris's proclamation of the "overwhelmingly strong evidence" that this was her source looking rather misplaced. His only other comments relate to her recollections of Agnes's tomb and of Coeur's house in Bourges, pictures and descriptions of which are reasonably widespread—especially of the latter, whose unusual mixture of architecture remains a significant tourist attraction. Given the wealth of other accurate information Jane provided, the explanations proffered by Harris in this instance are entirely unsatisfactory.

But before you carry on with the rest of the case, there is the matter of Jane's apparent ignorance of Coeur's family. It is certainly true that historians pay them scant regard, even though one of his daughters married the son of the Viscount of Bourges and a son became archbishop of the city. So it is entirely conceivable that he only married at an early age as an aid to social mobility and that his wife played little role in his later life before she died around the time of his arrest. As for his children, it is equally conceivable that a man with his widespread business interests and political responsibilities would have had little time for them. Alternatively, there are some subtle hints that Alison was very much in love with her master, although she flatly denied being his mistress, so Iverson's suggestion that perhaps she could not even bring herself to acknowledge his marriage may also have some merit.

First, Jane reported that the king's nickname was "heron legs," which Iverson confirmed in discussions with French historians. Second, she specifically commented on how his son Louis was "very wicked, very cruel and yet pious sometimes," which exactly matches the description by another French historian that his character consisted of "piety combined with ruthlessness." Third, she reported that Coeur suspected Louis had poisoned his wife Margaret, who was only twenty when she died, and again historians confirmed this was a popular rumor at the time. Fourth, she said that Coeur had been to Paris after its recapture from the English and had watched the king enter the city with both his queen and mistress in tow. He said Agnes was spat upon by the crowd because even her two beloved pet dogs were clothed in "coats of white fur with jeweled collars," after which the queen appeared with her on a balcony in a show of support. Jane talked about this happening some time after Louis' banishment but before Agnes's death, which places it somewhere between 1446 and 1450. Iverson was able to confirm that in her letters

Agnes often mentioned her two pampered pet greyhounds. More than this, though, he found a contemporary although anonymous account describing just such a visit to Paris, in April 1448, in which the queen and Agnes regularly appeared together much to the dismay of the people.

Jane also came up with rather more obscure information relating specifically to Coeur himself, and Iverson was again particularly thorough in his attempts to research at least the nonfictional sources for his life. What he found was that, despite his huge importance, only two detailed reference works about him existed in English at the time of Jane's sessions, and both were obscure books written in 1847 and 1927 that did not mention the facts that follow. Of course, skeptics might still point out that Jane learned some French at school and therefore must have read about Coeur's life in books from his homeland. But in fact, even French history books provide few details of this enigmatic character. So again Iverson had to spend considerable time with French scholars and historians, in Bourges and elsewhere, attempting to verify these seriously obscure aspects of Jane's recall.

Verifying the Story

First, she indicated that Coeur, who was very close to Agnes, gave her the first polished diamond in France on a chain with a sapphire clasp. Iverson was able to establish that he probably was the first person to have diamonds shaped and cut and that Agnes probably was the first person in France to model them for him. Second, Coeur's father is referred to in modern sources merely as a "rich merchant," but French historians told Iverson that there are two more detailed versions of his story, one that he was a furrier and the other that he was a goldsmith; while the former view is mentioned once in *The Moneyman*, Jane clearly stated the latter. Third, she discussed this in the context of rumors that Coeur was Jewish, and again historians were able to confirm that these were current during his life. Fourth, when describing how the king's men were coming to arrest her master, she showed extreme indignation at the ingratitude of it all that would have been entirely appropriate after everything Coeur did for him. Fifth, she reported that he was an avid collector of art and that in his main gallery hung paintings by "Fouquet," "van Eyck," "Giotto" and "John of Bruges." Iverson established that Jean Fouquet was the court painter to the king and that receipts show Coeur lent him money, that Jan van Eyck was the court painter to the nearby Duke of

Burgundy, and that Giotto was an Italian master who had lived in the previous century. John of Bruges, also known as "John Bondolf," was harder to trace, but a specialist art history book revealed him to have been a Flemish court painter for the king's grandfather, Charles V. Jane also mentioned a painting depicting Agnes with one of her babies and said that Coeur badly wanted to acquire it. She was wrong that this was by Van Eyck, but it is a reasonably renowned painting by Fouquet known as *Madonna and Child.* Sixth, Jane indicated that Coeur had a "body servant" called Abdul, who was "dressed differently from the others"; Iverson was able to establish from his trial records that he did indeed have an Egyptian body slave.

Yet the most impressive aspect of this case is Jane's recall of a "beautiful golden apple with jewels in it" that Coeur said had been given to him by the sultan of Turkey. All of Iverson's initial attempts to verify the existence of such a piece drew a blank, until his last night in Bourges when he returned to his hotel to find a message from a local historian, Pierre Bailly. The latter reported that he had been searching through contemporary archives when he found "an obscure list of items confiscated by the Treasury from Jacques Coeur"; in that list was a "grenade" of gold—a pomegranate. As Iverson points out, this is so like an apple in shape and size that the English word contains the French root, *pomme.* (© 2008 Ian Lawton)

Professional Mediums
and Organizations

Professional Mediums

Jock Brocas
Internationally renowned medium and researcher
www.jockbrocas.com

Joanne Brocas
Angelic communication expert
www.feelthevibes.org

Kai Muegge
http://felixcircle.blogspot.com

Robin Foy
www.scoleexperiment.com

Christine de Nucci
www.spirit-lodge-diary.blogspot.com

Professional Organizations

ASSMPI
American Society for Standards in Mediumship and Psychical Investigation
www.assmpi.org

Association for Research and Enlightenment
www.edgarcayce.com

The Bristol Spirit Lodge Circle
A small home circle for the support, development, and demonstration of
physical mediumship
www.spirit-lodge-diary.blogspot.com

Division of Perceptual Studies, University of Virginia
*www.medicine.virginia.edu/clinical/departments/psychiatry/sections/cspp/
dops/home-page*

FEG Group
The Felix Experimental Group: Applied spirituality and physical spirit
manifestation
http://felixcircle.blogspot.com

International Spiritualists Federation
www.theisf.com

The Rhine Research Center
www.rhine.org

The Scole Experiment
www.thescoleexperiment.com

Windbridge Institute
Applied research in human potential
www.windbridge.org

Additional Resources

Books

Retrocognitions: An Investigation into the Memories of Past Lives and the Periods Between Lives by Wagner Alegretti

Book of Six Rings by Jock Brocas

Dark Waters by Jock Brocas

Powers of the Sixth Sense: How to Keep Safe in a Hostile World by Jock Brocas

Is There an Afterlife? A Comprehensive Overview of the Evidence by David Fontana

Witnessing the Impossible by Robin P. Foy

The Golden Thread by Robert Goodwin

In the Presence of White Feather by Robert and Amanda Goodwin

The Collected Wisdom of White Feather by Robert and Amanda Goodwin

The Enlightened Soul by Robert and Amanda Goodwin

Answers for an Enquiring Mind by Robert Goodwin and Amanda Terrado

River Dreams by Dale E. Graff

Tracks in the Psychic Wilderness: An Exploration of ESP, Remote Viewing, Precognitive Dreaming, and Synchronicity by Dale E. Graff

Children Who Remember Past Lives, A Question of Reincarnation by Ian Stevenson

Reincarnation Cases of the Reincarnation Type by Ian Stevenson

Where Reincarnation and Biology Intersect by Ian Stevenson

Altered States of Consciousness by Charles T. Tart

Life Before Life: A Scientific Investigation of Children's Memories of Previous Lives by Jim Tucker

A Guide to Mediumship, and Psychical Unfoldment . . . : in Three Parts by E. W. Wallis and M. H. Wallis

Research

Richard Webster
Past life regressions
www.floraco.com/richard.htm

Andrea Greenwood, Hypnotherapist
Vision hypnotherapy
www.visionhypnotherapy.org

Dale E. Graff
PSI phenomena, seminars
mtnviewer@dalegraff.com
www.dalegraff.com

Circles of Wisdom Bookstore
90 Main Street
Andover, MA 01810
978-474-8010
www.circlesofwisdom.com

Shining Lotus Metaphysical Bookstore
2178 S. Colorado Boulevard
Denver, CO 80222
303-758-9113
http://shininglotus.com

Near-Death Experiences and the Afterlife
www.near-death.com

Selected Case Studies

The following case studies are taken from *Life Before Life: A Scientific Investigation of Children's Memories of Previous Lives* by Jim Tucker, and are kindly reprinted with his permission. These cases are an impressive overview of stories from all over the world, and provide insight into and proof of the existence of past lives.

The Case of Kemal Atasoy

Dr. Jürgen Keil, a psychologist from Australia, listened as Kemal Atasoy, a six-year-old boy in Turkey, confidently recounted details of a previous life that he claimed to remember. They were meeting in the boy's home, a comfortable house in an upper middle class neighborhood, and with them were Dr. Keil's interpreter and Kemal's parents, a well-educated couple who seemed amused at times by the enthusiasm that the little boy showed in describing his experiences. He said that he had lived in Istanbul, 500 miles away. He stated that his family's name had been Karakas and that he had been a rich Armenian Christian, who lived in a large three-story house. The house, he said, was next to the house of a woman named Aysegul, a well-known personality in Turkey, who had left the country because of legal problems. Kemal said that his house had been on the water, where boats were tied up, and a church was behind it. He said that people called him Fistik and that his wife and children had Greek first names. He also said that he often carried a large leather bag and that he only lived in the house for part of the year.

No one knew if Kemal's story was true when he met Dr. Keil in 1997. His parents did not know anyone in Istanbul. In fact, Kemal and his mother had never been there, and his father had only visited the city twice on business. In addition, the family knew no Armenians. His parents were Alevi Muslims, a group with a belief in reincarnation, but they did not seem to think that Kemal's statements, which he had been making from the time he was just a toddler at two years of age, were particularly important.

Dr. Keil set out to determine if the details that Kemal had given fit with someone who had actually lived. The great effort that this investigation took demonstrates that Kemal could not have come across the information by accident.

When Dr. Keil and his interpreter went to Istanbul, they found the house of Aysegul, the woman whom Kemal had named. Next to the house was an empty three-story residence that precisely matched Kemal's description—it was at the edge of the water, where boats were tied up, with a church behind it. Dr. Keil then had trouble finding any evidence that a person like the one Kemal described had ever lived there. No Armenians were living in that part of Istanbul at the time, and Dr. Keil could not find anyone who remembered any Armenians ever having lived there. When he returned to

Istanbul later that year, he talked with Armenian church officials, who told him that they were not aware that an Armenian had ever lived in the house. No church records indicated one had, but a fire had destroyed many of the records. Dr. Keil talked with an elderly man in the neighborhood, who said that an Armenian had definitely lived there many years before and that the church officials were simply too young to remember that long ago.

Armed with that report, Dr. Keil decided to continue his search for information. The next year, he made a third trip to the area and interviewed a well-respected local historian. During the interview, Dr. Keil made sure he did not prompt any answers or make any suggestions. The historian told a story strikingly similar to the one Kemal had told. The historian said that a rich Armenian Christian had, in fact, lived in that house. He had been the only Armenian in that area, and his family's name was Karakas. His wife was Greek Orthodox, and her family did not approve of the marriage. The couple had three children, but the historian did not know their names. He said that the Karakas clan lived in another part of Istanbul, that they dealt in leather goods, and that the deceased man in question often carried a large leather bag. He also said that the deceased man lived in the house only during the summer months of the year. He had died in 1940 or 1941.

Though Dr. Keil was not able to verify Kemal's statement that the wife and children had Greek first names, the wife came from a Greek family. The name that Kemal had given for the man, Fistik, turned out to be an Armenian term meaning "nice man." Dr. Keil could not confirm that people actually called Mr. Karakas that, but he was struck by the fact that, even though no one around him knew the expression, Kemal had given a name that could easily have been used to describe Mr. Karakas.

The Case of William

John McConnell, a retired New York City policeman working as a security guard, stopped at an electronics store after work one night in 1992. He saw two men robbing the store and pulled out his pistol. Another thief behind a counter began shooting at him. John tried to shoot back, and even after he fell, he got up and shot again. He was hit six times. One of the bullets entered his back and sliced through his left lung, his heart, and the main pulmonary artery, the blood vessel that takes blood from the right side of the heart to the lungs to receive oxygen. He was rushed to the hospital but did not survive.

John had been close to his family and had frequently told one of his daughters, Doreen, "No matter what, I'm always going to take care of you." Five years after John died, Doreen gave birth to a son named William. William began passing out soon after he was born. Doctors diagnosed him with a condition called pulmonary valve atresia, in which the valve of the pulmonary artery has not adequately formed, so blood cannot travel through it to the lungs. In addition, one of the chambers of his heart, the right ventricle, had not formed properly as a result of the problem with the valve. He underwent several surgeries. Although he will need to take medication indefinitely, he has done quite well.

William had birth defects that were very similar to the fatal wounds suffered by his grandfather. In addition, when he became old enough to talk, he began talking about his grandfather's life. One day when he was three years old, his mother was at home trying to work in her study when William kept acting up. Finally, she told him, "Sit down, or I'm going to spank you." William replied, "Mom, when you were a little girl, and I was your daddy, you were bad a lot of times, and I never hit you!"

His mother was initially taken aback by this. As William talked more about the life of his grandfather, she began to feel comforted by the idea that her father had returned. William talked about being his grandfather a number of times and discussed his death. He told his mother that several people were shooting during the incident when he was killed, and he asked a lot of questions about it.

One time, he said to his mother, "When you were a little girl and I was your daddy, what was my cat's name?"

She responded, "You mean Maniac?"

"No, not that one," William answered. "The white one."

"Boston?" his mom asked.

"Yeah," William responded. "I used to call him Boss, right?" That was correct. The family had two cats named Maniac and Boston, and only John referred to the white one as Boss.

One day, Doreen asked William if he remembered anything about the time before he was born. He said that he died on Thursday and went to heaven. He said that he saw animals there and also talked to God. He said, "I told God I was ready to come back, and I got born on Tuesday." Doreen was amazed that William mentioned days since he did not even know his days of the week without prompting. She tested him by saying, "So, you were born on a Thursday and died on Tuesday?" He quickly responded, "No, I died Thursday at night and was born Tuesday in the morning." He was correct on both counts—John died on a Thursday, and William was born on a Tuesday five years later.

He talked about the period between lives at other times. He told his mother, "When you die, you don't go right to heaven. You go to different levels—here, then here, then here" as he moved his hand up each time. He said that animals are reborn as well as humans and that the animals he saw in heaven did not bite or scratch.

John had been a practicing Roman Catholic, but he believed in reincarnation and said that he would take care of animals in his next life. His grandson, William, says that he will be an animal doctor and will take care of large animals at a zoo.

William reminds Doreen of her father in several ways. He loves books, as his grandfather did. When they visit William's grandmother, he can spend hours looking at books in John's study, duplicating his grandfather's behavior from years before. William, like his grandfather, is good at putting things together and can be a "non-stop talker."

William especially reminds Doreen of her father when he tells her, "Don't worry, Mom. I'll take care of you."

The Case of Patrick Christenson

Patrick Christenson is a boy who was born by cesarean section in Michigan in 1991. When the nurses brought him to his mother, she immediately felt that he was connected to her first son, who had died of cancer at the age of two in 1979, twelve years earlier. She soon noticed that Patrick displayed three defects that matched those of her other son when he died.

Her first son, Kevin, began to limp when he was one-and-a-half years old. One day, he fell and broke his left leg. This led to a medical work-up that included a biopsy of a nodule on his scalp above his right ear. Doctors diagnosed him with metastatic cancer. A bone scan showed many abnormal sites. His left eye was protruding and bruised due to a tumor. He received chemotherapy through a central line, a large IV line, in the right side of his neck. Though the site on his neck where the chemotherapy agents were entering his body became flushed and slightly swollen several times, he had no major problems with the treatment and was eventually discharged home. He received outpatient treatment but returned to the hospital five months later. At that point, he appeared blind in his left eye. He was admitted with a fever, treated with antibiotics, and discharged from the hospital. He died two days later, three weeks after his second birthday.

Kevin's parents had separated before his death, and his mother eventually remarried. She gave birth to a daughter and son before Patrick was born. At birth, he had a slanting birthmark with the appearance of a small cut on the right side of his neck, the same location of Kevin's central line, a nodule on his scalp above his right ear as Kevin's biopsied tumor had been, and an opacity in his left eye, diagnosed as a corneal leukoma, that caused him, like Kevin, to have very little vision in that eye. When he began walking, he limped, favoring his left leg.

When Patrick was almost four-and-a-half years old, he began telling his mother things that she felt were related to the life of Kevin. He talked for some time about wanting to go back to their previous home and told his mother that he had left her there. He said that the home was orange and brown, which was correct. He asked his mother if she remembered him having surgery, and when she replied that he had not had any surgery, he said that he had and pointed to the area above his right ear where Kevin had his nodule biopsied. He also said that he did not remember the actual surgery because he was asleep when it was done. At another time, Patrick saw a picture of Kevin, whose pictures were not normally displayed in the family's home, and said that the picture was of him.

After Patrick began making these statements, his mother contacted Carol Bowman, an author who has written two books about children who talk about previous lives—*Children's Past Lives* and *Return from Heaven*. They talked on the phone a number of times, with Carol offering guidance on how to deal with the past-life issues that seemed to be coming up. She eventually referred the case to us for investigation. Dr. Stevenson and I then visited the family when Patrick was five years old.

While we were there, we saw and photographed the birthmark on Patrick's neck, a 4-millimeter dark slanting line on the lower part of the right side of his neck that looked like a healed cut. The nodule on his head was very hard to see but easy to palpate, so we documented the small mass we felt there. We could see the opacity in Patrick's left eye and obtained copies of the eye exams he had received. We watched him walk and could easily determine that he had a slight limp, despite having no medical condition that would explain it. We obtained Kevin's medical records, and they documented the history described earlier, including the lesions that appeared to correspond to Patrick's subsequent birthmarks. We took Patrick to the home that Kevin had shared with his mother. Patrick, unfortunately, did not have great enunciation and could be difficult to understand at times, but he did not make any statements that definitely indicated that he recognized the home.

In summary, Patrick had three unusual lesions at birth that appeared to correspond to lesions that his half-brother Kevin had suffered. In addition, he limped when he began walking and also alluded to events in Kevin's life when talking to his mother.

The Case of Chanai Choomalaiwong

Chanai Choomalaiwong was born in central Thailand in 1967 with two birthmarks, one on the back of his head and one above his left eye. When he was born, his family did not think that his birthmarks were particularly significant, but when he was three years old, he began talking about a previous life. He said that he had been a schoolteacher named Bua Kai and that he had been shot and killed while on the way to school. He gave the names of his parents, his wife, and two of his children from that life, and he persistently begged his grandmother, with whom he lived, to take him to his previous parents' home in a place called Khao Phra.

Eventually, when he was still three years old, his grandmother did just that. She and Chanai took a bus to a town near Khao Phra, which was fifteen miles from their home village. After the two of them got off the bus, Chanai led the way to a house where he said his parents lived. The house belonged to an elderly couple whose son, Bua Kai Lawnak, had been a teacher who was murdered five years before Chanai was born. Chanai's grandmother, it turned out, had previously lived three miles away. Since she had a stall where she sold goods to many people in the surrounding area, she vaguely knew Bua Kai and his wife. She had never been to their home and had no idea to whose home Chanai was leading her. Once there, Chanai identified Bua Kai's parents, who were there with a number of other family members, as his own. They were impressed enough by his statements and his birthmarks to invite him to return a short time later. When he did, they tested him by asking him to pick out Bua Kai's belongings from others, and he was able to do that. He recognized one of Bua Kai's daughters and asked for the other one by name. Bua Kai's family accepted that Chanai was Bua Kai reborn, and he visited them a number of times. He insisted that Bua Kai's daughters call him "Father," and if they did not, he refused to talk to them.

As for Bua Kai's wounds, no autopsy report was available, but Dr. Stevenson talked with a number of family members about his injuries, and they said that he had two wounds on his head from being shot. His wife remembered that the doctor who examined Bua Kai's body said that the entrance wound was the one on the back of his head because it was much smaller than the wound on his forehead that would have been the exit wound. These matched Chanai's birthmarks, a small, circular one on the back of his head and a larger, more irregular one on the front. They were both hairless and puckered. No one photographed them until Chanai was eleven-and-a-half years old, so determining exactly where they were on his head at birth is difficult. In the photographs, the larger one is on the left toward the top of his head in front, but witnesses said that it had been lower on his forehead when he was younger.

In this case, a number of witnesses stated that a young child with birth-marks that matched the entrance and exit wounds on a deceased man had knowledge about that man's life that he seemingly could not have obtained through normal means, and he was able to pass tests that the man's family constructed for him.

The Case of Indika Ishwara

Indika Ishwara, an identical twin, was born in Sri Lanka in 1972. His brother talked about a previous life at an early age . . . When Indika was three years old, he also began talking about one. He said that he was from Balapitiya, a town nearly thirty miles from his hometown. He talked about his previous parents. He did not give their names but referred to them as his Ambalangoda mother and Ambalangoda father. He said that he attended a big school in Ambalangoda, a larger town near to Balapitiya, and that he traveled there by train. He said that he was called "Baby Mahattaya." *Mahattaya* means "master" or "boss" in Sinhalese, and Baby Mahattaya is a fairly common nickname in Sri Lanka. He claimed he had an older sister named Malkanthie, with whom he had bicycled. He described an uncle named Premasiri as well as a "Mudalali Bappa." *Mudalali* means an individual with a substantial business, and *bappa* means a paternal uncle. He mentioned that the family had a calf and a dog and said that a car and a truck were at the home.

In addition, he talked of going with his sister to the temple, where he said a red curtain hung in front of the Buddha image. He said that his previous father wore trousers; his own father wore a sarong. His previous home, where a wedding had taken place, had electricity. His family's home did not. He described his previous mother as being darker, taller, and fatter than his present one. He said that he had gone to school through the fourth grade and had a classmate named Sepali.

Indika's family did not know anyone who lived in Ambalangoda. His father had a friend who worked there, and he asked the friend to try to locate the previous personality's family based on what Indika had said. The friend quickly located a family in Balapitiya, who seemed to fit Indika's statements. Their oldest son, Dharshana, had died at ten of viral encephalitis four years before Indika was born.

The friend spoke with Dharshana's mother about Indika, since Dharshana's father was away at the time. When the father did learn what Indika had been saying, he was quite interested, and he soon made an unannounced trip to Indika's hometown. He went to the shop of Indika's father. While he was waiting there for someone to take him to the family's home, an employee asked him if he had a daughter named Malkanthie and a son called Mahatmaya, since Indika had been reporting these things. He did, and he then went to the family's home and met Indika, who was not yet four years old. People thought that Indika recognized him, because even though he did not call him by name directly, he said to his mother, "Father has come."

Shortly after that, various members of Dharshana's family made two trips to see Indika. Indika was thought to recognize several of them, but their interactions occurred in uncontrolled conditions with a lot of people around. Dr. Stevenson's long-time associate in Sri Lanka, Godwin Samararatne, later accompanied Indika to Balapitiya and Ambalangoda, but Indika did not say anything that suggested that he recognized anything he saw. At that point, most of Dharshana's family members had already met Indika, but Mr. Samararatne was able to set up controlled tests to see if Indika could recognize an additional uncle and cousin. He did not. On his second visit to Dharshana's family, he appeared to be looking for something outside a house in the family's compound. He discovered what he had been looking for and pointed out Dharshana's name and the date 1965 that had been scratched, presumably by Dharshana, in the wall of a concrete drain when the concrete was still wet. No one in Dharshana's family knew about this or had ever noticed the writing until Indika pointed it out to them.

Mr. Samararatne, Dr. Stevenson's associate, had learned of the case soon after it developed, and he conducted interviews with Indika's parents three weeks after the initial meeting between Indika and Dharshana's father and with Dharshana's father a week after that. All of Indika's statements about the previous life in these pages come from those initial interviews that occurred very soon after the families first met. The memory that Dharshana's father had of hearing the two names at the shop of Indika's father seems particularly striking, and I think we must conclude that Indika gave those names before the families ever met.

Almost all of the statements that Indika made proved to be correct for the life of Dharshana. Dharshana's family did live in Balapitiya, and he attended school in Ambalangoda. Dharshana was called "Baby Mahattaya" as a nickname. His older sister was named Malkanthie, and they did bicycle together. One of his uncles was named Premasiri (his full name was Sangama Premasiri de Silva), and a paternal uncle was a contractor and a timber merchant, thus a *mudalali*. Dharshana's family had a car and a dog. Though they did not own a truck, one was parked in the family's compound. Likewise, the family did not own a calf, but other people brought their calves to graze on the grass at the family's compound.

The temple that Indika's family attended had a white curtain in front of its image of Buddha, while the one that Dharshana's family attended had a red one. Dharshana's father did wear trousers, and the family's home did have electricity. Though Dharshana may not have witnessed a wedding directly in the family's home, several had taken place nearby, including one in a neighbor's house a few weeks before Dharshana died. Dharshana had fallen from a wall during the wedding, and his doctors later thought he might have sustained a head injury then that was related to his subsequent encephalitis. Indika's description of Dharshana's mother was accurate. Dharshana attended school through Grade 4. He was just starting Grade 5 when he became ill. As far as Dharshana's family and one of his classmates could recall, he did not have a classmate named Sepali.

How Indika could possibly have known all these details about an ordinary boy who died in another village almost thirty miles away is certainly worth wondering about. In addition, he had a nasal polyp his parents noticed when he was a year old. Though nasal polyps are not unusual in later ages, they are quite rare in infancy, and Indika's identical twin did not have one. So why did Indika have one? If we accept the possibility that some birthmarks and defects may arise through the process of reincarnation, one possibility to consider is that since Dharshana, the previous personality, had received both nasal oxygen and a nasal feeding tube during his illness, an irritation from one of those could have produced the subsequent polyp in Indika. The nasal polyp . . . is rare and has no known cause, and the explanation that it somehow mirrored irritation from the nasal tubes that Dharshana had is consistent with the numerous statements that Indika made that were correct for Dharshana's life.

The Case of Purnima Ekanayaka

Purnima Ekanayaka, a girl in Sri Lanka, was born with a group of light-colored birthmarks over the left side of her chest and her lower ribs. She began talking about a previous life when she was between two-and-a-half and three years old, but her parents did not initially pay much attention to her statements. When she was four years old, she saw a television program about the Kelaniya temple, a well-known temple that was 145 miles away, and said that she recognized it. Later, her father, a school principal, and her mother, a teacher, took a group of students to the Kelaniya temple. Purnima went with the group on the visit. While there, she said that she had lived on the other side of the river that flowed beside the temple grounds.

By the time she was six, Purnima had made some twenty statements about the previous life, describing a male incense maker who was killed in a traffic accident. She had mentioned the names of two incense brands, Ambiga and Geta Pichcha. Her parents had never heard of these, and when Dr. Haraldsson later checked the shops in their town, none of them sold those brands of incense.

A new teacher began working in Purnima's town. He spent his weekends in Kelaniya where his wife lived. Purnima's father told him what Purnima had said, and the teacher decided to check in Kelaniya to see if anyone had died there who matched her statements. The teacher said that Purnima's father gave him the following items to check:

- She had lived on the other side of the river from the Kelaniya temple.
- She had made Ambiga and Geta Pichcha incense sticks.
- She was selling incense sticks on a bicycle.
- She was killed in an accident with a big vehicle.

He then went with his brother-in-law, who did not believe in reincarnation, to see if a person matching those statements could be located. They went to the Kelaniya temple and took a ferry across the river. There, they asked about incense makers and found that three small family incense businesses were in the area. The owner of one of them called his brands Ambiga and Geta Pichcha. His brother-in-law and associate, Jinadasa Perera, had been killed by a bus when he was taking incense sticks to the market on his bicycle two years before Purnima was born.

Purnima's family visited the owner's home soon after. There, Purnima made various comments about family members and their business that were correct, and the family accepted her as being Jinadasa reborn. Dr. Haraldsson began investigating the case when Purnima was nine years old. He recorded the twenty statements that her parents said Purnima had made before the two families met. In addition to the ones already mentioned, they included the names of Jinadasa's mother and wife and the name of the school that Jinadasa had attended. Dr. Haraldsson verified that fourteen of the statements were accurate for the life of Jinadasa. Three were incorrect, and the accuracy of three of them could not be determined. He also obtained Jinadasa's autopsy report, which documented fractured ribs on the left, a ruptured spleen, and abrasions running diagonally from the right shoulder across the chest to the left lower abdomen. These corresponded to the birthmarks that Purnima had over her chest and ribs.

The Case of Sujith Jayaratne

Sujith Jayaratne, a boy from a suburb of the Sri Lanka capital Colombo, began showing an intense fear of trucks and even the word *lorry*, a British word for truck that has become part of the Sinhalese language, when he was only eight months old. When he became old enough to talk, he said that he had lived in Gorakana, a village seven miles away, and that he had died after being hit by a truck.

He made numerous statements about that life. His great-uncle, a monk at a nearby temple, heard some of them and mentioned Sujith to a younger monk at the temple. The story interested this monk, so he talked with Sujith, who was a little more than two-and-a-half years old at the time, about his memories, and then wrote up notes of the conversations before he attempted to verify any of the statements. His notes document that Sujith said that he was from Gorakana and lived in the section of Gorakawatte, that his father was named Jamis and had a bad right eye, that he had attended the *kabal iskole*, which means "dilapidated school," and had a teacher named Francis there, and that he gave money to a woman named Kusuma, who prepared string hoppers, a type of food, for him. He implied that he gave money to the Kale Pansala, or Forest Temple, and said two monks were there, one of whom was named Amitha. He said that his house was whitewashed, that its lavatory was beside a fence, and that he bathed in cool water.

Sujith had also told his mother and grandmother a number of other things about the previous life that no one wrote down until after the previous personality had been identified. He said his name was Sammy, and he sometimes called himself "Gorakana Sammy." Kusuma, the woman he had mentioned to the monk, was his younger sister's daughter, and she lived in Gorakana and had long, thick hair. He said that his wife's name was Maggie and their daughter's was Nandanie. He had worked for the railways and had once climbed Adam's Peak, a high mountain in central Sri Lanka. He had transported arrack, a liquor that was illegally traded, in a boat that had once capsized, causing him to lose his entire shipment of arrack. He said that on the day he died, he and Maggie had quarreled. She left the house, and he then went out to the store. While he was crossing the road, a truck ran over him, and he died.

The young monk went to Gorakana to look for a family who had a deceased member whose life matched Sujith's statements. After some effort, he discovered that a fifty-year-old man named Sammy Fernando, or "Gorakana Sammy" as he was sometimes called, had died after being hit by a truck six months before Sujith was born. All of Sujith's statements proved to be correct for Sammy Fernando, with the only exception being when he said that he had died immediately when the truck hit him. Sammy Fernando died one to two hours after being admitted to a hospital following the accident.

Once Sammy Fernando was identified as the previous personality, Sujith was able to recognize several people from Sammy's life and to comment on changes that had been made in the Fernando property. He made many of the recognitions when no witnesses outside of the two families were present, but the monk heard him give the name of Sammy Fernando's nephew.

Dr. Stevenson interviewed witnesses a year after Sammy Fernando had first been identified as the previous personality. He interviewed thirty-five people as part of his investigation of the case, including Sujith, who was still talking about the previous life at an age of three-and-a-half. Dr. Stevenson discovered that though Sujith's and Sammy's families had not known each other before the case developed, two people in Sujith's neighborhood had connections to Sammy Fernando. Sujith's family knew one of them, a former drinking buddy of Sammy, slightly, and the other one, Sammy's younger sister, not at all. The family had no idea of whom Sujith was talking until the monk went to Gorakana. In fact, neither Sujith's mother nor the monk had heard of Gorakana before the case developed, as it was a fairly small village some distance away from the Colombo area.

Sujith displayed other behaviors along with the phobia of trucks that were consistent with Sammy Fernando's life. He would pretend to drink arrack and then would act drunk. He also attempted to get arrack from neighbors, including one who obliged him until his grandmother intervened. In addition, he tried to smoke cigarettes. No one in his family drank arrack or smoked cigarettes, but Sammy Fernando consumed plenty of both. Sujith also asked for spicy foods Sammy Fernando frequently enjoyed, ones his family, who only ate them occasionally, would not normally have considered giving to a small child. In addition, he had a tendency as a toddler to be physically aggressive and to use obscenities, two habits that Sammy Fernando demonstrated when he was intoxicated. By the time Sujith was six years old, he had stopped talking about Sammy Fernando's life and displayed less of the unusual behaviors that he had shown earlier. He still continued to ask for arrack if he saw others drinking it.

The Case of Kumkum Verma

Kumkum Verma, a girl from in India, began talking about a previous life at the age of three-and-a-half. She said that she had lived in Darbhanga, a city of 200,000 people that was twenty-five miles away from her village, and that Urdu Bazar was the name of the section of the city where she had been. Her father, an educated man who was a landowner, homeopathic physician, and author, did not know anyone in Urdu Bazar, a commercial district where small businessmen, artisans, and craftsmen lived.

Kumkum asked her family to call her Sunnary, which means beautiful, and made many statements about the previous life. Her aunt made notes of some of them six months before anyone tried to identify the previous personality. Dr. Stevenson, who met Kumkum's family when she was nine years old, obtained an English translation of extracts of the notes, but he was unable to get the complete notebook, because it had been lost after being loaned to someone. The extracts listed eighteen statements that Kumkum made that all proved to be correct for the previous personality, including the name of Urdu Bazar, her son's name and the fact that he worked with a hammer, her grandson's name, the name of the town where her father lived, the location of his home near mango orchards, and the presence of a pond at her house. She had correctly stated that she had an iron safe at her house, a sword hanging near her cot, and a snake near the safe to which she fed milk.

Kumkum's father eventually talked about her statements to a friend who lived in Darbhanga. That friend had an employee from the Urdu Bazar section of the city, who was able to identify the previous personality, Sunnary or Sundari Mistry, whom Kumkum seemed to be describing. The previous personality's family belonged to a relatively low artisan class and would have been quite unlikely to have social contact with a family with the education and social status of Dr. Verma's family. In fact, they had little contact even after the case developed. The previous personality's grandson visited Kumkum's family twice. Dr. Verma went to Urdu Bazar once to meet the previous personality's family, but he never allowed Kumkum to go. Apparently he was not proud of his daughter's claim to have been a blacksmith's wife in her previous life.

One interesting note is that Kumkum said that she died during an altercation and that her stepson's wife had poisoned her. Sundari, who died quite unexpectedly five years before Kumkum was born, was preparing to be a witness for her son in his suit against her second husband, involving the son's belief that his stepfather had misappropriated his deceased father's money, when she died. No autopsy was performed, and Kumkum's statement that she was poisoned remained unverified.

Also of note is that Kumkum spoke with an accent different from that of her family. The family associated it with the lower classes of Darbhanga and reported that in addition, Kumkum used some unusual expressions that seemed related to them as well.

The Case of Jagdish Chandra

The case of Jagdish Chandra in India was quite old when Dr. Stevenson arrived on the scene. The subject was then in his late thirties. The subject's father, a prominent lawyer, had made a written record of the boy's statements and their verifications at the time that the case developed. Jagdish was born in a large city in northern India. When he was three-and-a-half years old, he began saying that he had lived in Benares, a city approximately 300 miles away. He gave a number of details, and his father had several friends and colleagues talk with Jagdish so that they could confirm that he was making those statements. His father then sent a letter to the chairman of the municipal board in Benares. The chairman wrote back that he could tell whom Jagdish was referring to as soon as he read the letter and that he had made inquiries and found that most of the boy's statements were quite accurate.

Jagdish's father then sent a letter to a national newspaper asking for help in verifying the child's statements. In the letter, he said that Jagdish stated that his father was named Babuji Pandey and had a house in Benares with a big gate, a sitting room, and an underground room with an iron safe fixed in one of the walls. *Ji* added to the end of a name means *respected*, so Jagdish was saying that his father was called Babu. He added that Jagdish described a courtyard in which Babuji sat in the evenings and people gathered to drink bhang, an Indian drink. He said that Babuji received massages and put powder or clay on his face after washing it. He described two cars—which were very unusual in India in those days—and a horse-drawn carriage and said that Babuji had two deceased sons and a deceased wife. The father added that his son "described many private and family matters."

The day after this was published, Jagdish's father went to a magistrate to have Jagdish's statements officially recorded before they traveled to Benares, where the previous personality had lived. The recorded statements, in addition to those listed in the paper, included that his name had been Jai Gopal, and that his brother, who was bigger than he was, had been named Jai Mangal and had died of poisoning. The Ganges River was near the house, and the Dash Ashwamadh Ghat was there. (Ghats are piers where people go to bathe, and Babu Pandey was the supervisor of one.) A prostitute named Bhagwati had sung for Babu.

Jagdish was then taken to Benares, where all of the above statements were verified, with the exception that Babu Pandey had used automobiles but not actually owned them. Jagdish appeared to recognize people and places there.

The Case of Ratana Wongsombat

Ratana Wongsombat was born in Bangkok in 1964. Her adoptive father meditated once a week at the Wat Mahathat, a large temple with more than 300 monks on the other side of Bangkok from the family's home. Ratana began asking to go there. When she was fourteen months old, her father took her for the first time. While they were there, she seemed to show knowledge of the buildings. After they returned home, her father asked her where she had been before this life. She began talking about a previous life at that point and eventually told the following story. She had been a Chinese woman named Kim Lan and had stayed at the temple, where she lived in a green hut with a nun named Mae Chan. After eventually being driven from there, she moved to a district of Bangkok named Banglampoo. She said that she had had only one daughter, who lived in Kim Lan's old hometown, which she named, and Kim Lan had returned there at the end of her life, where she died after surgery. Ratana expressed displeasure that after she died as Kim Lan, her ashes had been scattered rather than buried.

Ratana's father was not familiar with a woman named Kim Lan, and he apparently made no immediate attempts to verify Ratana's statements. When Ratana was two years old, he again took her to the temple. When they passed a large group of nuns there, Ratana appeared to recognize one and called out "Mae Chan" to her. The nun did not respond to her, but Ratana told her father that she had lived with that nun in her previous life. Ratana's father returned to the temple a few days later and spoke with the nun. Her name was Mae Chee Chan Suthipat (*Mae Chee* is an honorific for nuns in Thailand meaning "mother nun"), but some people, including the previous personality, called her Mae Chan. She confirmed that almost all of the statements that Ratana had made, including all the ones listed in this summary, were correct for the life of Kim Lan Prayoon Supamitr, who died one-and-a-half years before Ratana was born.

Kim Lan's daughter also confirmed Ratana's statements, including even the matter of her remains. Kim Lan had wanted her ashes to be buried under the Bo Tree at the temple complex, but when her daughter tried to honor her wish, the roots of the tree were so extensive that she ended up spreading the ashes rather than burying them.

The Case of Gamini Jayasena

Gamini Jayasena was born in Colombo, Sri Lanka, in 1962, and he began talking about a previous life before he was two years old. Over time, he gave details that included the following: He had another mother who was bigger than his present one. Someone named Nimal had bitten him. He had a schoolbag that was still sitting on a chair. He had a toy elephant that he bathed in a well. He had once fallen into a well. Someone named "Charlie Uncle" had a car in which he drove the subject to school, and "Charlie Uncle's" family also had a red motorcycle.

Since Gamini did not name a place or give a last name, the case might well have remained unsolved if his family had not taken a bus trip when he was two-and-a-half years old. When the bus stopped briefly at a place called Nittambuwe, Gamini told the person next to him, a family friend, that this had been his home. That person relayed the information to Gamini's parents, who in turn told his mother's cousin, a well-known monk.

The monk decided to look into the matter, and he took the family back to Nittambuwe. They got out of the car at the place where Gamini had made his comment and began walking toward the four houses that were down the road. Gamini said that his mother lived there, but the monk decided not to proceed further. He apparently was unsure if this was the correct place and was concerned that he would likely be entering the home of a Christian family. Gamini's family thought he was probably remembering the life of a Christian because he knelt during prayer with his trunk erect rather than with his buttocks resting on his heels in the typical Buddhist position, and because he had once asked his mother to hang up a wooden cross he had found. The family returned to Colombo, but some Nittambuwe villagers had recognized the monk during the family's stop and told a family living at the place indicated by Gamini. This family, which was in fact a Christian family, had lost a son two years before Gamini was born. The boy, named Palitha, had died after a short illness. Just before getting sick, he had returned from school on vacation and left his schoolbag on a chair, instead of putting it in the cupboard as he usually did, while announcing that he would not be going to school again. He had a younger brother named Nimal, who had once bitten him.

Palitha's parents visited the monk. They gave the monk a picture of Palitha that Gamini subsequently appeared to recognize. Following that,

Gamini's family returned to Nittambuwe to meet Palitha's parents. There, Gamini was judged to recognize a number of people and places. When he was taken to Palitha's school and the boardinghouse where Palitha stayed while attending school, he made additional recognitions and statements about Palitha's life.

All of Gamini's statements listed here proved to be correct for Palitha, except that Charles Senewiratne, Palitha's uncle, owned a car but did not drive Palitha to school. No possible connection could be found between Gamini's family in Colombo and Palitha's family in Nittambuwe, some twenty miles away.

The Case of Kendra Carter

Kendra Carter, a girl who lives in Florida, was four-and-a-half years old when she went to her first swimming lesson with a coach named Ginger. She immediately jumped into Ginger's lap and acted very lovingly toward her. When Ginger had to cancel a lesson three weeks later, Kendra sobbed uncontrollably. When she was able to have a lesson soon after, she was very happy and began talking about Ginger all the time.

A few weeks later, Kendra began saying that Ginger's baby had died and that Ginger had been sick and had pushed her baby out. When her mother asked her how she knew these things, Kendra replied, "I'm the baby that was in her tummy." At that point, Kendra had only seen Ginger at their lessons, and her mother knew that the two of them had never been alone. Kendra described an abortion, saying that Ginger had allowed a bad man to pull her out and that she had tried to hang on but could not. She described being scared in a dark and cold place afterwards. Kendra's mother eventually found out from Ginger that she had in fact had an abortion nine years before Kendra was born when she was unmarried, sick, and dealing with anorexia nervosa.

Kendra began saying that she would die, because Ginger had been unable to deliver her. She said, "I have to die, and I won't come back this time." This fear of dying became so severe that Kendra's mother took her to a therapist, who suggested a ceremony in which Kendra would be "born" to Ginger. Following this, her fear of dying seemed to resolve.

Even though Ginger was often cool toward her, Kendra began being very bubbly and happy when she was with Ginger but quiet and withdrawn otherwise. Her mother allowed her to spend more and more time with Ginger. Eventually, Ginger set up a room for Kendra in her home, and Kendra spent three nights a week there. Kendra's absences were hard for her mother, but she permitted them, because Kendra's wish to be with Ginger was so intense.

Unfortunately, Ginger and Kendra's mother eventually had a falling-out, and Ginger said that she did not want to see Kendra anymore. Following this, Kendra did not speak for four-and-a-half months. She showed no interest in activities, ate little, and slept a lot. At the end of that time, Ginger met with Kendra for two hours. During this meeting, Kendra talked again for the first time when she told Ginger that she loved her. Ginger began calling Kendra again, but Kendra did not feel comfortable going to her home. Kendra slowly began talking more, and she began participating more in activities.

Kendra's mother found all of this very troubling. Her daughter's struggle with the situation upset her, and the possibility of reincarnation troubled her as well. She attended a conservative Christian church, and she felt that she was committing a sin by merely buying a book on reincarnation during Kendra's troubles. She decided that perhaps Kendra's spirit had been looking for another body after Ginger's abortion, but she did not accept the idea that reincarnation is a process that normally occurs.

The Case of Sukla Gupta

Sukla Gupta in India is another subject who showed great emotion. She was less than two years old when she began the habit of cradling a block of wood or a pillow and calling it "Minu." She said that Minu was her daughter, and during the next three years, she gradually spoke more about a previous life. She gave a number of details, including the name and section of a village eleven miles away. A woman there who had an infant daughter named Minu had died six years before Sukla was born and was identified as the previous personality. When Sukla was five years old, her family went to meet the family of the previous personality. She cried when she met Minu, then eleven years old, and she appeared affectionate and maternal toward her. At one point, one of the previous personality's cousins tested Sukla by telling her falsely that Minu was sick with a high fever. Sukla began to weep, and she could not be comforted for some time. In another instance, Minu actually was sick, and when Sukla learned the news, she began crying and demanded to be taken to her. She remained agitated until the next day when her family took her to see Minu, who had improved by then.

Sukla also appeared deferential toward the previous personality's husband. After they met, she longed for him to visit her. He did so weekly for about a year, until his second wife complained about the visits, and he began to visit less frequently. Sukla talked less about the previous life after the age of seven, and she also gradually lost her feelings of attachment toward the previous personality's husband and Minu. By the time she was an early teen, she complained that they were pestering her when they came to visit.

The Case of Sam Taylor

Sam Taylor is a boy from Vermont who was born a year and a half after his paternal grandfather died. When Sam was one-and-a-half years old, his father was changing his diaper one day when Sam told him, "When I was your age, I used to change your diapers." After his mother saw the puzzled look on his father's face as he brought Sam out of his room, they discussed the comment, which they both found odd. Neither had ever given reincarnation much thought. Though Sam's mother was the daughter of a Southern Baptist minister, his parents were not religious.

Following that incident, Sam gradually began saying that he had been his grandfather. He also said, "I used to be big, and now I'm small." While his father was initially skeptical about such a possibility, his mother was more open to the idea, and she began asking him questions about the life of his paternal grandfather. At one point, she and Sam were talking about the fact that his grandmother had taken care of his grandfather before he died. Sam's mother asked him what his grandmother made every day for his grandfather to drink, and Sam correctly said that she had made milkshakes and that she had made them in a machine in the kitchen. He got up to show her the food processor on the kitchen counter. When his mother showed him the blender in the pantry and asked if he meant that his grandmother had made the milkshakes with it, he said no and pointed out the food processor instead. In fact, his grandmother had made milkshakes for his grandfather in the food processor. She had had a series of strokes after the death of his grandfather, and Sam had never seen her make milkshakes for anyone.

At another time, Sam's mother asked him if he had had any brothers or sisters when he lived before. He answered, "Yeah, I had a sister. She turned into a fish." When she asked him who turned her into a fish, he said, "Some bad guys. She died. You know what, when we die, God lets us come back again. I used to be big, and now I'm a kid again." The sister of Sam's grandfather, in fact, had been killed some sixty years before. Her husband killed her while she was sleeping, rolled her body up in a blanket, and dumped it in the bay.

At other times, Sam correctly said that his grandfather's favorite place in the home was the garage where he worked on "inventions" and that Sam's father had a small steering wheel of his own when they rode in the car.

When his father was a boy, he had a toy steering wheel that attached to the dashboard of a car by suction cups.

When Sam was four-and-a-half years old, his grandmother died. His father flew out to her home to take care of her belongings and returned with a box of family photographs. Sam's parents had not had any pictures of his father's family before then. When his mother spread them out on the coffee table one night, Sam came over and began pointing to the pictures of his grandfather and saying, "That's me!" When he saw a snapshot that just showed a car without any people, he said "Hey! That's my car!" This was a picture of the first new car that his grandfather ever purchased, a 1949 Pontiac that was very special to him.

His mother gave Sam a class picture from when his grandfather was in grammar school. The picture showed twenty-seven children, sixteen of them boys. Sam ran his finger over the faces, stopped it on his grandfather's face and said, "That's me."

His father says that Sam's grandfather did not communicate very well about emotional issues with his sons, particularly when they were adults. Sam's father let his own father know how he felt about him, but his father had great difficulty reciprocating. He feels that if his father has come back through Sam, then his deceased father is reaching out to return his love. Sam's father is very open with all of his children, and he and Sam seem to have a very good relationship.

The Case of Nazih Al-Danaf

One case that involved several recognitions is the case of Nazih Al-Danaf in Lebanon. At a very early age, Nazih described a past life to his parents and his seven siblings, all of whom were available for interviews. Nazih described the life of a man that his family did not know. He said that the man carried pistols and grenades, that he had a pretty wife and young children, that he had a two-story house with trees around it and a cave nearby, that he had a mute friend, and that he had been shot by a group of men.

His father reported that Nazih demanded that his parents take him to his previous house in a small town ten miles away. They took him to that town, along with two of his sisters and a brother, when he was six years old. About a half a mile from the town, Nazih asked them to stop at a dirt road running off the main road. He told them that the road came to a dead end where there was a cave, but they drove on without confirming this. When they got to the center of town, six roads converged, and Nazih's father asked him which way to go. Nazih pointed to one of the roads and said to go on it until they came to a road that forked off upward, where they would see his house. When they got to the first fork that went up, the family got out and began asking about anyone who had died in the way that Nazih had described.

They quickly discovered that a man named Fuad, who had a house on that road before dying ten years prior to Nazih's birth, seemed to fit Nazih's statements. Fuad's widow asked Nazih, "Who built the foundation of this gate at the entrance of the house?" and Nazih correctly answered, "A man from the Faraj family." The group then went into the house, where Nazih correctly described how Fuad had kept his weapons in a cupboard. The widow asked him if she had had an accident at their previous home, and Nazih gave accurate details of her accident. She also asked if he remembered what had made their young daughter seriously ill, and Nazih correctly responded that she had accidentally taken some of her father's pills. He also accurately described a couple of other incidents from the previous personality's life. The widow and her five children were all very impressed with the knowledge that Nazih demonstrated, and they were all convinced that he was the rebirth of Fuad.

Soon after that meeting, Nazih visited Fuad's brother, Sheikh Adeeb. When Nazih saw him, he ran up saying, "Here comes my brother Adeeb." Sheikh Adeeb asked Nazih for proof that he was his brother, and Nazih said, "I gave you a Checki 16." A Checki 16 is a type of pistol from Czechoslovakia that is not common in Lebanon, and Fuad had indeed given his brother one. Sheikh Adeeb then asked Nazih where his original house was, and Nazih led him down the road until he said correctly, "This is the house of my father and this [the next house] is my first house." They went in the latter house, where Fuad's first wife still lived, and when Sheikh Adeeb later asked who she was, Nazih correctly gave her name.

Sheikh Adeeb then showed Nazih a photograph of three men and asked him who they were. Nazih pointed to each and correctly gave the names of Adeeb, Fuad, and a deceased brother of theirs. Sheikh Adeeb showed Nazih another picture, and Nazih said correctly that the man in it was the father of those men. Later, Sheikh Adeeb visited Nazih's home, and he took a handgun with him. He asked Nazih if this was the gun that Fuad had given him, and Nazih correctly said that it was not.

Dr. Haraldsson investigated Nazih's case, and he was able to verify most of the statements that Nazih made, including the claim that the previous personality had a mute friend. He also found out that Nazih's description of Fuad's house matched another one in which Fuad lived for several years, including the time during which the house in town, which was not fully completed at the time of Fuad's death, was being built. The former house was by the dirt road that Nazih had pointed out during the family's first visit to the previous town, and a cave was also at the end of it as Nazih had said.

If the families in this case are remembering events correctly, then Nazih's statements are very difficult to explain by normal means. His spontaneous recognitions of the locations of two houses that the previous personality had owned are quite impressive just by themselves. Adding his ability to correctly point out the previous personality's first house makes coincidence seem an unlikely explanation. On top of these, his statements to Fuad's family about various small details are also notable. His statement about the Checki 16 pistol is particularly impressive in a number of ways, one being that this knowledge could not have arisen from any environmental cues. His ability to state the names of the men in a picture is more impressive than cases in which a child simply points to a member of the previous personality's family, since environmental cues would not lead him to know the names that he gave. The informants stated that Nazih had not seen pictures of the previous personality before he identified him in the group photograph, and Sheikh Adeeb was certain that with the possible exception of his wife, no one knew that Fuad had given him a Checki 16 pistol.

Index

A

Abuse
  and baggage, 105–6
  case study of, 34–35
  cycle of, 52, 72, 130
  and forgiveness, 106
Adam, 26
Affirmations
  and astral travel, 150
  and fears, 101–2, 126
  for intentions, 185
The After Death Experience, 234
Afterlife, 3–4
Akashic records, 203–12
Al-Danaf, Nazih, 281–83
Altered States, 97
Alternate reality, 6–7, 11. *See also* Reality
Amilius, 26
Ancient cultures, 4–6, 54
Angels, 167–72. *See also* Guides; Spirit guides
  and automatic writing, 196
  hierarchy of, 167–68
  meeting, 169–70
  recognizing, 171–72
  role of, 167–68
  signs from, 170–71
  understanding, 11, 159–74
Astral travel, 145–57
  desire for, 148–49
  exercise for, 151–53
  learning from, 153–57
  myths about, 146–48
  tips on, 149–51
  understanding, 146
Attraction, emotional, 41
Attraction, law of, 44–45, 154–55

Austen, A. W., 63
Automatic writing, 191–201
  dangers of, 193–94, 199–200
  exercise in, 198
  mechanics of, 192–93
  power of words, 200–201
  preparing for, 196–98
  and subconscious mind, 195–98

B

Baggage, releasing, 103–6
Baily, Alice, 204
Barbanel, Maurice, 58–59
Belief systems, 48–49, 54–58, 64–65, 217–18. *See also* Religion
Besant, Annie, 204
Bhagavad Gita, 4
Bible, 2, 14, 26, 210–11
Blavatsky, Helena, 208
Blockages, causes of, 22, 36, 112, 121, 127, 130, 138
Blockages, releasing, 66, 74–76, 86–87, 105, 164, 187–88, 198
Bloody Mary, 180–81
Bloxham, Arnall, 230–31
The Bloxham Tapes, 230–31
Book of Enoch, 168
Book of Life, 204–5, 207, 210–11
Book of Mormon, 178
Brahan Seer, 178–79
Brain, science of, 79
Brain wave entrainment, 91
Breath awareness, 101–2, 132–36
Brocas, Joanne, 229
Brocas, Jock, 19

Buddha, 2–3, 48–49
Buddhism, xii, 56–57, 68, 117

C

Candles, 49–50, 183
Carter, Kendra, 276–77
Case studies, 34–35, 156–57, 223–43, 253–83
Castle, visualizing, 124–28
Cayce, Edgar, 13, 14, 25–26, 72, 138, 204–6, 208–9
Chakras, 146, 149–51
Chandra, Jagdish, 272
Chemical substances, 91, 97
Children and past lives, 7–10. *See also* Past lives
Choomalaiwong, Chanai, 260–61
Christenson, Patrick, 258–59
Christianity, 3–4, 56. *See also* Religion
Clairalience, 120
Clairaudience, 117–19
Clairgustence, 120
Clairsentience, 119–20
Clairvoyance, 12, 115–17, 166, 176
Cognitive theory, 79
Coincidence, 41, 232, 240
Connections, identifying, 6–7. *See also* Past lives
Connections, making, 39–40
Conscious lucid visions, 47
Conscious mind, 80. *See also* Subconscious mind
Consciousness, 77–92
  altered states of, 88–92, 110–11

We Have
EVERYTHING®
on Anything!

With more than 19 million copies sold, the Everything® series has become one of America's favorite resources for solving problems, learning new skills, and organizing lives. Our brand is not only recognizable—it's also welcomed.

The series is a hand-in-hand partner for people who are ready to tackle new subjects—like you!

For more information on the Everything® series, please visit *www.adamsmedia.com*

The Everything® list spans a wide range of subjects, with more than 500 titles covering 25 different categories:

Business	History	Reference
Careers	Home Improvement	Religion
Children's Storybooks	Everything Kids	Self-Help
Computers	Languages	Sports & Fitness
Cooking	Music	Travel
Crafts and Hobbies	New Age	Wedding
Education/Schools	Parenting	Writing
Games and Puzzles	Personal Finance	
Health	Pets	